EARLY RECOLLECTIONS

EARLY RECOLLECTIONS
THEORY AND PRACTICE
IN COUNSELING AND PSYCHOTHERAPY

ARTHUR J. CLARK

BRUNNER-ROUTLEDGE
NEW YORK LONDON

The author wishes to acknowledge permission to reprint the following:

Table 2.1 Safeguarding Tendencies Categories with Definitions. "Safeguarding Tendencies: Implications for the Counseling Process" from *The Journal of Individual Psychology*, 56(2), 195. Copyright © 2000 by the University of Texas Press. All rights reserved.

Table 2.3 Defense Mechanisms with Definitions and Table 9.1 Sentence Completion. Arthur J. Clark, *Defense Mechanisms in the Counseling Process*, p. 21, 36, copyright © 1998 by Sage Publications. Reprinted by permission of Sage Publications.

Published in 2002 by
Brunner-Routledge
29 West 35th Street
New York, NY 10001

Published in Great Britain by
Brunner-Routledge
27 Church Street
Hove, East Sussex, BN3 2FA

10   9   8   7   6   5   4   3   2   1

Library of Congress Cataloging-In-Publication Data

Clark, Arthur J.
   Early recollections : theory and practice in counseling and psychotherapy / Arthur J. Clark.
     p. cm.
   Includes bibliographical references and index.
   ISBN 0–415–93499–0 — ISBN 1–58391–371–8 (pbk.)
   1. Counseling. 2. Psychotherapy. 3. Early memories. I. Title.

BF637.C6 C453 2002
158'.3—dc21
                                               2002020618

*Although they are not my earliest recollections,
the fondest memories of my life include my wife,
Marybeth, and my children, Heather, Tara, and Kayla.
It is to them that I dedicate this book.*

CONTENTS

ACKNOWLEDGMENTS

MANY PEOPLE CONTRIBUTED TO THE COMPLETION OF THIS BOOK, ranging from providing early recollections to assisting in the publication process. My graduate students in the Counseling and Development Program at St. Lawrence University encouraged me with their continuing interest in learning about early recollections. A mentor and friend, William "Bill" Brown, was steadfast with his incisive and perceptive critiques of the manuscript. Bill read every chapter with the enthusiasm and dedication of a lifelong Boston Red Sox fan. The professional staff at Brunner-Routledge was helpful at every turn in responding to the myriad details involved in publishing a book. It was a pleasure to work with Tim Julet, former Acquisitions Editor; Emily Epstein, Associate Editor; and Hope Breeman, Production Editor. I would also like to express my gratitude to the reviewers of my book. In particular, Thomas J. Sweeney, Jane E. Myers, Jon Carlson, and Rebecca LaFountain provided thoughtful insights. My graduate assistants, Amy Ploof-LaPage, Angela Kotz, and Arlene Dudley, were helpful in many ways and I thank them. Finally, I appreciate the assistance of Bonnie Enslow, University Senior Secretary, for her typing and logistical support.

ON A SUMMER EVENING 20 YEARS AGO, I WAS ENJOYING THE COMPANY OF my parents on the porch of our family home. Our conversation turned to memories of my younger days as a child, and it brought to mind a personality assessment instrument, early recollections, that I had recently begun using in my counseling practice. It was an ideal time for me to try out the projective technique with my parents, and I first asked my mother to try to recall one of her earliest childhood memories. My mother, who grew up in South Boston, Massachusetts, said, "I remember helping my mother hang out the laundry on a clothesline stretching from the window of our three-decker house to the corner of the house next door. We pulled on the line together to get it to move so that we could pin each piece of clothing, one after the other. It felt good to be able to help." Immediately, I was struck by how the memory captured the essential quality of my mother's positive outlook on life. In growing up, I recall her working hard with a family of six children, but she always seemed to be content. Her favorite saying as she went about completing household chores or doing whatever seemed necessary to care for the people she loved was, "There, now that's a little bit better."

In the years that have passed since asking my parents about their early recollections, I have elicited and interpreted a multitude of childhood memories from a diverse population of clients during my extensive experience as a counselor and psychologist in school and clinical positions. Initially, I used early memories only as a means to enhance the counseling relationship by building rapport, but with further experience, I began to employ the approach as a projective technique to understand client functioning and to integrate particular inferences in the counseling process. With rare exceptions, I found that persons openly narrate their first remembrances with a keen sense of interest and engagement. Through a relatively brief appraisal procedure, I learned that it is possible to illuminate ingrained convictions that individuals maintain about significant facets of life. In recent years, I have made numerous presentations on the function and application of early childhood memories in counseling through my work with graduate students and with practitioners in the field. I have also had an opportunity to reflect on early recollections in the course of my writings on the topic and related issues and through an examination of my own first memories (Clark, 1994a, 1995b, 1998a, 1999a, 1999b, 2000, 2001).

Although I found early recollections indispensable in my therapeutic work with clients, I also became aware that relatively few counselors and psy-

XIV   EARLY RECOLLECTIONS

chotherapists actually use the device in individual assessment. I was perplexed and disappointed that a method that seems so incisive in terms of capturing the personality dynamics of individuals, and economical in terms of time efficiency, was apparently so minimally employed (Piotrowski, Sherry, & Keller, 1985). Through my continuing research, I began to recognize several prominent factors that appear to have limited greater professional use of early recollections as a projective technique. Significantly, many individuals primarily associate childhood memories with a classic psychoanalytic orientation. A model postulating that manifest memories frequently conceal perceptions of infantile sexual experiences may not be of particular interest to a broad range of practitioners and possibly restricts their exploration of the topic. Further, organized training opportunities in early recollections and projective techniques in general are limited for students in advanced higher education courses and for practitioners in continuing education programs. Finally, and perhaps most importantly, there is a lack of a coherent and practical publication that enables individuals to understand and integrate early recollections in counseling and psychotherapy.

Unlike other more highly recognized projective techniques—such as the Rorschach, Thematic Apperception Test, and human figure drawings—that are described in detail in multiple texts, there is no book-length volume in print focusing specifically on the systematic interpretation and application of early recollections as a projective technique in the therapeutic process. A number of years ago, Olson (1979a) edited a volume of a collection of papers that provided an annotated bibliography and broad coverage on a variety of topics relating to early recollection use in diagnosis and psychotherapy. In a more recent work, Bruhn (1990b), who has written extensively and discernibly on the subject of early memories, published a book describing an interpretive system based on a cognitive-perceptual theory of personality. Unfortunately, a second planned volume focusing on a review of the research of early memories and illustrations of autobiographical memories in the psychotherapy process was never published.

The interest in early childhood recollections has been broad and enduring as is demonstrated by the vast number of relevant theoretical and research investigations published for more than a century. Reichlin and Niederehe (1980) provided an inclusive bibliography relating to early memories since the initial publication on the topic in 1893. The present volume further expands and updates titles in a comprehensive review of the literature on early childhood memories. With the ascendance and prominence of cognitive theory over the past three decades, writings on early recollections have further escalated, particularly from an Adlerian perspective (Watkins, 1992a, 1992b; Watkins & Guarnaccia, 1999). Bibliographic entries in the current

text number approximately 350 investigations in the literature directly relating to early recollections, early memories, or autobiographical memories.
Autobiographical memory involves specific personal and enduring memories
that are usually significant to the self-system of an individual (Nelson, 1993).
Additional sources contribute to an understanding of the theoretical and
practice implications of early recollections in the counseling process.

This book constitutes a systematic effort to integrate the substantial body
of research material on early recollections as a projective technique within a
contemporary treatment framework of counseling and psychotherapy. The
text is organized in three parts: (1) Introduction of Early Recollections
Theory and Research, (2) Scoring Approaches, Administration, and Interpretation, and (3) Applications in Counseling and Psychotherapy. After the
introduction, Part I continues with a focus on the formative literature on
childhood memories involving the salient perspectives of Adler and Freud.
Other topics in this section include taxonomic considerations, personality
dimensions, and diagnostic impressions. Part II articulates diverse methodological procedures in eliciting and interpreting early recollections. Various
scoring and interpretive systems are also reviewed that contribute to a synthesizing framework and practical assessment guidelines. Part III concerns
the functional role of early recollections in the counseling process in working
with clients in a contextural and developmental model. A contextural model
emphasizes integrating conclusions from client assessment procedures into a
coherent whole. A three-stage conceptualization of the counseling experience
integrates humanistic, psychodynamic, and cognitive-behavioral orientations
in the service of client development. In addition to pertinent therapeutic issues in the application of early recollections, discussion also focuses on the
creative and wide-ranging use of first memories beyond traditional assessment procedures. This section of the book concludes with a chapter-length
case study integrating theory and practice.

Both Sigmund Freud and Alfred Adler initiated pioneering investigations
into the psychological significance of early childhood memories that have resulted in clearly different points of view and practice implications (Ansbacher, 1947; Last, 1997). Although Freud's theoretical perspectives
contribute to a comprehensive and dynamic formulation of early memories
in a psychoanalytic treatment approach, it is Adler's theory of Individual Psychology that represents the central focus in understanding early recollections
as a projective technique within the counseling process. At the same time,
the therapeutic use of early recollections in counseling and psychotherapy is
applicable to practitioners from a broad range of theoretical approaches beyond Individual Psychology. Accordingly, this book is written for direct service professionals including counselors, psychologists, social workers, and

psychotherapists. In academic settings, the text would augment courses in evaluation and appraisal techniques, counseling and psychotherapy, and the counseling practicum and internship.

1 EARLY RECOLLECTIONS

INTRODUCTION, THEORETICAL PERSPECTIVES, AND RESEARCH

Introduction of Early Recollections

"Our earliest childhood memories have a magical quality
about them, if for no other reason than their being the
apparent beginnings of our conscious lives."
            —Patrick Huyghe (1985, p. 48)

INTRODUCTION

IN RESPONSE TO A COUNSELOR'S REQUEST TO RECALL ONE OF HIS EARLIEST
memories, a 23-year-old client states, "I remember my mother picking up
my clothes that I had pulled out of my dresser and thrown all over my room.
She put them all away while I watched. It felt good that I didn't have to do it
myself." This reminiscence supports the counselor's initial inference or impression relating to the client's lack of accountability for his behavior. As
counseling progresses, the therapist empathizes with the individual's desire
for others to be in his service and to rectify his misbehavior. An understanding of the client's conceptualization of life contributes to a guiding
structure for formulating specific interventions in the counseling process. In
time, the client's assumption of increased responsibility becomes a mutual
and central therapeutic goal. This brief scenario highlights both the strengths
and limitations of early recollections as a projective technique in counseling
and psychotherapy. In a positive direction, early recollections offer a potential for fostering the counseling relationship in the context of integrating the
technique in the counseling process. The disguised quality of the instrument
also minimizes response distortion while enabling the counselor to understand ingrained convictions of an individual. Yet, despite the apparent therapeutic strengths of the device, questionable psychometric and methodological
properties continue to cast doubt on the viability of the use of early memories for personality assessment among practitioners (Anastasi & Urbina,
1997). As with most projective techniques, early recollections lack adequate
normative data, and there is an absence of consensus on a particular interpretation approach (Rabin, 1986). In practice, early memories tend to be subjectively scored, and the accuracy of findings rests on the clinical
sophistication and experience of the examiner.

In response to skepticism proceeding from inadequate norms and methodological limitations, however, it is possible to view early recollections as a functional counseling tool that is germane to a comprehensive personality assessment (Clark, 1994a, 1995c, 1998a, 2001). In this regard, the counselor may generate tenable hypotheses based on early memory inferences that are subject to verification and augmentation with further information from various sources (Anastasi & Urbina, 1997). In this volume, perspectives from subjective, interpersonal, and objective data (Rogers, 1964) provide broad-based support for a practitioner's contextual interpretation of early recollections into a coherent whole. Employing early recollections with corroborating information—such as other projective techniques, objective tests, behavioral observations, reports from a parent, teacher, or spouse, and dream material—enables practitioners to critically seek consistency and order from multiple perspectives (Faidely & Leitner, 1993; Goldman, 1990). The process of assembling conclusions from comprehensive procedures represents a contextual assessment model.

ADVANTAGES OF EARLY RECOLLECTIONS IN COUNSELING AND PSYCHOTHERAPY

COUNSELING RELATIONSHIP

As a relatively nonthreatening and open-ended procedure, early recollections of childhood almost invariably enhance the therapeutic alliance. Eliciting several early memories tends to involve clients in an intrinsically interesting and engrossing task. In what appears to be a mere recounting of objective and fairly innocuous material, individuals typically become absorbed in narrating their early childhood memories (Janoe & Janoe, 1979; Korner, 1965). Consequently, client defensiveness frequently diminishes through the participatory and unintrusive nature of the inquiry, which assumes no right or wrong answers. Resistant clients, children, and other persons may be uncomfortable with spontaneous verbal disclosure, and the structured procedure of eliciting early recollections serves as an intermediate counseling activity (Clark, 1994a, 1995c, 1998a). Significantly, the counselor may empathize with clients' feelings and perceptions evoked by narrating early memories, and this nonjudgmental response engenders rapport and trust. Recalling early memories may also be an appealing and manageable task for clients who experience difficulty with assessment procedures requiring specific skill levels in reading or other developmental functions. Further, many clients representing non-Anglo cultures respond more positively to mental health services offered on an informal and personal basis. The interactive quality of early recollections allows for a therapeutic exchange that can be sensitive to the task orientation and cultural frameworks of individuals from diverse backgrounds (Dana, 1995, 2000; Ivey, D'Andrea, Ivey, & Simek-Morgan, 2002).

COUNSELING INTEGRATION

As with other projective techniques, early recollections may be integrated into the counseling process without clients perceiving the procedure as an interruption (Hood & Johnson, 2002; Pepinsky, 1947). There is an intimate connection between assessment and counseling, as the focus of early memories is closely related to the immediate experiencing of individuals (Goldman, 1990; Watkins, 2000). The collaborative effort of clients speaking with a freedom of expression and the therapist empathically listening and making written notations models effective counseling, particularly in the initial relationship-building stage. Thus, the interaction of eliciting and reporting of early recollections does not interfere with the continuity of the therapeutic experience (Mosak, 1958). It is likely to be understandable to clients that the role of the counselor is to inquire about their past, and the procedure is therefore a "natural bridge" to the areas of social history and childhood background for discussion at a later point (Mosak, 1958). Requesting a reasonable number of reminiscences, perhaps three, maintains client interest and involvement within a relatively brief time allocation. Practitioners may also employ other types of projective and objective test procedures that are compatible with early recollections in order to develop more comprehensive perspectives of individuals (Clark, 1995c, 1998a; Watkins, Campbell, Hollifield, & Duckworth, 1989).

RESPONSE DISTORTION

With infrequent exceptions, individuals are willing to express their early remembrances in an open and uninhibited manner, as they are usually unaware of the possible hidden meanings and implications inherent in their disclosures (Adler, 1931/1958). Although early memories are consciously acknowledged and expressed, their purpose and orientation primarily involve covert or unconscious aspects of personality functioning. Consequently, a client is less likely to strive to offer socially acceptable responses and attempt to manipulate memory renderings to fit a predetermined self-image (Eckstein, Baruth, & Mahrer, 1982; Levy, 1965). The relatively unstructured and ambiguous nature of the task makes faking and distorting results difficult given the virtually unlimited variety of possible responses. In contrast, self-report scales tend to evoke defensive answers to particular transparent questions and produce a facade of mental health for a sizeable group of distressed individuals (Shedler, Mayman, & Manis, 1993). Unlike some other projective techniques, such as the Rorschach and Thematic Apperception Test, the lack of structured visual stimuli of early recollections does not raise the issue of the client's familiarity with stimulus cards (Lord, 1971). Additionally, considering the unique nature and minimal language requirements of the early memories, the projective technique may provide a relatively sensitive instrument for assessing personality functioning of individuals from diverse cultural backgrounds (Lord, 1971; Wohl, 1989).

CLIENT UNDERSTANDING

Saul, Snyder, and Sheppard (1956) observed that the first memories of life are absolutely specific and distinctive, and probably reveal the core of each person's psychodynamics more clearly than any other psychological datum. Out of innumerable incidents in childhood, individuals tend to recall a small number of memories consistent with their long-held beliefs about life or schemas of apperception (Adler, 1937b). From countless early experiences, persons create private worlds of meaning through the construction of enduring basic personality structures (Adcock & Ross, 1983; Bruhn, 1990a; McNamee, 1996). Such core convictions are largely influenced by the perceptions of individuals in diverse social or interpersonal contexts. From an appraisal perspective, the relatively coherent meaning structures constitute a theoretical schema model (Singer & Salovey, 1991). Distinctive client perspectives of self, the world, and life may be organized through a schema-based framework, and in this regard, early recollective data present a global or composite view of personality rather than a measurement of specific traits (Bruhn, 1990a). A schema conceptualization closely relates to Adler's lifestyle construct, and construing client meaning and subjective functioning is prominent in a range of contemporary theories of counseling and psychotherapy (Capuzzi & Gross, 1999; Corsini & Wedding, 2000). It is also in the context of a comprehensive evaluation involving multiple dimensions of functioning that early recollections contribute to clarifying client understanding.

THERAPEUTIC PROGRESS

Although a contextural assessment of early recollections is somewhat complex and time-consuming, an understanding of enduring client perspectives may actually enhance sound therapeutic planning and ultimately accelerate the counseling process. Clarifying significant issues early in therapy enables the counselor to focus on material that might otherwise take several sessions or more to uncover (Binder & Smokler, 1980; Lieberman, 1957). It is also possible for the counselor to foresee potential concerns relating to client resistance, transference, and interpersonal conflicts. The quality of the relationship with either a male or female therapist, for example, may be predicted, and this factor may be significant for the development of the working alliance (Mosak, 1965). The counselor is also in a position to rapidly determine initial hypotheses about clients in order to provide a therapeutic focus that is open to corroboration or modification as counseling progresses. The global quality of early recollections may also serve as a unifying framework for other projective techniques and assessment data from various sources. Finally, although it is not a direct therapeutic benefit, the cost of early recollections as an appraisal instrument is negligible in terms of material expenditures.

COUNSELING PROCESS

Beyond treatment planning, early recollections in a contextural and developmental model potentially contribute to strategic considerations throughout the therapeutic experience. In a three-stage conceptual process, the initial period focuses on establishing a supportive counseling relationship and clarifying client understanding. Early recollections are integral as a basis for knowing an individual and empathically responding through pertinent counselor strategies and interventions. In the middle stage of counseling, through collaborative participation with a therapist, clients are in a position to examine and modify core convictions that relate to early recollection perspectives. In conjunction with the core level of client functioning, an intermediate level or a "protective-belt" response to threat is vital to consider in counseling (Liotti, 1987). Specifically, defense mechanisms (Clark, 1991, 1998a) and safeguarding tendencies (Clark, 1999a, 2000) become manifest as a means of warding off threat and conflict relating to ingrained beliefs and maintaining psychological equilibrium. At both levels of response, a prominent counseling emphasis is to challenge clients to reduce self-deception and construct new meanings and perspectives. In the final stage of counseling, as a consequence of the emergence of more purposeful core schemas and reactions to threat, clients assume a readiness to instrumentally act in more adaptive ways. In an evolving assessment, selected components of contemporary theories of counseling and psychotherapy provide a theoretical and functional basis for client change and development.

DISADVANTAGES OF EARLY RECOLLECTIONS IN COUNSELING AND PSYCHOTHERAPY

PSYCHOMETRIC PROPERTIES

The elicitation of open-ended and wide-ranging early childhood reminiscences often captures the subjective functioning of clients in the counseling experience (Taylor, 1975). In a less favorable direction, however, the individu-

alistic nature of early memories reduces the possibility of devising a more psychometrically precise appraisal instrument. As with most projective techniques, early recollection methodology lacks adequate standardization and
clear procedural guidelines for both administration and scoring (Anastasi &
Urbina, 1997; Rabin, 1981). Practitioners typically interpret early memories
without the benefit of a structured and coherent scoring system, and consequently, problems of subjectivity and nonreplicable procedures appear to be
inherent weaknesses in regard to this approach (Nikelly & Verger, 1971). Individuals who prefer clearly established statistical standards and normative
data will likely be adverse to an evaluation method that essentially rests on the
varying accuracy of clinical opinion. In spite of endorsements from reputable
sources (e.g., "It is truly an X ray into the human mind," Manaster & Corsini,
1982, p. 188), other scientist–practitioners are skeptical and tentative about
meanings in test interpretation that are not supported through verification in
the empirical literature (Allison, Lichtenberg, & Goodyear, 1999). Equally serious is the possibility that practitioners with inadequate training and experience in interpreting early recollections may misuse the technique with clients
in the absence of explicit and systematic early memories appraisal guidelines.

INTERPRETIVE APPROACHES

Alfred Adler's routine elicitation of an individual's early memories in the treatment process is recognized as the first procedural use of the approach as a projective technique designed to illuminate enduring personality trends
(Munroe, 1955). Adler (1920/1968, 1927, 1929, 1931/1958, 1933/1964,
1937b, 1947) described the therapeutic application of early recollections from
an ideographic perspective through numerous illustrative case studies and the
presentation of informal guidelines. Since Adler's original formulations, researchers have attempted to devise scoring approaches that systematically evaluate early memories from Adlerian, psychoanalytic, and cognitive-perceptual
memory theoretical frameworks (Bruhn, 1990b; Langs, Rothenberg,
Fishman, & Reiser, 1960; Levy & Grigg, 1962; Manaster & Perryman, 1974;
Mayman, 1968). None of the procedures, however, has been validated statistically using normative data, and the coding methods tend to be criticized for
either insufficient comprehensiveness or excessive length and cumbersome-
ness (Rabin, 1986). Although there is a lack of consensus on a scoring and interpretive system, the Manaster–Perryman (1974) procedure has generated
the most research interest as an early recollection appraisal approach.

PRACTICE EMPHASIS

As with other projective techniques, early recollection assessment with individuals requires training and experience to develop a sufficient degree of ex-

aminer competency. Training, however, is limited at the master's degree level, and among counseling program directors surveyed (Piotrowski & Keller, 1984), a clear majority reported that they did not offer courses in projective techniques within their curriculum. In a national survey of counseling psychologists, respondents ranked several projective techniques among the top 10 appraisal instruments in frequency of use, but early recollections was not listed in this group. In a related survey of members of the Society for Personality Assessment, Piotrowski, Sherry, and Keller (1985) found that less than four percent of the Society members even occasionally employed early memories as a part of their psychological assessment of individuals. Although a lack of training opportunities with projective techniques and infrequent use of early recollections among practitioners is not a weakness of the device per se, both conditions restrict its general acceptance as an assessment instrument in instructional and practice contexts. Table 1.1 presents a summary of the advantages and disadvantages of early recollections in counseling and psychotherapy.

TABLE I.I: ADVANTAGES AND DISADVANTAGES OF EARLY RECOLLECTIONS
IN COUNSELING AND PSYCHOTHERAPY

Advantages

1. Promotes the counseling relationship
2. Contiguous with the counseling process
3. Minimal intentional client response distortion
4. Enhances client understanding
5. Accelerates treatment planning and interventions
6. Contributes to strategic therapeutic considerations

Disadvantages

1. Questionable psychometric properties
2. Lack of consensus on an interpretive system
3. Limited use and training opportunities

EARLY RECOLLECTIONS IN A CONTEXTURAL AND DEVELOPMENTAL MODEL

HYPOTHESES DEVELOPMENT

In order to address the debatable value of early recollections as a projective technique in counseling and psychotherapy, it is advantageous to view the procedure as a counseling tool that generates hypotheses for subsequent verification (Anastasi & Urbina, 1997; Clark, 1995c). In reference to projective techniques, this approach is endorsed in the 1985 edition of the *Standards for Educational and Psychological Testing* as one of the methods that "yields multiple hypotheses regarding the behavior of the subject in various situations as they arise, with each hypothesis modifiable on the basis of further information" (American Educational Research Association, American Psychological Association, & National Council on Measurement in Education, 1985, p. 45). After interpreting early memories and integrating findings with other relevant resources, a therapist is in a position to formulate client hypotheses that serve as a coherent framework and stimulus for therapeutic intervention and development. Through the construction of a schematic of a client's functioning or a working "model of a person," the counselor is able to call upon tentative conclusions that inform practice in each stage of the counseling process (Pepinsky & Pepinsky, 1954; Watkins, 2000). Thus, counseling decisions are not exclusively based on early memories, but the data provides an organizing structure in a contextural assessment that is open to refinement or revision.

ASSESSMENT INTEGRATION

Pepinsky and Pepinsky (1954) proposed a sequential method of counseling involving observation, inference, and hypotheses testing in interactions with clients. Elaborating on the Pepinskys' classic approach, Spengler, Strohmer, Dixon, and Shivy (1995) emphasized critical thinking and multiple methods of hypotheses testing that reflect contemporary views on the influence process of counseling (Claiborn & Hanson, 1999). Extending the classic and influence process, in the contextural model of this book, data from early recollections contributes to the formulation of an overarching framework for synthesizing various hypotheses through a schematic client conceptualization. In addition to the traditional information-generating focus of testing, contextural assessment also facilitates the development of more purposeful client self-schemas through the counseling process (Finn & Tonsager, 1997). From the perspective of Individual Psychology, the lifestyle syllogism depicts convictions or schemas that an individual maintains about oneself, the world (people and events), and conclusions about life (Manaster & Corsini, 1982). Carl Rogers (1964) conceptualized another framework that also contributes to organizing client data and constructing a rubric of a lifestyle syllogism. Through three ways of knowing involving subjective, interpersonal, and objective perspectives, the counselor is in a position to direct his or her capacity for empathy to comprehensively understand individuals on the basis of multiple points of view.

COUNSELING PROCESS

In a productive therapeutic counseling experience, clients often examine and modify assumptions about themselves and develop alternative ways of construing their relationships to people and experiences (McNamee, 1996; Spengler et al., 1995). Generating a model of a person in the initial period of counseling enables the counselor to influence clients in constructing more purposeful schemas in subsequent stages of the therapeutic process. As individuals begin to internalize more constructive perspectives, they frequently assume a readiness to act in ways that are increasingly adaptive. Contemporary research focuses on the ability of counselors to conceptualize models of clients and their concerns, which, in turn, serve as guides to strategic interventions in progressive stages of counseling (Jones & Lyddon, 1997; Morran, Kurpius, Brack, & Rozecki, 1994). In a study involving graduate counseling students, Morran et al. (1994) found that counselors who were able to formulate multidimensional and comprehensive conceptualizations of clients were viewed as more effective during sessions by stimulating individuals to disclose in greater depth. Additionally, integrating data from various sources often reveals inconsistencies in client functioning, which become appropriate for challenge and confrontation at a subsequent time in counseling (Pepinsky & Pepinsky, 1954). A three-stage sequence of the counseling process also provides a conceptual framework for employing intentional therapist interventions and evaluating client change and development (Clark, 1998a; Ivey & Ivey, 1999; Patterson & Welfel, 2000).

PRACTICE IMPLICATIONS

In order to suggest viable training and application directions for early recollections, it is necessary to make explicit assumptions relating to the function and value of the procedure in the context of appraisal in the counseling process. Hayes, Nelson, and Jarrett (1987) introduced the phrase "the treatment utility of assessment" to refer to the contribution that assessment makes to beneficial and functional outcomes in counseling and psychotherapy. Conceptually, aspects of treatment utility involve assessment devices, theoretical distinctions, and treatment approaches (Hayes et al., 1987), and each particular component has direct relevance to the therapeutic application of early recollections. As an appraisal device, early memories can serve as a linchpin for organizing and integrating multidimensional client data from various sources. Theoretical distinctions of early recollections emphasize the construction of meaning structures specific to Individual Psychology, cognitive therapies, and other schema-based modalities. Treatment approaches for early recollections encompass a sequential stage process involving client development through contemporary interventions from diverse psychotherapies. Thus, for practice purposes, early memories appraisal involves a contextural assessment and developmental client model emphasizing treatment utility throughout the counseling process. Although this conceptualization is distinct from procedures that tend to separate assessment from treatment, the approach represents emerging integrative trends in counseling and psychotherapy. Table 1.2 provides a summary of the Early Recollections Contextural and Development Model. In the next section, a case example with an adolescent client will illustrate the assessment process and its treatment function in promoting individual development.

TABLE 1.2: EARLY RECOLLECTIONS CONTEXTURAL AND DEVELOPMENTAL MODEL

1. Generates client hypotheses as a counseling tool.
2. Contributes to the formulation of schematic client conceptualizations.
3. Provides an integrative framework for organizing multiple sources of client data.
4. Functions as a guide for utilizing various therapeutic interventions in the counseling process.
5. Facilitates the development of more purposeful client schemas through a model of a person.

EARLY RECOLLECTIONS IN A CASE ILLUSTRATION

Early one morning, I received an unsettling telephone call in my position as a counselor in a program for at-risk adolescents. An unidentified person warned me that it was "a waste of time" for me to see Crystal Lynn, a student in the school program, for counseling because she was a "worthless person." Although I had not yet begun to meet with Crystal, I had heard about her a few days before in a staff meeting. Her educational record reflected a pattern of disciplinary infractions, truancy, and suspensions. Results from standardized testing indicated that Crystal's intelligence functioning was in the average range, with below average academic achievement. She had also been referred by the courts for shoplifting, running away from home, and extensive marijuana use. Based on several evaluative measures, Crystal's behavior was summarized in a psychological report as "impulsive, immature, and lacking assumption of responsibility." The report on Crystal concluded with a diagnostic impression with an onset in adolescence: Conduct Disorder (American Psychiatric Association, 2000, *Diagnostic and Statistical Manual of*

Mental Disorders–Text Revision, 4th ed.). The final piece of background information made available to me was that Crystal lived with her mother, Mrs. Lynn, and her mother's boyfriend. The staff meeting concluded with a recommendation that Crystal should meet with me on a weekly basis for individual counseling.

Prior to my first session with Crystal, I reviewed the appraisal material from the staffing. It was intriguing to me that in all the varied data on Crystal, there was not a single reference relating to her capabilities. My hope was that I would be able to build upon Crystal's strengths by emphasizing an encouraging approach through the counseling process. I did not have long to ponder my observation, though, because Crystal promptly appeared at my office door. She wore a full-length multicolored dress and began throwing a few small balls in the air. In a dismissive tone, Crystal stated that she did not have any reason to meet with me and preferred to go back to her classroom where she could practice juggling. I informed her that she was required to see me and that returning to her class was not an immediate option. With that, Crystal began to roll the balls across my desk and asked me if I wanted to play a game. At this point, I recalled both the "wasting my time" warning and the omission of any redemptive qualities of Crystal from the reported data, and thought that sometimes there is a justification for certain perspectives, however unprofessional.

Instead of succumbing to such thinking, however, I instead attempted to empathize with Crystal by reflecting her feelings:

AC: I guess it's a relief for you to play with those balls.
CL: Hey, there's nothing wrong with having a little fun.
AC: It would be a little more enjoyable if I joined you in your game.
CL: Yeah. You look like you could use a little loosening up.

Our discussion went on this way for a few minutes until I decided to use reflection of meaning:

AC: When I said that it was time to put the balls away, you appeared uncertain about what to do.
CL: Well, I'm getting a little tired of these things, and I think that maybe I've had enough.
AC: It's important for you to be able to make up your own mind about things.
CL: I hate it when people tell me what to do because that takes all the fun out of it.

I asked Crystal to expand on her last statement, but instead she went back to playing with the balls. Crystal only became involved in discussion once again when we focused on the topic of her interests and their relation to artwork. Our session concluded as Crystal described several pottery items that she recently had completed.

Our second session began when Crystal appeared holding a purple vase. After briefly describing how she made the piece, Crystal began putting small beads into the jar. As in our initial meeting, I acknowledged her feelings relating to her determination to choose what to do. This did not seem to deter Crystal from dropping more beads in the vase. After a few minutes of talking about her artwork, I wished to begin the projective assessments and thought that asking Crystal to complete a human figure drawing would appeal to her artistic interests. As I expected, Crystal eagerly began to draw. After drawing a small figure and scribbling around the body, Crystal abruptly dropped her pencil. Next, I requested that she complete a 25-item sentence completion task that I have used with clients for many years (Clark, 1998a). Crystal looked the sheet over and said that since the sentences were listed on only one side of the paper, she would work quickly and get it over with. Interestingly, Crystal took an above average amount of time to finish the procedure, and several of her responses were revealing of her personality dynamics. Crystal, who is 16 years old, completed the following sentence stems: "I regret . . . getting caught." "The happiest time . . . is when I'm with my boyfriend." "I failed . . . nothing." "School . . . is boring." "I need . . . excitement." "I wish . . . I could be little again."

After finishing the sentence completion tasks, I asked Crystal to provide an early recollection. She proceeded to relate a reminiscence with minimal hesitation in an appropriate response to my directions: "Think back to a long time ago when you were little and try to recall one of your earliest memories, one of the first things that you can remember." Crystal stated: "I was at a birthday party and there were a lot of kids running around. One of the boys threw ice cream at another kid and I laughed. It was so much fun." In response to my question about anything else that she could recall in the memory, Crystal mentioned the orange and blue balloons attached to the party chairs. Responding to another follow-up question, Crystal said that the boy throwing the ice cream stood out the most in the recollection. My last question related to Crystal's feelings regarding the most vivid part of the memory; her response was that she "felt excited." Crystal's next early recollection included a visualization of her mother: "I took some candy from a store and walked out. My mother told me that I shouldn't take the candy, but she was sort of smiling and didn't tell me to put it back." The most vivid part of the memory related to her mother's smiling, and at that point, Crystal felt "relieved and happy." Our counseling session concluded as Crystal shared her third early memory, which was much like the content of her initial recollection involving peers in a disruptive experience.

After Crystal left my office, I had time to look over her assessment materials and begin exploring their possible patterns of meaning. From my subjective frame of reference, I was able to empathize with Crystal by experiencing visual and sensual imaging of her early memories. As an overall impressionistic pattern, I sensed the excitement that she revels in while engaging in unrestricted experiences. She participates in situations involving misbehavior for which individuals experience minimal or no consequences for their actions. At the same time, I also felt uncomfortable with the disregard for self-restraint and responsibility in each of Crystal's early recollections.

From an interpersonal perspective, in terms of a way of knowing, I next attempted to develop further inferences from Crystal's first memories. I began by considering thematic variables and details in assessing Crystal's phenomenological experiencing. In an analysis of thematic possibilities, I employed a set of binary variables organized in a lifestyle syllogism format. As an example, the lifestyle rubric begins with "I am. . . ." This sentence stem may be completed with descriptors that appear to represent the client's self-perception or self-representation. For Crystal I chose the variables of defiant and independent. In Crystal's early memories, she found excitement by defying or rejecting convention. The rubric continues with "Others are. . . ." Other persons involved in her memories either participate in irresponsible acts or are ineffectual in limiting their occurrence. The next part of the syllogism focuses on "Events are. . . ." Events or experiences in Crystal's memories depict turbulent or unrestricted situations of inappropriate behavior. Another interpretive emphasis addresses memory details. Although there were only a few details in Crystal's early recollections, they generally seemed related to her pursuit of "fun" activities: food, candy, and party balloons. Crystal's mention of color in the balloons possibly reflects an appreciation of colors in her environment or in artistic interests. As I turned to a consideration of her early memories from an objective perspective relating to the literature on early recollections, I recognized a familiar trend of rule breaking without sanctions, which frequently occurs in populations demonstrating conduct disturbance and juvenile delinquency (Bruhn & Davidow, 1983; Davidow & Bruhn, 1990).

After reaching this point in the assessment process, I was able to construct schemas of Crystal's perceptions developed from the three ways of knowing: "I am . . . determined to act as I choose." "Other people . . . enable me to do what I wish." "Events are . . . exciting when they involve rule breaking." The methodological procedures for evaluating early recollections will be comprehensively reviewed in the next section of the book.

These assumptions regarding Crystal's core convictions are tentative and serve only as a point of reference as further appraisal data from the three ways of knowing are considered. In terms of an interpersonal perspective, Crystal's playful interactions in counseling and observations provided by her classroom teachers confirm her tendencies toward a disregard for rules and restrictions. In attempting to understand Crystal's phenomenological perceptions from material gleaned from other projective techniques, I thought that her sentence completion responses suggest an immature quality and possible use of denial. The rendering of a small human figure often relates to reduced self-esteem, and scribbling has an association with regressive behavior (Cummings, 1986). In a consideration of an objective way of knowing, results from the Millon Adolescent Clinical Inventory (Hood & Johnson, 2002) presented at the staffing indicated that Crystal showed scale elevations in social (histrionic) personality patterns, identity diffusion, academic noncompliance, and an impulsive propensity. Consistent with the diagnosis of conduct disorder from the *DSM–IV–TR* (2000), Crystal demonstrated a pattern of stealing without confronting a victim, use of illegal substances, and school suspensions. Finally, from a subjective perspective through my interactions with Crystal, I intuitively sensed that she had some ambivalence about rejecting responsibility and might be receptive to change. Is this, however, biased or wishful thinking, I wondered as I prepared for my next counseling session with Crystal?

As Crystal entered my office, I felt more prepared in terms of understanding her outlook on life as a result of the assessment process. Crystal stood by my door playing with a yo-yo, but she was having a difficult time negotiating the toy. Recognizing an opportunity for self-disclosure, I told her about the yo-yo contests that I entered as a young person. Crystal then asked me to demonstrate the use of the yo-yo, and I eagerly showed her several tricks. In this instance, I purposefully engaged Crystal's playful tendencies in the interest of developing an improved counseling relationship. After several minutes, Crystal asked me, "Why did you give up playing with the yo-yo when you seemed to enjoy it so much?" This provocative question led to a discussion of growing up and assuming new responsibilities, and it was a topic that we returned to at various points in counseling. Our discussion prompted Crystal to raise the subject of a dream that she had the previous night, which intrigued her. Realizing the reverie-like quality of dreams that relate to Crystal's lifestyle and their value in relationship building, I listened carefully as she reported her dream. In this initial period and in later stages of counseling, Crystal shared several of her dreams with me. We also began to focus on issues relating to school and peers, and despite Crystal's use of denial and her tendency to minimize her difficulties, she started to disclose on a more personal level.

After about six counseling sessions, although Crystal had developed more openness and trust, I knew that I had to assume a more challenging role in order to clarify her pattern of conflicted functioning. As an example, as we entered the middle or integration stage of counseling, Crystal stated that she did not wish to be dismissed from her school program due to excessive absences, yet she tended to deny the importance of regular attendance. In a supportive tone, I confronted Crystal in her expression of contradictory or inconsistent statements, and continued to do so in subsequent instances of her avoidant behavior. This intervention was an uneven process, as Crystal accused me of "taking all the fun out of things." Beyond clarifying Crystal's conflicted behavior, it was also necessary to begin to challenge her self-defeating belief system as she continued to express an apparent level of satisfaction in life with respect to her ability to avoid controlling influences and act in an impulsive way. My efforts to promote change were guided by cognitive restructuring procedures (Cormier & Cormier, 1998; Meichenbaum, 1977).

Perhaps through my pursuit of the possibility of schema change, or simply because Crystal was becoming tired of listening to me, she began to consider that life can be at least tolerable with certain restrictions and responsibilities. As counseling continued through our tenth session, Crystal seemed to grasp that, paradoxically, her potential for choice and freedom may actually increase by accepting limits on her behavior. Consideration of this reframing intervention was soon followed by Crystal's probing question, "Why do I always feel that I have to find excitement?" We explored the developmental aspects of her generalization by suggesting a possible relationship between feeling intensely alive and breaking rules or violating conventions. This interpretation (Clark, 1995a) led us back to generating change in Crystal's belief system toward alternative and more purposeful schemas.

As we approached the final or accomplishment stage of counseling, Crystal began to follow through on action-oriented techniques designed to assist her in consolidating perspective change and performing more purposeful instrumental actions. Crystal also worked on limiting her habitual denial of the need to accept limits and her tendency toward regressive functioning. In our final and sixteenth counseling session, she delighted me with a demonstration of her recently developed yo-yo skills. One of Crystal's last comments to me was, "I just wanted to show you that it's possible to have fun along with putting up with the discipline required to learn something."

SUMMARY

Early recollections present advantages and disadvantages as a projective technique in counseling and psychotherapy. Potentially, first memories enhance the therapeutic relationship between a client and practitioner while being integral to the continuity of the counseling process. In empathic interactions, early recollection assessment typically provides incisive client understandings with minimal intentional distortion of memory productions. The projective device often accelerates counseling progress and contributes to guiding purposeful intervention practices. In a less favorable direction, early childhood appraisals generally involve questionable psychometric qualities and the approach is limited in terms of the development of viable and comprehensive interpretive procedures. Another drawback relates to the infrequent use of the instrument among practitioners, which persists, in addition to limited training opportunities.

In order to address particular concerns about early recollections, while maintaining advantageous aspects of the assessment approach, the focus of this book emphasizes a contextural and developmental model. As a counseling tool, it is possible to formulate hypotheses in the construction of a schema that reflects an individual's unique outlook on life. This conception provides an overarching framework for synthesizing multi-element client data through three ways of knowing—subjective, interpersonal, and objective. The schema or "model of a person" also serves as a functional and evolving guide for strategic interventions and client development through three progressive stages of the counseling process. The treatment utility of early recollections in a systematic and integrative process also encompasses contemporary goals and practices in counseling and psychotherapy. A case study concludes the chapter by illustrating the integration of early recollections in the counseling experience with an adolescent demonstrating conduct issues.

2

THEORETICAL PERSPECTIVES OF EARLY MEMORIES

"Early recollections have especial significance. To begin
with, they show the style of life in its origins and in its sim-
plest expressions."
—Alfred Adler (1931/1958, p. 74)

"The indifferent memories of childhood owe their existence
to a process of displacement: they are substitutes, in
[mnemic] reproduction, for other impressions which are really significant."
—Sigmund Freud (1901/1960, p. 43)

INTRODUCTION

ALTHOUGH ADLER AND FREUD'S VIEWS OF EARLY CHILDHOOD MEMORIES
are not mutually exclusive, their perspectives emphasize clearly different psychological meanings and treatment practices. The selective quality and importance of early memories are prominent in the writings of both Freud and
Adler, and each agree that it is comparatively immaterial whether the remembrances correspond to historical fact or not (Ansbacher, 1947). Fundamental differences in their approaches to conceptualizing early memories do
exist, however, which ultimately result in divergent methods in their therapeutic applications. Freud felt that seemingly innocuous manifest memories
function as a screen for more emotionally charged and disturbing traumatic
experiences at a latent level (Mosak, 1958). By ascribing a screening quality
to early childhood memories, their interpretation through free association
and other depth-oriented techniques became integral to working through
conflicted material in Freud's psychoanalytic treatment approach (Kahana,
Weiland, Snyder, & Rosenbaum, 1953). In contrast, Adler believed that
manifest early recollections are never indifferent in treatment practice because they illuminate an individual's unique outlook on life. In recognizing
the profound effect of early recollections in understanding a person's lifestyle,
Adler's approach to discerning their meaning is comparatively unambiguous
within the assessment and therapeutic treatment process.

ALFRED ADLER'S PERSPECTIVES ON
EARLY MEMORIES

In a presentation to the Vienna Psychoanalytic Society in 1911, Adler commented on the significance of early recollections: "A person's true attitude toward life can be discerned from his earliest dreams and recollected experiences, proving that such memories are also constructed according to a planful procedure" (Ansbacher, 1973, pp. 135–136). This observation was a part of a longer address that marked Adler's formal separation from the Society, and recognizes the value of early dreams and recollections for clarifying fundamental life perspectives. During the same time period, in an article on sleep disturbances, Adler (1913) again mentioned dreams in connection with a series of early memories. In one of the paper's case studies, Adler discussed a physician who recalled from his early childhood several encounters with sickness and death, and the resultant deep impression of those memories. As later revealed, the physician in the case was Adler, and he subsequently wrote about the influence of the remembrances in his life and his career choice in particular (Adler, 1947). It is interesting to note that whereas Adler analyzed the projective function of his early childhood memories for self-understanding, Freud primarily devoted his attention to the interpretation of his own dreams. In each pursuit, the approaches became a central focus of their respective therapeutic orientations (Ansbacher, 1973).

From his perspective as an adult, Adler recalled a life-threatening case of pneumonia at the age of five: "A doctor, who had suddenly been called in, told my father that there was no point in going to the trouble of looking after me as there was no hope of my living. At once a frightful terror came over me" (Adler, 1947, pp. 10–11). Adler went on to state how a few days after the incident he became determined to become a physician in order to combat death and illness more successfully than the doctor who had treated him. Phyllis Bottome (1937/1957), a biographer of Adler, suggests that the memory reveals how terrified Adler felt when confronted with people who have lost hope or become pessimistic. Adler's quest to find solutions and improve such situations and to fully realize his capacities is also apparent in his reactions to his own first memories. Much of what Adler theorizes about the relevance of early recollections clearly proceeds from the impact of his personal memories recalled from childhood. The goal-directive and motivational quality of these remembrances combine to bring forth a vital focus. For Adler, first memories are purposeful and reflect a broad pattern of functioning consistent with one's perception of life (Kadis, Greene, & Freedman, 1952; Kadis & Lazarsfeld, 1948). The next section is designed to introduce basic conceptualizations of Adler that relate to early recollections and provide a fundamental understanding of Adlerian theory that is essential for effectively using the memories as a projective technique in counseling and psychotherapy.

ADLER'S BASIC CONCEPTUALIZATIONS

Adler referred to his theoretical orientation as "Individual Psychology," a term connoting the uniqueness, indivisibility, and intrinsic value of each human being. Adler viewed persons as self-determining and striving toward goals that provide a motivational direction to patterns of behavior. In this respect, individuals construct an enduring outlook on life in early childhood that is consistent with basic convictions toward themselves and the world. In his writings, Adler emphasized that persons seek to actualize their capacities as they strive for self-fulfillment and seek to dispel feelings of inferiority. In Adler's view, the measure of compassion, cooperation, and contribution that an individual expresses in relationship to others enhances mental health and meaning in life. There is also a continuity and unity to behavior that enables people to be understood in a holistic context. Adler thought that one's early environment is crucial in terms of its influence on psychological development and is integral to the manner in which a person interprets his or her situation in a family constellation and a cultural context. Individuals protect themselves from threat to their self-esteem, according to Adler, through evasive and maladaptive actions that conceal feelings of inferiority. Adler felt that early recollections illuminate the totality of an individual's functioning and are indispensable for understanding personality dynamics and patterns of behavior.

PURPOSE OF BEHAVIOR. Central to Adler's formulations is the goal-striving nature of individuals that provides an organizing and controlling function to all behaviors (Carlson & Sperry, 2000; Dowd & Kelly, 1980). Adler (1914a) wrote, "We cannot think, feel, will, or act without the perception of some goal" (p. 77). In order to more fully understand a person it is essential to grasp what he or she anticipates from a purposeful or teleological perspective. Adler's view in this respect is consistent with recognizing that the most fundamental general function of memory for an individual or any organism is to provide guidance for action in the present and in the future (Nelson, 1990). Although Adler also recognized and acknowledged causal influences in childhood, such as neglectful parental relationships, he primarily emphasized the capacity of persons to strive for goals in a subjective and self-determining manner. In this regard, Adler (1914b) stated, "We must remember that the most important question for the sound or diseased psyche to answer is not the where from? But whither?" (p. 13). Thus, Adler (1929/1969) felt that an individual's early recollections justify or validate current movement in a purposeful and emotionally stabilizing direction, rather than merely function as a reaction to events recalled. Postulating that there are no indifferent or nonsensical first remembrances, Adler pointed out the importance of evaluating the memories in the context of the life of the individual. In a counseling example, the chronic dependency demands of a middle adulthood client become more understandable with the perspective of an early childhood recollection in which the individual expresses relief and satisfaction while being dressed and taken care of by an older sister.

LIFESTYLE.   Perhaps the most well-known of Adler's conceptualizations, the lifestyle constitutes ingrained beliefs that individuals maintain about life that are consistent with early childhood memories (Gushurst, 1971; Manaster & Corsini, 1982; Thorne, 1975). Although the lifestyle is primarily an unconscious process, it serves as a master plan or cognitive blueprint by providing a direction for living life (Eckstein et al., 1982; Shulman, 1985). In terms of an outlook on life, each person constructs a "lens" for perceiving that is unique and self-consistent. Adler introduced the term "life style" in 1926, after using other designations earlier in his writings, including lifeline, line of movement, and life plan (Ansbacher, 1967; Ansbacher & Ansbacher, 1956). Adler felt that, after acquiring the lifestyle in early childhood through experiences of the first five years (1931/1958), the belief system then remains constant without an individual's insight into the self. Adler (1937b) stated that first recollections illuminate the origins of the lifestyle by suggesting invaluable hints about a person's goals, values, and cautions.

As a schema of apperception, early remembrances provide an axiomatic structure from which private meanings proceed (Powers & Griffith, 1987). With respect to an individual's lifestyle, there is a latitude for behavioral choice (Sweeney, 1998), but behaviors will always be consistent with fundamental beliefs. As an example, in therapy a late adulthood client diagnosed with an anxiety disorder describes an early recollection: "I remember crossing a busy street with my mother, when suddenly she let go of my hand. I was terribly frightened and I can't remember what happened next." In this instance, the person's current sense of anticipatory danger is apparent in her unwillingness to leave her room in an assisted living facility and is consistent with her core convictions formed decades earlier.

STRIVING FOR SUPERIORITY.   A central dynamic force in Adler's theory is the individual's constant striving for significance or superiority (Shulman, 1985). Seeking to actualize potentialities serves as a master motive for all individuals as they progress from one stage of life to the next (Manaster & Corsini, 1982; Mosak, 2000). Striving for higher levels of development is consistent with a fulfillment model of personality, as Adler expressed in his statement, "To live means to develop" (Ansbacher & Ansbacher, 1979, p. 31). In his early writings, Adler gave prominence to feelings of inferiority as a means for stimulating persons to overcome felt deficits through compensatory responses. In a more pathological direction, some individuals become overwhelmed with inferiority feelings, and this condition, referred to as an inferiority complex, largely hinders further emotional development. Although Adler subsequently continued to recognize the influence of inferiority feelings as a catalyst for personal growth, he placed primary emphasis on striving for superiority as a developmental stimulant (Carlson & Sperry, 2000; Ellenberger, 1970). Relatedly, the direction of individual development is psychologically healthy or maladaptive dependent on one's level of social interest or kinship with humanity (Ewen, 1998). In order to clarify this distinction, consider, for example, the individual who perceives life as means to give and receive affection and support. This person strives for goals that are primarily social and constructive. On the other hand, another individual's outlook on life and goal-striving is oriented to manipulating and taking advantage of others. Both persons maintain contrasting lifestyles, while striving for self-realization in different directions.

SOCIAL INTEREST. As a visible indication of community feeling, social interest becomes manifest through cooperation and emotional involvement identification with others (Ansbacher, 1992; Powers & Griffith, 1987). Adler gave particular attention to the importance of social interest for engendering a person's perceptions of self-worth, well-being, and meaning of life. As individuals strive to develop their potential, while advancing the welfare of others, they enhance their sense of purpose and meaning in life (Adler, 1927, 1931/1958). Participating as an active and contributing member of the human community promotes feelings of significance and realization that the person matters in a broader sense (LaFountain, 1996). According to Adler, as an individual focuses on others through self-transcendent interactions, his or her debilitative preoccupations and dysphoric feelings tend to diminish. Relatedly, the expression of social interest often mitigates feelings of inferiority and alienation, as persons expand their sense of belonging as a part of a whole (Adler, 1933/1964). In Adler's view, people have an innate potentiality or capacity for social interest that needs to be nurtured early in life in order to develop. A lack of social interest coincides with numerous psychological disorders representing the "useless side of life" (Adler, 1927). Adler recognized that largely through an early recollections appraisal it is possible to discover the lack or presence of social interest within the expression of the lifestyle of an individual. As an example, consider implications for human kinship in the first remembrances of two different persons. One individual relates: "I remember being at a birthday party with a bunch of other kids, and we were playing pin the tail on the donkey. When it was time, I took my turn and we all had a lot of fun." Another person recalls: "I was at a birthday party and we were playing pin the tail on the donkey. I hated it that I had to wait while other kids took their turns."

HOLISM.   An Adlerian assumption from a holistic perspective is that there is a unity and constancy of personality functioning (Dreikurs, 1967). In this regard, the thematic pattern of a person's behavior may be more accurately understood from a global rather than partial framework. In Adler's (1914a) view, dynamic psychological processes, including feeling, thinking, and acting, operate in concert and constitute an expression of an individual's unique and indivisible strivings. Persons exemplify this organismic consistency through their cognitive structures as well as expressions of their affective and overt behaviors (Slavik, 1991). As an example, consider counseling a late adolescent who demonstrates withdrawal and avoidant actions, and maintains an ingrained belief of "I am inadequate and worthless." This core conviction is evident in the individual's expressed statements of private logic—"I can't do anything right" and "Nobody will ever love me." To continue with the cited example, the client's early recollections also reflect a continuity and totality of behavior. The client states an early remembrance: "I was in the first grade and we were playing show and tell. I started to talk about a pet rock that my older brother had given me and everybody, including my teacher, started laughing at me. I felt so embarrassed and foolish." This memory, as with other early recollections, substantiates the unity of the personality (Plewa, 1935).

BIRTH ORDER.   For Adler, a child's order of birth in a family is significant because it reveals subjective perceptions relating to the individual's early environment (Adler, 1937a; Shulman, 1962). Adler (1929/1969), however, cautioned that predictions based on birth order are expressed in the form of tendencies, and "there is no necessity about them" (p. 92). In a family constellation there are five possible birth order positions: first, second, middle, youngest, and only child. Adler (1927, 1929/1969, 1931/1958,1937a) presented personality inferences relative to birth order, and various other pertinent sources are available on the topic (Forer, 1977; Manaster, 1977; Mosak, 2000; Shulman, 1962; Shulman & Mosak, 1977; Sulloway, 1996). Briefly, the oldest child learns the advantages of authority and seeks to maintain his or her perceived position of power and recognition. The first born often stimulates the second child to keep up with him or her. If this is not possible, that individual may rebel or withdraw. The middle child has a number of competitors, but also learns how to relate to others in terms of negotiating and cooperative functioning. The youngest child has many pacemakers and may develop extraordinary qualities in order to be noticed. Finally, the only child, who typically associates with adults more frequently, may be particularly affectionate and mature more quickly.

Numerous variations exist among birth order positions, such as the oldest child's perception of being dethroned by the next born and consequently feeling deprived and resentful. The validity of birth order inferences is debatable due to a relative lack of empirical evidence, and the minimal attention given to such areas as gender differences, blended families, and death and survivorship (Shulman & Mosak, 1977). In recent years, however, birth order has been given more credence among professionals and the general public as research on the subject expands (Mosak, 2000; Sulloway, 1996; Watkins & Guarnaccia, 1999). As an example, in a cross-cultural study involving college students and adults, Mullen (1994) reported a significant linear trend, with first borns having the earliest memories in terms of age followed by second, and third or later-born individuals. From a counseling perspective, a counselor may use birth order information as a basis for developing hypotheses about a client's lifestyle (Forer, 1977), and the use of early recollections can contribute to this effort. As an example, an adult client, who is a second-born child, recounts one of his earliest memories: "I was with my mother and father in the backyard of our house. They were teaching my older brother how to hit a ball with a bat. He started to hit the ball all by himself, and my parents got really excited. I felt ignored."

SAFEGUARDING TENDENCIES.   In order to forestall anticipated failure, individuals may conceal assumed deficiencies by evading responsibilities and problems. Adler (1912/1917, 1914b, 1929/1969, 1935) recognized this pattern of behavior as safeguarding tendencies that function to protect an individual's self-esteem from perceived threat. A contemporary definition of the construct involves a self-deceptive evasion that deters functioning in those experiences that evoke feelings of inferiority (Clark, 1999a, 2000). A person, for instance, repeatedly avoids making decisions because he or she dreads selecting what ultimately may prove to be the wrong choices. Individuals may also endure a range of suffering that tends to evoke sympathy and service from others, while retreating from the demands and responsibilities of life. Although Adler did not establish a systematic categorization of safeguarding tendencies, he does suggest four "movements" that either avoid, restrict, divert, or hinder active problem solving (Adler, 1935). It is possible in counseling, through the use of early recollections, to clarify the biased apperceptions in the lifestyle that a client attempts to obscure through safeguarding

tendencies. As an example, a middle adulthood individual relates the following early memory, which reflects a sense of shame: "I was in church and I
had to go to the bathroom. I desperately wanted to leave and I asked my
mother, but she said no. I went in my pants and everybody smelled it and
looked at me. I felt so humiliated and started to cry." Perhaps to avoid the
anticipation of failure and shame, the client has held the same menial job for
a number of years, while rejecting numerous opportunities for career ad-
vancement. Table 2.1 presents safeguarding tendencies categories with definitions (Clark, 2000).

TABLE 2.1: SAFEGUARDING TENDENCIES CATEGORIES WITH DEFINITIONS

Distancing Complex	Avoiding challenges and problems through disaffiliation from perceived obstacles, and expressing doubts and uncertainties that preclude the possibility of active problem solving.
Hesitating Attitude	Justifying restricted activity and involvement with problems due to various obstacles and misfortunes, and blaming others for hardships and impeding problem solutions.
Detouring Around	Diverting attention to less significant concerns, and expending an extraordinary amount of energy on matters of secondary importance in comparison to central problems and challenges.
Narrowed Path of Approach	Hindering the pursuit of prominent problems by not completing tasks, or making meager commitments to challenges outside of highly circumscribed or predictable endeavors.

ADLERIAN AND CONTEMPORARY PERSPECTIVES

Theoretical perspectives pertaining to schema theory, cognitive theory, and
social constructionism are prominent in contemporary literature and relate
to various aspects of Adler's conceptualizations. Schemas are meaning structures that organize and guide life experiences and are intrinsic to Adler's concept of lifestyle. Cognitive theory emphasizes individuals' belief systems that
broadly impact and influence their behavioral patterns. Social constructionism also relates to how persons construe meaning in particular life contexts, while emphasizing the prominent influence of interpersonal forces on
behavior.

SCHEMA THEORY.   In his writings, Adler (1929/1969, 1931/1958) referred
to a "schema of apperception," a term he related to the meaning individuals
attribute to their subjective perceptions. Introduced by Piaget (1929) as developmental constructions in infancy and childhood, schemas as structures

of the mind are widely known in cognitive and clinical sciences (Horowitz, 1991; Kelly, 1955/1991a, 1955/1991b; Slap & Saykin, 1983; Stein, 1992). In a classic text on memory, Bartlett (1932) observed that individuals actively create memory and construct schemas that serve a dynamic and instrumental function for organizing specific information. Bartlett's view is in essential agreement with Adler, as both theorists recognize that schemas represent knowledge or cognitive structures that provide a consistency to life experiences and that memory is not merely a reproduction of the past (Barclay, 1986; Purcell, 1952; Segal, 1988; Singer & Salovey, 1991). Containing conceptually similar or related material, schemas can function as a guideline or a cognitive map for organizing or interpreting incoming data (Marcus, 1980). From an Adlerian perspective, Manaster and Corsini (1982) conceptualized the lifestyle syllogism consisting of schemas of the self, the world, and life. The deeply established views are referred to as "private logic" (Manaster & Corsini, 1982; Sweeney, 1998). As an example of the lifestyle syllogism, a client diagnosed with a mood disorder maintains the following schemas or private logic: "I am worthless." "The world offers me no support or understanding." Therefore, "Life is intolerable." Another Adlerian term, "basic mistakes," refers to the specific content of the faulty or mistaken conclusions (Dreikurs, 1961; Manaster & Corsini, 1982).

COGNITIVE THEORY.   Similarities also exist between Adler's views and cognitive theory, which emphasizes cognitive structures relating to core beliefs (Beck, 1995; Safran, Vallis, Segal, & Shaw, 1986). In terms of a cognitive structural model, the core level of a person's functioning maintains unquestionable assumptions that serve to organize and guide behavior (Liotti, 1987). The cognitive model also conceptualizes an intermediate level that protects core beliefs and prevents a critical appraisal of assumptions that would potentially disrupt psychological equilibrium (Kelly, 1955/1991a, 1955/1991b; Liotti, 1987). This "protective-belt" at the intermediate position relates to safeguarding tendencies that provide a buffer to threat. In addition to core and intermediate functioning, a peripheral level in the system focuses on how individuals negotiate the demands of life through instrumental actions and problem solving (Liotti, 1987). This action-oriented conceptualization is similar to Adler's "degree of activity," which involves the persistence of effort and energy that individuals expend toward the pursuit of goals and meeting challenges of life (Adler, 1927; Mosak & Maniacci, 1999).

Considering the three operational levels in a counseling example, an early adulthood client repeatedly complains to a college counselor about students in his college dormitory. At the peripheral level, Jim insists that the school administration should investigate the "disgusting and wanton ways" of the student residents who are extremely messy and rarely sleep at night. In regard to the intermediate level, Jim claims that he is unable to concentrate and his grades are poor due to the constant distractions in his residence hall. The operation of safeguarding tendencies seems probable, because Jim totally dismisses the possibility of finding alternative sites in which to study. At the core level, Jim maintains an ingrained schema or private logic that he is incapable of succeeding on his own, yet others are not available for support. This schema or lifestyle perspective may be recognizable in one of Jim's early recollections: "When I was about six years old, I was at the beach with some of my relatives. When I came out of the water I was really cold and asked my aunt for a towel. She told me that I should have taken one from home, and then she just ignored me. I felt so cold and angry."

In regard to core beliefs, a central assumption is that the cognitive structure of an individual maintains a consistent degree of stability over an extended period of time (Horner, 1997). Consequently, if early recollections reflect a person's belief system, the memories should be relatively stable in terms of basic thematic material. Several investigators have considered this proposition by evaluating the early memories of groups of individuals. Hedvig (1963) designed a study to assess the stability of early recollections following the manipulation of the experimental conditions of success–failure and friendliness–hostility. Immediately preceding reporting early recollections and completing stories in response to the Thematic Apperception Test (TAT), college students were subjected to the experimental variables. Hedvig reported that the thematic content of the TAT was significantly influenced by the differing conditions of the study but not early recollections. The stable quality of the early memories, according to Hedvig, provides support for the instrument as a projective technique and for assessing personality characteristics of an enduring or trait nature. In a related study, Langs (1967) evaluated the stability of early recollections of underemployed male actors under LSD-25 and a placebo. After reporting a low stability of early memories after drug consumption, Langs concluded that his experimental instructions may have influenced findings to an unknown extent. Plutchik, Platman, and Fieve (1970) assessed the early recollections of a group of adult patients diagnosed with manic depression and a group of college students. The authors reported a relatively constant level of early recollections content and affect scores over an average period of seven weeks for both groups. Finally, Josselson (2000) conducted a longitudinal study of early memories with 24 female college students over a period of 22 years. After eliciting the individuals' remembrances at three chronological points (ages 21, 33, and 43), Josselson concluded that early recollections are largely stable, highly individual, and portray very subtle change over time.

SOCIAL CONSTRUCTIONISM.   Adler's viewpoints are also compatible with social constructionism, as both theoretical approaches recognize that human life takes place in and is most understandable in interpersonal and social contexts (Adler, 1927; Jones & Lyddon, 1997). Individuals actively create meaning in their personal existence, and a social relational engagement with others is inseparable from this experience (Faidley & Leitner, 1993; Mahoney, 2000; McNamee, 1996). In particular, Adler focused on the importance of social interest as a means for persons to find purpose and sense of well-being through sustained empathic interactions with others. Both perspectives also stress the developmental and cultural influences of early childhood experiences in shaping enduring aspects of behavior (Jones & Lyddon, 1997). An individual's subjective perceptions are also crucial for construing reality and evoking early recollections, which is a premise consistent with Adlerian and social constructionist positions. Various aspects of social constructionism are recognizable in the following early recollection of a late adulthood individual: "I was with my father in the chicken coop in our backyard, and we were feeding the chickens. I was little but he let me help out. When I threw the feed on the floor the chickens ran to it. It felt good to see the chickens eat because they were hungry."

IMPLICATIONS FOR COUNSELING AND PSYCHOTHERAPY

Challenging an individual's maladaptive lifestyle is a prominent transaction for Adler in his therapeutic process. As a treatment goal, Adler primarily focuses on fostering fundamental structural change in a client's dysfunctional belief system. In a contemporary framework, Adlerian counseling and psychotherapy emphasizes second-order change relating to the construction of new core level assumptions about the self and the world (Lyddon, 1990). In contrast to second-order change, first-order change typically involves immediate symptom relief and situational problem solving (Lyddon, 1990; Lyddon & Satterfield, 1994).

Adlerian therapy is also similar to cognitive behavior therapy models in terms of altering self-defeating thought patterns and stimulating new ways of behaving (Freeman & Urschel, 1997). As a human encounter, engendering trust and a sense of equality is crucial to the development of a therapeutic alliance. In this regard, the use of early recollections as an assessment tool enhances the counseling relationship through the counselor's empathic interactions with the client. The use of encouragement is also prominent, as the therapist recognizes a client's abilities, control, and effort in effecting personal change (Sweeney, 1998). Dreams are another frequent component of Adlerian therapy, particularly recurrent dreams that may relate to lifestyle functioning. Understanding the development of the individual in the con-

text of his or her family constellation is yet another primary treatment consideration. Numerous current works (i.e., Dinkmeyer & Sperry, 2000;
Mosak & Maniacci, 1999; Sperry & Carlson, 1996; Sweeney 1998; Watts &
Carlson, 1999) clarify and expand on Adler's conceptualizations and practices. In the third section of this book, additional sources will augment
Adlerian approaches relating to the use of early recollections in counseling
and psychotherapy.

SIGMUND FREUD'S PERSPECTIVES ON EARLY MEMORIES

In contrast with Adler's view that early childhood memories are revealing of
personality, Freud thought that early memories potentially conceal troubling
conflicts relating primarily to sexual abuse (Glover, 1929; Schachtel, 1947).
Freud (1901/1960) wrote, "It may very well be that forgetting of childhood
can supply us with the key to understanding of those amnesias which lie, according to our most recent discoveries, at the basis of formation of all neurotic symptoms" (pp. 46–47). Initially, Freud claimed that individuals may
experience early sexual trauma, but then he subsequently proposed a position
that the abuse is fantasy-based (Bowers & Farvolden 1996; Masson, 1984).
Freud (1901/1960) also conceptualized a "screen" function in which manifest and indifferent memories conceal significant latent memories from a
person's childhood (Chess, 1951; Katan, 1975). Relatedly, throughout his
decades of childhood memory investigations, Freud is generally constant in
his assertion of the determining and causal influence of early experiences on
later personality development (McCabe, Capron, & Peterson, 1991). Consequently, unlike Adler's position centering on early recollections as a projective technique, Freud provides an alternative view that has clinical utility in a
different context. Clarifying Freud's initial and subsequent extensions of his
psychoanalytic approach contributes to a broader perspective for understanding the projective quality of early memories.

TRAUMA THEORY

In *The Aetiology of Hysteria*, published in 1896, Freud proposed that previously forgotten memories of early childhood sexual abuse constitute primary
factors in the development of hysteria as well as other forms of neurosis and
psychological disorders (Bowers & Farvolden, 1996; Freud, 1896/1962;
Powell & Boer, 1994). Freud verified his trauma or seduction theory on the
accounts of some 18 patients who claimed to remember repressed scenes of
sexual trauma. For Freud the patients uniformly expressed specific details of
infantile scenes, which appeared to confirm the authenticity of the sexual en-

counters. In Freud's evolving views, he conceptualized "screen memories" as representing indifferent events concealing early impressions that are often sexual in nature (Freud, 1899/1962, 1901/1960). Although largely innocuous at the time of the occurrence of the incidents in early childhood, memories of the sexual experiences often produce damaging psychological effects in later life. Consequently, psychoanalytic treatment focuses on tracing a hysterical symptom through a thread of associations to the more significant sexual episodes (Freud, 1896/1962). It is anticipated that the patients will experience catharsis or an emotional reaction and alleviation of their symptoms after revealing their seductions during psychoanalytic treatment.

FANTASY-BASED THEORY

In 1905, in a major shift of opinion, Freud (1905/1953) recanted his trauma theory and adopted a fantasy-based theory of infantile sexual abuse. Freud

TABLE 2.2: ADLER'S AND FREUD'S PERSPECTIVES OF EARLY MEMORIES

FACTOR	ADLER	FREUD
1. Importance	Significant	Significant
2. Selective Quality	Prominent	Prominent
3. Corresponds to Historical Fact	Comparatively immaterial	Comparatively immaterial
4. Dynamic Aspect	Revealing of personality	Concealing of significant repressed events
5. Function	Goal-directive influence on personality	Determining influence on character formation
6. Manifest Memories	Illuminate outlook on life	Indifferent or innocuous
7. Latent Memories	Not distinguished	Source of perceived trauma, which is often sexual in nature
8. Screen Function	Not distinguished	Manifest memories obscure perceived trauma
9. Therapeutic Applications	Projective technique	Uncover perceived trauma
10. Interpretation Process	Comparatively unambiguous	Complex
11. Treatment Outcome	Understanding individuals and indicating therapy goals	Catharsis of traumatic memories
12. Primary Orientation	Teleological	Causation

found that in the treatment of his patients, the analysis of early childhood memories was not in itself curative, and he became aware of his own overestimation of the reality of traumatic events (Edwards, 1990). In a framework similar to his dream approach, Freud proposed that manifest memories obscure and distort fantasies of sexual abuse (Lehmann, 1966). The fantasies emanate from conflict-laden repressed incestuous desires in the early childhood period (Martin, 1959; Powell & Boer, 1994). The repression of significant latent memory content in the unconscious represents "infantile amnesia," and a concomitant defense system restricts threatening and anxiety-provoking material from breaking through to consciousness (Greenacre, 1949; Kennedy, 1950; Schachtel, 1947). In terms of therapeutic interventions, psychoanalytic treatment, emphasizing free association, dream interpretation, and processing transference patterns enable a patient's infantile conflicts to emerge through rigid defenses (Berdach & Bakan, 1967; Oberholzer, 1931; Simmel, 1925; Wolfman & Friedman, 1964). Table 2.2 presents a summary of Adler's and Freud's perspectives of early memories.

EXTENSIONS OF PSYCHOANALYTIC THEORY

Since the seminal work of Freud, psychoanalytic thought has retained an essential assumption relating to the importance of the past, via memory structures, for determining a person's pattern of behavior (Hadfield, 1928; Ivimey, 1950; Lewy & Rapaport, 1944; Tuch, 1999). At the same time, contemporary psychodynamic theory significantly broadens and expands on Freud's foundational positions, and it is interesting to observe the convergence of the views with those of Adler. Ego psychology emphasizes the value of both manifest and latent childhood memories, while recognizing the influence of social forces on a person's functioning. Object relations theory gives further prominence to the significance of interpersonal relationships in the formative development of a person's perceptual framework. Self psychology also attempts to understand and reconstruct a patient's representation of self and others while providing particular emphasis to the importance of the therapeutic relationship.

EGO PSYCHOLOGY.   In a change of emphasis occurring in the latter years of Freud's life, ego psychologists in the 1930s began to recognize the importance of the manifest content of early memories, particularly as a means for understanding how individuals manage forces involving latent content (Bruhn, 1990b). A key assumption in their theses is that childhood memories, as an expression of ego functioning, are attempts to integrate, synthesize, and resolve current conflicts (Burnell & Solomon, 1964). While not abandoning the significance of intrapsychic processing, understanding how individuals cope with interpersonal and environmental influences assumes a prominent role. Therapeutic focus also turns to evaluating specific deficits and arrests that occur in the development of ego functions, and both manifest and latent memory content is crucial in uncovering these dynamic concerns (Kris, 1956; Niederland, 1965; Ross, 1991). In a similar direction, the conceptualization of defense mechanisms expands from Freud's emphasis on drive and anxiety control to a broad inclusion of emotional reactions to challenging social encounters. In particular, defenses emerge when individuals experience threat and react with feelings such as shame, humiliation, and embarrassment (Clark, 1992, 1998a, 2002). Anna Freud (1936/1966), Sigmund Freud's daughter, was instrumental in clarifying and categorizing the mechanisms of defense and recognizing their impact relating to both internal and external forces. Table 2.3 presents a list of the defense mechanisms with definitions (Clark, 1998a).

TABLE 2.3: DEFENSE MECHANISMS WITH DEFINITIONS	
Denial	Negating the meanings or existence of perceptions
Displacement	Redirecting feelings to a vulnerable substitute
Identification	Assuming desired attributes of another person through fantasized associations
Isolation	Severing verbalized cognitions from associated affect
Projection	Attributing intolerable behavior to others that is characteristic of oneself
Rationalization	Justifying objectionable behavior through the use of plausible statements
Reaction formation	Demonstrating exaggerated moralistic actions that are directly contrary to cognitive and affective functioning
Regression	Reverting to developmentally immature behavior
Repression	Excluding from awareness intolerable cognitions and affect
Undoing	Nullifying a perceived transgression through a reverse action

OBJECT RELATIONS.   Although ego psychologists recognize the importance of social influences, object relations theorists explicitly emphasize the primacy of developmental and current relationships with others (Auld & Hyman, 1991). Attending to the capacity for individuals in forming and maintaining intimate relationships becomes a predominant therapeutic focus (Westen, 1998). Formative interpersonal experiences crystallize in psychic representations of the self and others, which potentially play a crucial role in subsequent interpersonal relationships and psychopathology. Early childhood memories are integral to understanding internal structures, and analytic change entails altering the mental images in the context of relationships with others (Mitchell, 1988; St. Claire, 2000). When faced with social interactions that are perceived as threatening, patients will typically respond with various defense mechanisms both inside and outside of therapy. The processes ward off disturbing affect and conflict, especially when the therapist probes schemas and the personal core of the individual (Maslow, 1966). In particular, the defense mechanism of projective identification involves clients' distorting boundaries between the self and the therapist in a manipulative and provocative interaction (Clark, 1995b, 1997; Ginter & Bonney, 1993).

SELF PSYCHOLOGY.   By therapeutically focusing on the experiencing self, self psychology attempts to understand the shaping of a person's development and rectify stereotyped and maladaptive schemas (Auld & Hyman, 1991; Knapp, 1991). Individuals may have lacked the constancy and care of a nurturing person in early childhood years, resulting in a sense of fragmentation and a primary defect in the self (Kohut, 1977). In analysis, therapeutically exploring early memories provides one means of evaluating a patient's perception of his or her formative relationships that contribute to the development of the self. In this uncovering type of treatment, patients typically mobilize defenses to protect the vulnerable self from overwhelming threat in both interpersonal and therapeutic experiences. As an essential empathic response, the analyst strives to provide a predictable and secure environment that enhances the self-esteem and psychological stability of the patient. As individuals experience support and understanding, they are more able to tolerate transactions involving the scrutiny of schemas relating to self and others.

RECOVERED MEMORIES, FALSE MEMORIES, AND EARLY RECOLLECTIONS

Since Freud first presented his provocative and evolving views on early childhood memories, they have dominated popular and professional opinion on the topic. His conceptualization of screen memories concealing latent content has been particularly influential with practitioners as they have considered the treatment decision to explore recollected memories that potentially involve threatening and emotionally damaging content. The continuing controversy over the therapeutic management of recovered memories has further escalated with accusations that therapists may inadvertently suggest or implant false memories of trauma in the minds of their patients. In contrast to procedures employing more directive measures, the use of early recollections as a projective technique is qualitatively different and involves less risk with clients than approaches that explicitly attempt to recover assumed memories of trauma.

RECOVERED MEMORIES

When Freud shifted his original conceptualization from trauma theory to a fantasy-based theory of infantile sexual abuse, he set the stage for a controversy that continues today with respect to the veracity of memories of abuse (Masson, 1984; Melchert, 1996, 1998). With Freud's perspective change, it has become far more difficult to distinguish a critical difference between objective reality and subjective reality in regard to establishing the accuracy of a history of trauma (Person & Klar, 1994). Freud further theorized that a repression or dissociation of perceived trauma generally occurs in childhood, resulting in a patient's behavioral functioning becoming largely devoid of affect or fragmentary in nature. Relatedly, Freud's concept of a screen memory involves a cover of significant latent trauma content that becomes difficult to access or to understand. Psychoanalytic treatment consequently emphasizes uncovering perceived traumatic memories, which are a basis for symptomatic behavior. In this context, the term "recovered memories" relates to the process of individuals recalling traumatic content that has not previously been remembered (Berliner & Briere, 1999; Knapp & VandeCreek, 2000). The popularity of Freud's positions involving the pervasive and traumatic quality of childhood memories is reflected among significant sectors of the general public and therapeutic community who share his views. This common perception frequently results in a reluctance of professionals to pursue the recovery of early memories, which by definition involves material that is affectivity-loaded with a potential to overwhelm a person's psychological integrity. In this regard, memory recovery techniques may evoke varied emotional reactions, which include, but are not limited to, depression, rage, fear, and anxiety (Roland, 1993). On the other hand, others maintain that it is crucial to recover memories that may involve painful trauma in order to possibly resolve damaging and seemingly intractable conflicts.

FALSE MEMORIES

Related to the issue of recovered memories is another controversy pertaining to the creation of false memories of abuse. In this instance, individuals presumably distort past events and create inaccurate memories of abuse, which they perceive as real (Searleman & Herrmann, 1994). This viewpoint also holds that most often a patient's false memories are an inadvertent product of suggestion on the part of the therapist who unwittingly pursues a perceived trauma source. Prompting of patients by the therapist to imagine or repeatedly think about suggested incidents may engender inaccurate beliefs

(Berliner & Briere, 1999; Enns, 2001). In particular, children and impressionable adults may be disposed to comply with suggestions of authority figures that influence responses in a predetermined direction. Leading questions, guided imagery, and hypnosis have all come under attack as techniques that may generate mistaken or false beliefs of abuse (Arbuthnott, Arbuthnott, & Rossiter, 2001). Although Freud rejected the possibility of a psychoanalyst planting the idea of abuse in the mind of a patient, he has been accused of an apparent tendency to inform patients of his abuse hypothesis and then aggressively pursue the possibility through psychoanalytic interactions (Powell & Boer, 1994). At the same time, the complex therapeutic problems that Freud was willing to take up the challenge of and critically evaluate in his professional work persist today with respect to the perplexing task of evaluating memories of abuse.

EARLY RECOLLECTIONS

The treatment options of overlooking the possibility of trauma history or attempting to reconstruct dubious client memories may not be appealing to many practitioners. In order to assume a broader perspective beyond this dilemma, it is essential to understand the particular frame of reference of an individual in relationship to early memory recall. When clients are asked about their first memories, they generally express recollections that are consistent with the organizing principles of their personality or the lifestyle (Orgler, 1952; Piers, 1999). The significance of any experience is primarily influenced by the perspective on life that a person applies or brings to an event. In this respect, early recollections tend to have contemporary meaning and are largely conscious and accessible, and generally lack threat. As most persons do not maintain a trauma-laden perspective of life, it is unlikely that a request to recall manifest early recollections without additional probing or associative procedures will produce trauma content. Thus, a misapprehension exists that most or even a significant percentage of early memories involve trauma (Bruhn, 1990b). Consequently, asking clients to relate their early recollections in the assessment context of a projective technique poses a minimal risk because this procedure elicits material that typically reflects belief system perspectives. At the same time, this view does not rule out recollections that are consistent with trauma perspectives or the possible revelation of trauma that is available to consciousness and that a client feels sufficiently secure in disclosing. Even though these occurrences may be relatively infrequent, it is imperative that practitioners be prepared to effectively respond in the event of client disclosure of current or past trauma (Terr, 1988). In response to this potential concern, the administration guidelines presented in chapter 6 of this text include suggestions relating to the issue.

In addition to the premise that eliciting early recollections as a projective technique tends to evoke enduring lifestyle perspectives, the procedure is also qualitatively different from other more extensive treatment methods that involve depthful clinical exploration and probing of client experiencing. In particular, the psychoanalytic orientation intentionally attempts to uncover developmental material through techniques such as free association, dream interpretation, and transference processing. These interventions are explicitly established to therapeutically address perspectives of patients that may or may not include trauma. Any practitioner who subscribes to a treatment approach focusing on addressing early life experiences and the possibility of memory recovery must be alert to the suggestibility of perceived trauma and the urgency of avoiding confirmatory bias. In sum, the projective use of early recollections clearly differs from the more probing and uncovering treatment practices, and it is understandable that assessment findings between the two approaches typically produce divergent outcomes.

SUMMARY

Adler's and Freud's approaches to early memories largely reflect a different set of assumptions relating to theory and practice. Adler recognizes that early childhood recollections are revealing of an individual's functioning, whereas Freud believes that the memories primarily serve to conceal conflicted material. Adler's system of Individual Psychology emphasizes the goal-oriented and social nature of persons. Basic conceptualizations of Adler relate to early recollections and contribute to understanding effective applications of the projective technique in the counseling process. Contemporary perspectives relating to schema theory, cognitive theory, and social constructionism are compatible with Adlerian theoretical positions. The psychoanalytic tradition of Freud emphasizes the developmental prominence of sexuality and conceptualizes a screening function of early memories. Within the Freudian orientation, the principle of the determining effect of the past on development and the influence of the unconscious becomes foundational. Extensions of psychoanalytic thinking focus on the significance of manifest and latent early memories and the impact of interpersonal relationships on development and psychopathology. Clarifying the dynamics of recovered memories, false memories, and early recollections is crucial for understanding and responding to the phenomena in counseling and psychotherapy.

3

Taxonomic Considerations and Personality Dimensions of Early Memories

"My first memories are fragmented and isolated and con-
temporaneous, as though one remembered some first moments of the Seven Days. It seems as if time had not yet
been created, for all the thoughts connected with emotion
and place are without sequence."
— William Butler Yeats (1916/1927, p. 5)

INTRODUCTION

SINCE THE FIRST PUBLISHED STUDY IN 1893, RESEARCH RELATING TO
early memories of childhood has been continuous and wide-ranging in
scope. Investigations from Adlerian and Freudian perspectives have remained
prominent throughout the twentieth century and to the present. Emerging
as an initial line of inquiry, taxonomic studies categorized such variables as
age, emotions, and sense modalities. The evaluation of early memories in
terms of personality dimensions encompasses another major research focus.
A further broad area of study relates to diagnostic impressions of early remembrances, which will receive extensive consideration in the next chapter
of the text. A comprehensive review of the literature provides a broad historical context and specific data resources when considering early recollections
as a projective technique in counseling and psychotherapy.

TAXONOMIC INVESTIGATIONS

Various methods have been used for assessing early memories since Miles
(1893) first asked college students and adults to complete a mailed questionnaire relating to life functioning, which included among other questions,
"What is the earliest thing you are sure you can remember?" Two years later,
a questionnaire devised by Henri (1895a, 1895b) focused exclusively on
early recollections and was printed in two psychological journals. The survey

findings, which considered queries such as age, clarity, and significance of the first remembrances, were subsequently published (Henri & Henri 1896, 1898). In another mailed questionnaire, Colegrove (1899) comprehensively evaluated the early experiences and first memories of over 1,600 culturally diverse individuals across the life span. A number of years later in 1928, Gordon administered a brief questionnaire to college students, and this approach of asking assembled groups to respond to early memory inquiries became popular among researchers (Dudycha & Dudycha, 1933b; Heinemann, 1939; Hersztejn-Korzeniowa, 1935; Waldfogel, 1948).

In a study published in 1901, Potwin reported the results of a direct-question method in which he asked a group of college students to state their early memories and relevant data. Potwin then tabulated the responses under 17 predetermined categories, which included frequency, nature of the events, and sense types. Henderson (1911) employed a similar approach with college students and adults, focusing on the relative frequency of pleasant and unpleasant experiences. Other researchers (Benoschofsky, 1938; Blonsky, 1929; Dudycha & Dudycha, 1933a; Murray, 1938) also used this procedure in evaluating early memory data. Through the use of reminiscing, G. Stanley Hall (1899) returned to where he grew up in rural Western Massachusetts and recalled a large number of memories as he walked around retracing paths and locations he had experienced in his youth. In a brief review, Titchener (1900) expressed praise for Hall's innovative paper as it related to genetic and structural psychology. In other instances using the reminiscence method for evaluating early memories, Crook (1925) and Hennig (1937) reflected back on their childhood experiences and first recollections. Plank (1959) discussed Crook's first memories in terms of their possible authenticity.

Crook and Harden (1931) initiated another approach for the assessment of early memories by asking adult respondents to simply provide a check on a chart for each experience recalled. Child (1940) was the only other researcher to use this checklist method, as the results are commonly viewed as being subject to quantitative falsification and appear statistically unreliable (Ansbacher, 1947; Waldfogel, 1948). Dudycha and Dudycha (1941) and Waldfogel (1948) published extensive literature reviews of the research on early memories through mid-century. After this active period of general investigations, with notable exceptions (e.g., Howes, Siegel, & Brown, 1993; Kihlstrom & Harackiewicz, 1982; Weiland & Steisel, 1958), taxonomic research tended to emphasize more particular and directed areas of inquiry. For example, Usher and Neisser (1993) focused specifically on the earliest age that an event can be recalled. Using a questionnaire method, college students were asked about their earliest memories of discrete events, including the birth of a younger sibling, hospitalization, death of a family member, and a family move to a new home. In another study, Gold and Neisser (1980) asked children and adolescents specific queries relating to their remembrances of persons and experiences in kindergarten. This procedure of providing a cued recall has become more common among contemporary researchers (Eacott & Crawley, 1998; Rubin & Schulkind, 1997) and differs from the earlier generation of investigations, which almost exclusively employed a free recall of early memories. Since the inception of taxonomic studies, particular variables have been the focus of sustained research interests, and these topics will be considered next.

AGE

There is widespread agreement among researchers that most individuals recall their earliest memories between their third and fourth year of life, although the age range of recollection varies between two and eight years (Eacott, 1999). This finding is consistent with numerous surveys and reviews of the literature over a 100-year period (Bruhn, 1998; Dudycha & Dudycha, 1941; Howes et al., 1993; Kihlstrom & Harackiewicz, 1982). Published studies on first memories indicate that approximately one percent of individuals are able to recount recollections from a period prior to their third birthday, with a sharp rise after that date (Rubin, 2000). There are also isolated reported instances of memories dating back to the first year of life, with the average age of recall of early childhood remembrances tending to be slightly lower for females than for males (Howe, 2000; Rubin, 2000; Waldfogel, 1948). In the early taxonomic investigations (Colegrove, 1899; Crook & Harden, 1931; Henri & Henri, 1896, 1898), there are accounts of a very small percentage of persons recalling memories prior to their first birthday. Crook (1925) reminisced about a personal memory of being breast-fed by a neighbor, who visited his family home on only one occasion, before he turned one year of age. Among others, Schmideberg (1950) expressed skepticism about infant memories attributed to the first year, as they are personal constructions and difficult to confirm. Contemporary research suggests that the earliest memories of individuals appear to be from a period of two to three years of age, and even these findings were determined with the aid of cued responses (Crovitz & Quina-Holland, 1976; Eacott & Crawley, 1998; Howe, 2000; Markowsky & Pence, 1997; Usher & Neisser, 1993). In a study with college students, Westman (1995) reported that the mention of when an early recollection occurred, either in terms of calendar time or event time, was significantly less frequent than other aspects of a first memory.

Intelligence, level of adjustment, and cross-cultural considerations have also been a focus of research interest relating to the age of first memories recall. In regard to intelligence functioning, persons with higher measures of intelligence typically report chronologically earlier first memories (Pustel, Stern-licht, & Siegel, 1969; Rabbit & McInnis, 1988; Rule & Jarrell, 1983). In contrast to these findings, earlier investigators (Dudycha & Dudycha, 1933b; Waldfogel, 1948) found relatively little relationship between the age of recall of early memories and intelligence. In an investigation with college students, Spirrison, Schneider, Hartwell, Carmack, and D'Reaux (1997) reported that individuals relating first memories prior to four years of age tended to have significantly higher scores on general maladjustment than did persons with early memories occurring later. Bruhn (1998) observed that the first remem-brance of early memories is likely related to a number of psychological and demographic variables, and he called for further research on factors affecting the age of first recall in order to avoid questionable attributions of pathology. From a cross-cultural perspective involving four studies with college students and adults in the United States, Mullen (1994) reported that Caucasians have earlier memories than Asians by approximately six months. In a related study with American and Chinese college students, Wang (2001) found that the earliest childhood recollection of Americans was 3.5 years, which was approx-imately six months earlier than those of the Chinese students.

EMOTIONS

Varying in degrees of intensity, emotional reactions almost always accom-pany the report of early childhood memories (Blonsky, 1929; Dudycha & Dudycha, 1933a, 1933b; Westman and Westman, 1993; Westman & Wau-tier, 1994a, 1994b). At the same time, however, some individuals in recalling their first memories may lack awareness of their feelings, experience indif-ferent emotions, or simply fail to report their affective states. When consid-ering emotions relating to early recollections, the range is broad, yet particular affective categories emerge among groups of individuals (Waldfogel, 1948). Dudycha and Dudycha (1933a) reported prominent emotions accompa-nying early memories in descending order of frequency: fear, joy, anger, sorrow and disappointment, and wonder and awe. In a related study, Dudycha and Dudycha (1933b) found similar results in terms of relative ex-pression of emotions with another sample of college students. Joy was the dominant emotion reported by Waldfogel (1948), followed by fear, in an in-vestigation with college students that focused only on the first memory. The proportional frequency of other emotions observed by Waldfogel closely par-alleled studies reported by Dudycha and Dudycha. In regard to the domi-nant emotion of fear, numerous experiences such as punishment, strange situations, and being left alone understandably tend to evoke the response. Various other situations, such as receiving gifts, gaining attention, and playing a game, often give rise to the emotion of joy.

Relating to gender differences, Dudycha and Dudycha (1933b) found that females more often recall joyful than fearful memories, and males more frequently report memories involving fear than joy. In contrast to these findings, in a study with college students, Adcock (1975) reported that females recall frightening experiences more frequently than males. Schwartz (1984–1985) found that female graduate students related significantly more fear and anxiety in their early memories than males, but there were no significant differences relating to these emotions among undergraduate students. In a contemporary study with college students, Tylenda and Dollinger (1987) observed that individuals reporting such emotions as pain, guilt, or shame in their earliest memory were also likely to experience these feelings in their recent memory. The authors concluded that in terms of affective characteristics, the earliest memory is no more significant than recent memory, and may be even less important.

PLEASANTNESS AND UNPLEASANTNESS

Pleasant early memories generally comprise a higher proportion of recollections than unpleasant ones. As early as 1899, Colegrove asked the survey question, "Do you recall pleasant or unpleasant experiences better?" and this type of inquiry has remained prominent in early memory research. Colegrove reported that persons tend to recall pleasant recollections more frequently, an observation that has been supported in various other studies (Henderson, 1911; Kihlstrom & Harackiewicz, 1982; Potwin, 1901; Waldfogel, 1948). It is also noteworthy that a sizeable number of individuals express neutral reactions in their early childhood memories. As an example, Waldfogel (1948) stated, in round numbers, that pleasant recollections comprised about 50 percent of the total among persons surveyed, unpleasant about 30 percent, and neutral about 20 percent. Not all researchers, however, are in agreement that pleasant memories outnumber unpleasant ones. Gordon (1928), in a study involving college students, reported a preponderance of unpleasant early memories and further concluded that this trend occurred even more frequently among males. In a more recent study, Cowan and Davidson (1984) found the majority of college students providing "unhappy" responses to the request for, "early memories in which you had a strong emotional reaction to another human being." Chance (1957) reported the percentage of pleasant and unpleasant early memories to be about equal among college students that he surveyed. Unpleasant memories from early childhood were more prevalent than those representing middle childhood and adolescence for college females in a study conducted by Thompson and Witryol (1948).

In investigations considering social and cultural forces, Epstein (1963) found that lower class adolescents had significantly more early memories involving angry feelings, while middle class adolescents had significantly more memories relating to euphoric affect. In a related study, boys experiencing favorable home and school environments were more than twice as likely to have pleasant early memories than boys living in unfavorable environments involving poverty, violence, and neglect (Pattie & Cornett, 1952). Pustel et al. (1969) evaluated the early childhood recollections of a group of adolescents and adults who were measured within the mild range of mental retardation. The individuals were residents of a state school. The authors assumed that the vast majority of institutionalized persons were drawn from lower socioeconomic groups and that their emotional experiences would have been of a generally negative nature. Pustel et al. (1969) found that the institutionalized adults and female adolescents reported a significantly greater number of unpleasant early memories than pleasant ones. The male adolescent residents, however, recalled about an equal number of pleasant and unpleasant memories.

SENSORY MODALITIES

Visual images dominate in the early memories of individuals, as other sensory functions occur far less often (Westman & Orellana, 1996; Westman, Westman, & Orellana, 1996). Henri and Henri (1896, 1898) found that most people responding to their questionnaire on early recollections had clear visual and in contrast weaker and less distinct auditory images. Other early researchers report that the majority of childhood memories are visual and often involve movement, with far fewer sensory representations of auditory, tactile, gustatory, and olfactory functioning (Colegrove, 1899; Dudycha & Dudycha, 1933a; Potwin, 1901). Potwin cited a relatively rare instance of an olfactory memory of a person sitting under an apple tree on a sunny autumn day, with a fragrance in the air and experiencing a feeling of happiness. As an example of an infrequent report of an early recollection with an auditory focus, my wife, Marybeth, remembers listening to her father reading a bedtime story to her. Williams and Bonvillian (1989) evaluated early childhood memories in deaf and hearing college students. Positive recollections were significantly higher among two deaf groups in comparison to a hearing group, and the mean age of the earliest memory reported did not differ across the three subject groups.

In more recent studies, Kihlstrom and Harackiewicz (1982) stated that visual memories were reported by three quarters of a high school and college age student sample, followed by kinesthetic and tactile; auditory was rather rare, with gustatory and olfactory expressions virtually absent. Reporting similar findings with college students, Saunders and Norcross (1988) found visual imagery and motor activity early memories in the majority, seven percent tactile, auditory and gustatory two percent respectively, and no olfactory sensations. In their study, Westman and Westman (1993) observed that only one college student reported a memory associated with an odor, even though it has long been recognized that odors have a strong capacity to trigger particular memories. In this regard, Laird (1935) reported that smell-stimulated memories are often vivid and frequently evoke an emotional response. Laird (1935) wrote of the poignancy of smell-revived recollections: "It is now shown that these memories of the past that have a particularly haunting, emotional grip over us are often aroused by some fleeting odor" (p. 126).

PERSONALITY DIMENSIONS

After establishing an extensive data base, researchers expanded beyond a taxonomic focus and began to explore the relationship of personality dimensions and early memories. Proceeding from the assumption that early childhood memories reflect aspects of a person's personality structure, numerous investigations evaluate characteristics such as security–insecurity, explanatory style, and interpersonal functioning. In other instances, research focuses on the role of early recollections in illuminating various expressions of personality in the lives of individuals. Occupational choice, historical figures, and a range of diverse topics relating to personality dimensions are prominent in these investigations of early memories.

SECURITY–INSECURITY

In an early personality study, Ansbacher (1953) administered the Maslow Security–Insecurity Test to male college students and found a relationship between security scores and particular types of early recollections. Maslow's inventory defines insecurity in terms of such feelings as rejection, isolation, threat, and mistrust, while associating security with feelings of being liked, belonging, safety, and happiness (Maslow, 1942). Ansbacher reported that individuals with high security scores typically described early recollections involving participation in group activities, being more active in general, and receiving kind treatment by others. In contrast, persons with low security scores often related early recollections reflecting a sense of being cut off from the larger group, getting or losing prestige, having done something bad, remembering others receiving kindness or attention, or suffering or inflicting harm. In an interesting finding, individuals receiving presents in their childhood memories were almost always among those found in the secure category, and those persons observing harm suffered by others in their early recollections were generally in the insecure range. In a related study also using Maslow's inventory, Purcell (1952) reported that secure college students had significantly more pleasant early memories than persons with scores reflecting insecurity in their recollections. Through the use of questionnaires with female college students, Holmes (1965) reported a continuous measure of affective tone of early memories from positive to negative in relationship to security. Holmes also observed that individuals in the middle range of security manifested a distinct need to psychologically defend their self-esteem in order to maintain feelings of security. Relatedly, highly secure persons find no need to defend themselves in regard to their self-esteem, and individuals maintaining low feelings of security cannot defend themselves or have given up all attempts to make an effort to offer a defense.

EXPLANATORY STYLE

As a psychological construct, explanatory style involves the way people have a tendency to habitually express similar explanations for the causes of good or bad events that involve themselves (Peterson, Buchanan, & Seligman, 1995). In this regard, when bad events occur to them, individuals with a pessimistic outlook tend to blame themselves and believe that the experiences are enduring and global in terms of effect. In contrast, when bad events occur to them, persons with an optimistic outlook tend to look for causes outside of themselves and recognize that experiences are time-limited and circumscribed in terms of effect. From a research perspective, in a study with college students, Nichols and Feist (1994) evaluated explanatory style as a personality predictor of early memories by considering the question: Do optimistic individuals report different early recollections than pessimists? The results of the study suggested that differences exist between both groups in regard to explanatory style and early childhood memories. Optimists are more likely to include the presence of others with more sustained interactions in their early memories. Optimists also tended to perceive themselves as active and generally competent, whereas pessimists typically viewed themselves as passive and assuming the roles of victims, followers, and servers. Finally, early recollections of optimists were more pleasant than the memories of the pessimistic participants, while appearing comparatively more distinct and clear. A more circumscribed concept, locus of control, relates to expectations about the future in terms of an internality–externality dimension on the part of an individual.

With respect to the active–passive aspect of explanatory style, Fried (1970/1989) considered the variable to be a crucial psychological dimension. Persons with an active orientation tend to be problem-focused and demonstrate inventive thinking. Such individuals "live passionately, creatively, and in the spirit of youthfulness that is not tied to chronological age" (Fried, 1970/1989, p. 208). In contrast, others who maintain a passive stance gravitate toward procrastination and mental immobility. Inertness, rumination, and wishful thinking are common among such persons. Yet, in spite of these evasive behaviors, there may be some quasi-advantages for inaction and prolonged curtailment of emotions and capabilities. Individuals frequently elicit compassion and assistance from others in response to their continuous claims for sympathy. Developmentally, Fried (1970/1989) felt that persons forfeit a pursuit of activeness and living affirmatively out of habit, and that it is possible to engender these behaviors through psychotherapy. In particular, she maintained that persons who are evasive, fearful, and inert become strong and independent when they make an effort to do what is difficult in terms of emotional and mental challenges.

From another theoretical position, Adler (1920/1968) emphasized active–passive dimensions in his constructs of degree of activity and safeguarding tendencies, which entail the operation of evasive and avoidant functioning by individuals. In a study with adolescents, Kopp and Der (1982) reported that the degree of activity and type of role that individuals assume in early recollections correlate with clinical assessments based on parental descriptions and an activity dimension. Finally, Lord (1971) reported that the dimensions of activity and positive affect in the early memories of adolescent males were significantly related to elevated measures of self-concept and sense of coping effectiveness.

INTERPERSONAL FUNCTIONING

Researchers have shown interest in various facets of interpersonal behavior relating to early recollections. Barrett (1983) examined the factor of self-disclosure by correlating self-disclosure and interpersonal functioning inventories with early recollections reported by college students. Barrett found that the greater length in words of the early recollection reports correlated with dominance ratings for males and friendliness for females. Self-disclosure questionnaire scores correlated with the number of words and an earlier age of the early recollections. Barrett concluded that a negative relationship in regard to age and length of early recollections suggests a reduced openness to self-disclosure and a guarded interpersonal style. In an earlier study, Barrett (1980) evaluated the prediction of personality traits and early recollections. A group of college students completed three personality scales and written reports of their early memories. Barrett reported findings of significant correlations with the personality scales and the factors of anxiety, locus of control, and need for approval determined through the early memories. In a related study also with college students, Sattler and Brandon (1967) reported significant correlations for personality measures of manifest anxiety and introversion–extroversion in relation to early recollections content.

SOCIAL INTEREST

Visible indicators of social interest involve an expression of community feeling through constructive interpersonal relationships and an emotional identification with other persons (Powers & Griffith, 1987). Various research studies have evaluated the lack or presence of social interest as a variable within particular populations. McCarter, Schiffman, and Tomkins (1961) used early recollections with male college students to predict performance on a variety of the Tomkins–Horn Picture Arrangement Test (PAT) scales, which involve cartoon-like drawings. Predictions of scale arrangements based on the early recollections of participants were compared to results obtained on the PAT. The authors concluded that early recollections are a valid method of personality appraisal in regard to social interest and degree of activity. Another study investigated the relationship between social interest dimensions of early recollections and selected variables (Altman & Rule, 1980). Early recollections of graduate students participating in a summer guidance institute were evaluated for social interest content using The Early Recollections Rating Scale of Social Interest Characteristics (Altman, 1973). Three judges also rated each participant for the expression of empathy using audiotape communication excerpts generated during the first week of the institute. Significant correlations were obtained between selected social interest dimensions reflected in the early recollections and the participants' levels of expressed empathy. Altman and Rule cautioned, however, that a "well-rounded" understanding of an individual's social interest is probably not possible from early recollections alone, and other background information is needed relating to developmental and behavioral functioning.

In a related study, Marcus, Manaster, and Spencer (1999) assessed dimensions of social interest by comparing the early recollections of graduate counseling students and clients in psychotherapy. The results indicated that clients were more likely than counseling students to mention nonfamily members, illnesses or injuries, and significantly more negative and passive early recollections. Finally, evaluating the early recollections of college students through Altman's (1973) scale, Eckstein and Springer (1981) found that psychology majors had higher levels of social interest in comparison to nonpsychology majors and people in general.

BIRTH ORDER

Published studies show mixed relationships between the birth order position of individuals and the content of their early recollections. Fakouri and

Hafner (1984) employed the Manaster–Perryman (1974) scoring system to evaluate the early recollections of first-born and later-born college students. General findings indicate that the first-born early recollections were more similar than dissimilar in comparison to childhood memories of other ordinal positions. Significant differences, however, were found in several variables that Fakouri and Hafner felt were consistent with Adlerian theory. Siblings were mentioned more frequently in early recollections by later borns than by first borns. This result suggests that later-born individuals have experienced more comparative and competitive lives, which in turn has influenced the interpersonal content of their early memories. Reports of parents, siblings, and other relatives were conspicuously absent in the early recollections of first borns. The authors attribute these frequent omissions to the possibility of a perceived dethronement and accompanying loss of attention due to the birth of later borns. Finally, in comparison to later borns, first borns expressed more themes involving traumatic events, such as injuries and accidents. A possible function of these perceptions, in the view of Fakouri and Hafner, is that the first-born individuals perceive unpleasant aspects of life as a warning or caution. A related study considered ordinal position among other factors in relationship to the early recollections of college students. Employing the Comprehensive Early Memory Scoring System (Last & Bruhn, 1983) and two self-report instruments, Saunders and Norcross (1988) reported no significant differences on any of the early childhood memories variables relating to ordinal position. Consequently, the authors concluded that the early recollections of first borns were indistinguishable from later borns in terms of personality characteristics.

OCCUPATIONAL CHOICE

Adler first recognized the value of early recollections in relationship to his career choice as a physician. Soon after recovering from a near fatal illness, Adler remembers being asked by another child what he planned to do with his life. In reaction to Adler's reply of becoming a doctor, the young person remarked, "Then you should be strung up on the nearest lamp post" (Adler, 1947, p. 11). Unphased by the remark, Adler thought that the boy had encountered a bad experience under medical care with a doctor. Adler felt determined to become a competent physician in order to be in a position to solve difficult and challenging problems. Since the time of Adler's original inquiries, numerous researchers have evaluated the role of early recollections and the potential of individuals' memories for making a contribution to vocational and career guidance (LaFountain & Garner, 1998; Watts & Engels, 1995). A basic assumption in using early recollections in career exploration and planning is that it is more likely that an individual will find satisfaction in an occupation that is compatible with the goals and outlook on life that are reflected in his or her first memories (McFarland, 1988).

A series of investigations has attempted to discriminate among persons preparing for or employed in different occupations based on their early recollections. Researchers exploring this proposition almost exclusively have used the Manaster–Perryman (1974) early recollections scoring system, which includes such variables as concern with detail, activity–passivity, and setting. In one study, Hafner and Fakouri (1984b) compared the content of early recollections of college students majoring in accounting, secondary education, and psychology. Results indicated that the early recollections of accounting students reflected more internal control, and education students mentioned "school" as a setting more often than the other two groups. Psychology students more frequently expressed negative affect, including a marked trend to recall the dysphorias of life. In a related study, the content of early recollections was compared for differentiation purposes among students preparing for careers in clinical psychology, dentistry, and law (Hafner & Fakouri, 1984a). The relative degree of activity or initiation of patterns of action was highest among law students and least common among students in dentistry. Psychology students more frequently expressed themes in their early recollections relating to fear and anxiety. The authors suggest that clinical psychology students may be motivated as a function of career choice to become better equipped to manage anxiety-provoking or threatening situations. In another study, Hafner, Fakouri, and Etzler (1986) found that first recollections were of some value in differentiating among college students preparing for careers in chemical, electrical, and mechanical engineering.

In a related occupational study, Fakouri, Fakouri, and Hafner (1986) compared the early recollections of nursing students with students in college programs other than nursing. Nursing students expressed significantly more themes involving mastery, concern with details, motor activity, and initiation of activity in comparison to the control group. In a comparable study, Coram and Shields (1987) found significant differences between the early recollections of criminal justice majors and majors in other fields of college study. One interesting finding is that criminal justice majors reported significantly more visual details in their early memories, suggesting the possible operation of more precise sensory processing. In a study considering employed individuals, the early recollections of medical technologists and nurses were compared in order to differentiate personality factors between their early recollections (McFarland, 1988). Specific scoring variables reached significance between the two groups. McFarland concluded that early recollections may be a useful tool in career guidance, and he suggested the possibility of developing computerized empirical matches relating to lifestyle and major occupations.

Manaster and Perryman (1974) evaluated the early recollections of undergraduate and graduate students on the basis of a scoring manual devised for vocational guidance purposes. The Manaster–Perryman Manifest Content Scoring Manual includes seven variables or categories: characters, themes, concern with detail, setting, active–passive, internal–external control, and affect. The authors found that several of the variables showed significant differences or trends among students in teaching, counseling, nursing or medicine, biological science, and business or accounting. As an example, students in the nursing and medical group mentioned the character "mother" in their written early recollections significantly more frequently than subjects in any other group except counseling. Manaster and Perryman observed that the presence of a "mother" or maternal character type was understandable for students preparing for work in the helping professions.

Using a questionnaire, Holmes and Watson (1965) reported data findings that differentiated the early recollections of teaching and nursing students. Carson (1994) investigated the early recollections of physicists, mathematicians, and psychologists. Interestingly, some of the themes uncovered in the early recollections of the scientists related to curiosity, independence of thought, and skepticism of news received from authority figures. Two studies combined early recollections with vocational assessment instruments developed by John Holland. In correlating responses from the Vocational Preference Inventory with early recollections of young adults, Elliot, Amerikaner, and Swank (1987) endorsed the combined use of these two appraisal devices in vocational counseling. Attarian (1978) administered the Self-Directed Search and elicited early recollections in research with college students. While cautioning that judges were highly skilled in the interpretation of early recollections, Attarian concluded that there was sufficient correlational agreement between the two instruments to substantiate the use of early memories in vocational or educational guidance.

In order to provide a sufficiently broad context, McKelvie (1979) advised that career counseling should be viewed as a particular part of a comprehensive counseling process. As one aspect of this experience, early recollections can assist in clarifying major goals implicit in the lifestyle of individuals. From a related perspective, Watkins (1984) suggested that on an individualized basis, early recollections can provide a vast amount of career-related information relating to client dispositions in such areas of occupational focus; activity/passivity; affiliation/isolation; desire for superior, inferior, or egalitarian work relationships; and orientation toward people, data, or things. A concluding consideration is that while early recollections may contribute valuable or even unique perspectives, multiple sources of information are an essential aspect of sound decision making in career and vocational counseling.

HISTORICAL FIGURES

Another direction for understanding personality dimensions is to explore early recollections through biographical and autobiographical accounts of historical figures. As Yeats conveys in his quoted reflections at the beginning of the chapter, childhood memories are intriguing, and individuals occasionally record their first remembrances as a part of personal life reflections. From a psychohistorical perspective, Freud analyzed the early memories of Leonardo da Vinci and Goethe and applied his theoretical insights without the benefit of clinical treatment (Plank, 1953). In a full-length biographical study, Freud recounted an early memory of da Vinci, "It seems that I was always destined to be deeply concerned with vultures; for I recall as one of my very earliest memories that while I was in my cradle a vulture came down to me and opened my mouth with its tail, and struck me many times with its tail against my lips" (Freud, 1910/1957, p. 82). Recognizing the importance of the memory for understanding da Vinci's development and personality functioning, Freud also acknowledged its improbable fantasy quality. Observing that the tail striking corresponds to the act of fellatio, Freud regarded the memory as a starting point to substantiate a case for da Vinci's homosexuality.

As another subject of Freud's biographical analysis, Goethe, who was born in 1749, described an early memory. Goethe wrote, "One fine afternoon when all was quiet in the house, I was playing with the dishes and pots in the hall, and since this seemed to lead to nothing (opening to the street), I threw the plate into the street, and was overjoyed to see it go to bits so merrily" (Freud, 1917/1955, pp. 147–148). Goethe went on to explain how three neighbor brothers urged him on to break more dishes and he found delight in throwing more earthenware out to the street until they were all gone. Freud inferred that Goethe's throwing the crockery out of the window is a symbolic action in which he gave violent expression to a wish to get rid of a recently born younger brother. Freud believed that Goethe's mischievous and destructive actions represent a screen memory concealing bitterness inherent in a sibling rivalry.

In contrast with Freud's psychoanalytic analysis of Goethe's early memory, Rom (1965), from an Adlerian perspective, suggested a markedly different interpretation of the memory. Rom refuted Freud's analysis of a sibling rivalry position, and observed that Goethe's early reminiscence is consistent with acute visual and acoustic sensitivities that later emerge in the expressions of his greatness as a poet and dramatist. Goethe's delight in entertaining audiences and receiving applause for extraordinary actions is also apparent in his early recollection and in the chronicles of his life as an artist and statesman. In another account of a statesman, McLaughlin and Ansbacher (1971) evaluated the early recollections of Benjamin Franklin through his well-known autobiographical writings. From an earlier period, Schrecker (1973) recounted an early memory that St. Augustine wrote in his *Confessions*. Presenting an Adlerian perspective, Schrecker believed that the memory represents the basic tendency of most early recollections, which is to safeguard and reinforce the life plan or lifestyle. In particular, Schrecker viewed St. Augustine's reminiscence as a desire for power or domination:

> I fidgeted and cried and gave through the few clumsy signs at my disposal only unclear expression to my wishes. When my will was not fulfilled because one could not understand me, I became angry at the adults who did not wish to be subservient to me, and at the free people who did not want to be subordinated to me. By crying, I sought to revenge myself on them. This is the way of all children. (Schrecker, 1973, pp. 149–150)

Representing a more contemporary era, Bruhn and Bellow (1987) described Golda Meir's early memory from a period in her poverty-stricken childhood in Russia. At about age three-and-a-half or four, Meir recalls her father and other fathers trying to barricade doors with boards of wood to prevent their families from being rounded up by the oppressive authorities. Meir felt scared and angry that others were ineffectual in protecting her, and she was aware that her persecution had something to do with being Jewish. The reminiscence also conveys a determination to survive, which was evident in her life as she worked toward becoming Prime Minister of Israel. Relating to another early recollection involving a political luminary, Lyndon Johnson recalled disobeying his parents by wandering from a dirt path to go to a river and falling and hitting his head. His parents carried Johnson home and put him to bed, and Johnson stated, "I remember thinking that being hurt and frightened was worth it so long as it ended this way" (Ansbacher, 1978, p. 29). Ansbacher recognized the strong social interest theme in the memory, as well as a reflection on the independent and active nature of Johnson. Each of these qualities was apparent in Johnson's public service capacity as he rose to the position of President of the United States. In another evaluation of a President, Bruhn and Bellow (1984) reviewed the early memories of Dwight David Eisenhower in relationship to his career prominence in the military and government. Outside the political field, an early memory of the composer Stravinsky involves music and the sensory experiences of hearing and smell (Plank, 1953). From a literary and psychological perspective, the French writer Stendhal's early recollections relate to particular themes, characters, and scenes prominently represented in his nineteenth-century novels (Merler, 1992).

To conclude this section, Mosak and Kopp (1973) published an analysis of the early recollections of Adler, Freud, and Jung that reflects aspects of their personalities and theoretical positions. Among the numerous early memories presented, a selection of a representative memory from each theorist is suggestive of the authors' findings. Adler recalls at age two:

> I remember sitting on a beach bandaged up on account of rickets, with my healthy elder brother sitting opposite me. He could run, jump, and move about quite effortlessly, while for me, movement of any sort was a strain and an effort. Everyone went to great pains to help me and my mother and father did all that was in their power to do. (Mosak & Kopp, 1973, p. 158)

The memory suggests that Adler felt deficient, particularly in comparison to his older brother. He received attention for his physical ailments, and other people demonstrated social interest and concern for his well-being.

Also at age two, after wetting his bed and being reproved by his father, Freud recalled saying on one of the occasions, "Don't worry Papa. I will buy you a beautiful new red bed" (Mosak & Kopp, 1973, p. 160). Freud's recollection emphasizes his willingness to make amends for a transgression, and involves an organic function as a part of conflicted father–son encounter. Freud also mentions a color, which connotes an aesthetic interest that is clearly represented in personal accounts of his life. When he was four years old, Jung recollects:

> I am restive, feverish, unable to sleep. My father carries me in his arms, paces up and down singing his old student songs. I particularly remember one I was especially fond of and which always used to soothe me. To this day I can remember my father's voice, singing over me in the stillness of the night. (Mosak & Kopp, 1973, p. 163)

The memory has a clear sensual quality, including the soothing touch and singing by Jung's father. A contrast exists between discomfort of sickness and comfort in the expression of touch and song. In Jung's analytic treatment, he utilized various means of sensory expression, including the therapeutic use of singing, and his theoretical system emphasizes an extensive use of symbols and the importance of balance in expressive functioning (Douglas, 2000).

OTHER PERSONALITY DIMENSIONS

The range of topics relating to personality dimensions is vast, as is apparent in the chapter to this point and through a listing of other variables that have been a focus of research. Relationships have been established between early recollections and the following: "accidents" and reading difficulties (Wagenheim, 1960), anomie (Reimanis, 1965, 1974), college achievement (Rogers, 1977, 1982; Tolor & Fazzone, 1966), expected leisure activities (Rule & Traver, 1982), homosexuality (Farrell, 1984; Friedberg, 1975; Manaster & King, 1973), identity status (Josselson, 1982; Kroger, 1990; Neimeyer & Rareshide, 1991; Orlofsky & Frank, 1986), learning to read and write (Morawski, 1990; Morawski & Brunhuber, 1993), obesity and lifestyle (Laser, 1984), parental strictness–permissiveness (Rule, 1991–1992), stress (Burnell & Solomon, 1964; Tobin & Etigson, 1968), and work-stress burnout (Vettor & Kosinski, 2000).

SUMMARY

For over 100 years there has been extensive and continuous research activity in investigating the relationship of early recollections to taxonomic and personality dimensions. Taxonomic or classification studies have been conducted through various methods including questionnaires, direct questions, checklists, and reminiscences. Current research often features a cued recall procedure in eliciting first memories. Particular variables have been the subject of numerous studies relating to age, emotions, pleasantness and unpleasantness, and sensory modalities. Another broad line of inquiry involves personality dimensions and early recollections. Specific characteristics of personality functioning that have received prominent research focus include security–insecurity, explanatory style, and interpersonal functioning. Investigations relating expressions of personality to early recollections encompass social interest, birth order, occupational choice, historical figures, and other dimensions. Although deficiencies are apparent in the research on early recollections, such as an overemphasis on using college students as sample groups and a lack of control groups when pertinent (Bruhn & Schiffman, 1982a; Malinoski, Lynn, & Sivec, 1998; Watkins, 1992a), it is clearly possible to discern viable trends and patterns in the data that can provide a historical perspective and a reference base for applications in counseling and psychotherapy (Fakouri & Hafner, 1994).

4

Diagnostic Impressions of Early Recollections

"Memory is not just the imprint of the past time upon us; it is the keeper of what is meaningful for our deepest hopes and fears."

—Rollo May (1953, p. 258)

INTRODUCTION

AN EXTENSIVE NUMBER OF RESEARCHERS HAVE ATTEMPTED TO DETERmine a relationship between early recollections and particular clinical and personality disorders. Investigations have been robust in evaluating the first memories of patients and clients representing diverse clinical populations. Efforts to clarify the degree and type of psychopathology are based on the assumption that characteristics of early recollections can be linked to specific diagnostic categories or impressions. At the same time, the inquiries involving normative data and the employment of various early memory scoring systems restrict comparisons across psychological disorders (Malinoski, Lynn, & Sivec, 1998). A specific proposition that some researchers have pursued is the possibility of making a diagnosis of individual disorders on the basis of early recollections content without the benefit of additional assessment information. Understandably, various categories and clinical descriptors used in the diagnostic research reflect respective time periods in which particular studies were conducted. In some instances outdated terminology, such as the multiple types of neurosis, makes it difficult to organize research findings in a coherent manner that is consistent with contemporary categorization standards. In order to enhance understanding and accessibility, the research data is divided into sections that broadly conform to Axis I and Axis II of the multiaxial system of the *DSM–IV–TR* (2000). A consideration of the affinity of early recollections to specific disorders contributes to the identification of characteristic themes that can be of diagnostic value in individual assessment.

CLINICAL DISORDERS

A broad range of investigations has been conducted relating the content of early recollections of persons to clinical disorders represented on Axis I of the *DSM–IV–TR* (2000). Most of the studies compared the early recollections of treatment groups of individuals diagnosed with different disorders or with the early memories of designated comparison or control groups. To date, the focus of early recollections research has included the clinical classifications of substance-related disorders; schizophrenia and other psychotic disorders; mood disorders; anxiety disorders; dissociative disorders; eating disorders; disorders of infancy, childhood, and adolescence; and conduct disorder. A discussion of the findings proceeding from this research will include representative examples of early recollections of persons diagnosed with each respective disorder. Early childhood recollection investigations focusing on Axis II of the *DSM–IV–TR* personality disorders will be considered in the concluding section of the chapter.

SUBSTANCE-RELATED DISORDERS

The focus of several studies has been to discern common characteristics of individuals with substance abuse issues by evaluating their early recollections. Hafner, Fakouri, and Labrentz (1982) compared the early memories of 30 adults in treatment for alcoholism at a mental health outpatient unit with 30 other "normal" adults who had not been in treatment for psychological problems. Using an early recollections scoring system (Manaster–Perryman, 1974), the authors found that the normal group expressed memories with a higher frequency of the theme of mutuality, which relates to feelings of acceptance, friendliness, and cooperation with others in social situations. In contrast, the early memories of alcoholic individuals were characterized by interpersonal relationships involving fear, anxiety, threat, and an external locus of control. In a comparable study, Hafner, Fakouri, and Chesney (1988) reported that 27 adult females in treatment for alcoholism at a mental health center recalled significantly more early recollections with themes involving fear and anxiety than 30 females in a control group.

In a related study, Chaplin and Orlofsky (1991) evaluated the early memories of 45 adult males in an alcoholism treatment program in comparison with 45 males not in treatment. The authors reported that the alcoholism treatment sample in comparison to the nontreatment group reported early recollections reflecting more negative affect, greater passivity, a reduced self-concept, and an external locus of control. Through an analysis of early recollections content, Chesney, Fakouri, and Hafner (1986) were able to differentiate between adults in treatment for alcoholism in regard to their willingness or unwillingness to continue treatment. An example of a patient's early recollection in treatment for alcoholism reflects representative characteristics suggested in the research literature. The individual recalls: "I was about six years old when my father made me help him wash his car. I was sick of working so I pushed soapy water through the window. My father yelled at me and grabbed me by the neck. I felt scared and mad."

From a substance dependence perspective, Laskowitz (1961) evaluated the thematic content of early recollections of adolescents in an inpatient facility for addictions treatment. Laskowitz found that the early memories of the patients generally reflected feelings of inadequacy, isolation, and fear. The adolescents' early memories also tended to involve the expression of withdrawal or hostility in response to a perceived hostile environment. In other instances, individuals reported memory recall relating to personal infractions and rule breaking with only minimal consequences. As an example, a patient shared the following early recollection: "I gave away two of my father's ties to some kids in the street. Don't remember why. When my father found out he yelled and yelled. But even then I knew his screaming was a lot of crap, all bark and no bite" (Laskowitz, 1961, p. 72). In a related study, researchers attempted to thematically appraise common features in early recollections among young adult males in addictions treatment (Lombardi & Angers, 1967). Individuals in treatment tended to express themes involving low social interest, dependence in learning, a perception of the world as hostile and dangerous, and a lack of goals and direction in life. The following examples illustrate early recollections of the addicted population: "I remember when I was about six, my grandfather—well, I had this whistle and I was blowing it and stopping cars and he came and hit me." "I was about seven, I got hit by a car. I ran upstairs into the hallway and started crying. I didn't tell my mother. I wasn't hurt but scared" (Lombardi & Angers, 1967, p. 9). In a study involving adults with at least two years of opiate abuse (Colker and Slaymaker, 1984), two judges evaluated their early recollections in comparison to a control group. The group in addictions treatment demonstrated a significantly reduced level of social interest relative to the control group.

SCHIZOPHRENIA AND OTHER PSYCHOTIC DISORDERS

An effort to differentiate among various types of psychoses has been a focus that has generated some research interest involving early recollections. Friedman and Schiffman (1962) attempted to distinguish differences between 20 adult patients with a diagnosis of paranoid schizophrenia and 20 other patients with a psychotic depression diagnosis. The authors reported that with the paranoid schizophrenic group, fear and concerns about bodily harm were prominent in their early recollections, and the memories of the psychotic depressive group frequently involved illness and reflections on good times lost. A patient diagnosed with paranoid schizophrenia related the following early recollection: "I was frightened, didn't want to go to school, don't know why. Just feared it for a couple of days and weeks. My mother brought me a box of Chiclets to pacify my fear" (Friedman & Schiffman, 1962, p. 60). In another study evaluating the early memories of 20 adult female inpatients with a diagnosis of paranoid schizophrenia, Langs et al. (1960) reported common thematic findings. The individuals' memories tended to be relatively barren, including a lack of interaction between persons or a high frequency of being alone. The memories were also varied in feeling tone, but the patients generally perceived their recollections as pleasant or neutral.

From a case study perspective, Olson (1979a) provided an analysis of the developmental background and early recollections of "Robert" who was diagnosed with schizoaffective disorder. According to Olson, Robert was sheltered and overprotected by his parents and had developed hallucinations in college. Olson observed that Robert's early recollections emphasized a self-boundedness and a barrenness, implying that human contact is uncomfortable or threatening. Robert related the following early recollection:

> I remember seeing a tremendous blue rocking chair with polka dots, also a red toy box. These seemed huge. The rest of the room seemed out of focus, hazy and black-like. No light from outside, space that seemed consumed, as if there were no door or windows. Remember being there, not wanting to know what was on the outside, not caring. (Olson, 1979b, p. 316)

In other investigations involving multiple cases, which include schizophrenic patients, Friedmann (1950, 1952) reported the early recollections of a number of adults. She related an early memory of a patient diagnosed with hebephrenic (disorganized type) schizophrenia: "Being chased by a wild dog; being paralyzed, unable to move" (Friedmann, 1952, p. 267). In his delusion, the patient recognizes President Wilson as a wild dog. In other cases that do not specify the schizophrenia type, persons reported their early recollections, which tended to reflect solitary and distressful experiences. One patient stated, "I'm in my crib, wet, soiled, screaming. My parents arrive, scold me, beat me, hit me over the head" (Friedmann, 1950, p. 113). In another instance, a patient describes a depersonalized early memory depicting an ice-cold day, with fog outside, and icicles on trees. A further example that is characteristic of the schizophrenia group includes the early recollections of a patient involving perceived episodes of drowning, losing control, getting lost, and being lost (Friedmann, 1950).

In another direction in terms of diagnostic impressions, Ferguson (1964) found that experienced clinicians using early recollections were not able to make valid diagnoses between groups of adult inpatients with a diagnosis of schizophrenia and outpatients with a diagnosis of neurosis at a level better than chance. At the same time, the judges using Adlerian summaries of lifestyle formulations were able to reliably differentiate specific personality traits among the patients. Hafner, Corotto, and Fakouri (1980) attempted to differentiate hospitalized adult patients diagnosed with paranoid and undifferentiated schizophrenia types and schizoaffective disorder on the basis of their early recollections. Employing an early recollections scoring system (Manaster & Perryman, 1974), the only theme reaching significance involved paranoid schizophrenia groups mentioning "new situations" more frequently. In another study comparing early recollections of "normal" adults and adults with a diagnosis of paranoid schizophrenia, Hafner, Fakouri, Ollendick, and Corotto (1979) evaluated differences relating to diagnosis and lifestyle. The only theme cluster reaching significance level occurred in the early recollections of the normal group who reported memories involving more illness or injury and more attention-getting behavior than the paranoid schizophrenic group. The authors concluded that a differential diagnosis of early recollections cannot be determined actuarially, and instead should be made clinically and phenomenologically in conjunction with other assessment data. Finally, evaluating the early recollections of patients with a diagnosis of various types of schizophrenia, Hafner and Fakouri (1978) reported a pronounced continuity from memories of the past and the present crises that brought the individuals to the hospital.

MOOD DISORDERS

A number of investigations have explored the possibility of using early recollections for diagnostic purposes in regard to depression or mood disorders (Brewin, Andrews, & Gotlib, 1993). One study compared the early recollections of a group of 25 "normal" adults and the first memories of 25 patients diagnosed with neurotic depression in treatment at a mental health center (Fakouri, Hartung, & Hafner, 1985). Each subject in the study completed two written early recollections that were systematically evaluated (Manaster & Perryman, 1974). In comparison to the normal group, patients diagnosed with depression recalled significantly more early recollections involving anxiety, threat, and an external locus of control. In another study, correlating the early recollections of a small group of late adulthood individuals with scores on the Beck Depression Inventory (Hood & Johnson, 2002), Allers, White, and Hornbuckle (1990) reported significant relationships between depression level scores on the inventory and particular early recollections variables.

Subjects with scores in the depressed range reported early recollections content relating to negative affect, an external locus of control, and a passive versus active orientation. As an example of the variable of passivity, an elderly person with an inventory score indicating depression related the following early recollection:

> The very earliest thing I ever remember is looking out the window. We lived in the country in a little red house, and I had an older brother and sister. And I was lookin' out the window, and it had been snowin'. It snows a lot in Kentucky. And I was looking out the window, and they were out there with my Dad building a snowman. And that's the first thing I recall and I must have been, maybe, three or four years old. (Allers et al., 1990, p. 64)

It may be noted here that the individual's feelings are not reported in conjunction with the early recollection, and this omission leaves the interpretation of the memory tentative at best.

Employing a similar method with their study involving late adulthood individuals, Allers, White, and Hornbuckle (1992) evaluated the early recollections of graduate level counseling students in relationship to depression. Of the three variables selected for examination, depressed subjects reported significantly more early memories relating to passivity, an external locus of control, and negative affective tone. As an example, a subject related the following early recollection: "I was five years old when playing in the back yard. My dad came into the yard and let our two pointers out of their dog pen. They headed straight for me and kept chasing me. They caught me and knocked me down and I couldn't get away" (Allers et al., 1992, p. 326).

In a related study, Acklin, Sauer, Alexander, and Dugoni (1989) evaluated the hypothesis that certain variables should be present in the early recollections of depressed individuals. Using the Beck Depression Inventory (Hood & Johnson, 2002) among other standardized measures and an early recollections scoring system (Last & Bruhn, 1983), the authors found significant relationships associated with predicted early memories variables obtained through a self-administered questionnaire with college students. Depressed individuals reported significantly more recollections involving the following perceptions: self—passive, ineffectual, and damaged; others—need-frustrators; environment—threatening, unpredictable or unsafe; peer/sibling interactions—involving a higher frequency of defeat. The early memories of the depressed subjects were also rated significantly more unpleasant in comparison to nondepressed individuals. In a contrasting direction in terms of outcome, Robbins and Tanck (1994) evaluated the early recollections of a group of college students relating to pleasant versus unpleasant experiences. On the basis of responses to the Beck Depression Inventory, participants were categorized as depressed or nondepressed. Although the tendency was to rate more early memories as pleasant than unpleasant, there was no difference between the two categorized samples in the recall of unpleasant early memories.

From a case study perspective, Ilgenfritz (1979) discussed the course of treatment for a client, Ann, in her early 20s, who found life empty, meaningless, and almost unbearable. Ann believed that others have more than she has and she felt fearful and uncertain, particularly in regard to accepting responsibility. Ann, diagnosed with depression, reported the following early memory in which prominent personal themes are identifiable: "I went to the hospital for my tonsils. I didn't want to leave home but once I got there I was okay. I had a crib; everybody else had a bed. That really bothered me." Ann was five years old at the time of the recollection. The most vivid part of the memory for Ann was that she "didn't want to leave home," and at that point she felt scared. Eisenstein and Ryerson (1951) recounted the first memories of clinically depressed adult patients and found a common theme of being abandoned. The following are early memories of two female patients: "Mother and father went out and left us children alone in the house." "Mother left us sleeping all alone in the afternoon in the store; I got scared and ran out" (p. 217).

Considering the acknowledged relationship between depression and suicide, evaluating the early recollections of individuals with suicidal ideation may be a therapeutically useful pursuit. With this in mind, Monahan (1983) assessed the early memories of suicidal and nonsuicidal children and adolescents at an inpatient psychiatric setting. Monahan hypothesized that there would be differences in the ratings of ego functions and object relations proceeding from the early recollections of subjects who talk about taking their own lives and those persons who actually attempt suicide. In comparison to individuals who attempt suicide, subjects who talk about suicide were predicted to demonstrate higher levels of self-restraint through an ability to delay action and a willingness to initiate communication with others by seeking help or through the means of a threat. Results indicated that the suicidal group provided significantly more early memories than a control group of nonsuicidal children and adolescents. Subjects who talk about suicide had more pleasant memories and described people as more caring and less often injured or ill than those subjects who attempt suicide or controls. Monahan concluded that on the basis of frequency and content of early memories, practitioners should not assume that suicidal behavior implies a lack of connectedness or relationships with others.

ANXIETY DISORDERS

Early investigations of neuroticism focused on the total number of early memories that individuals express. From a psychoanalytic perspective, it was assumed that persons with a diagnosis of neurosis would tend to repress unpleasant and disturbing early memories, and a higher frequency of recalls should indicate greater emotional stability. Crook and Harden (1931) reported results that tended to confirm this hypothesis with a small number of adult subjects. In contrast to their finding, other researchers using much larger sample sizes found no statistical association for relatively low reportings of early memories and degree of neuroticism (Child, 1940; Waldfogel, 1948). In a contemporary study involving college students, Caruso and Spirrison (1996) found that individuals with more pervasive childhood amnesia were less neurotic and less self-conscious than persons who were more able to recall early childhood memories. From another perspective, Feichtinger (1943) discussed several case studies pertaining to the early memories of adult individuals involving prominent fearful situations that relate to a contemporary diagnosis of anxiety disorders. In a more recent study, Langs (1965b) evaluated the early memories of adult male patients in addition to considering the assessment results from a battery of other psychological assessments. With the group of patients diagnosed with obsessive-compulsive disorder, the most distinguishing features in their early memories were passivity, voyeuristic content, a paucity of people, and a relative absence of people with active roles.

In an attempt to substantiate the hypothesis that particular neurotic categories would involve certain themes in childhood memories, Jackson and Sechrest (1962) assessed the early recollections of adults in outpatient treatment. The authors reported that patients diagnosed with anxiety neurosis reported memories in which fear and threat are prominent, and others with gastrointestinal symptoms recalled memories relating to gastrointestinal distress. In another study, assessing the early recollections of college students and adults, Warren (1982) found significant correlations with self-report inventories measuring major personality dimensions, including obsessive-compulsive functioning and early recollections. Focusing on a group of male Vietnam veterans diagnosed with posttraumatic stress disorder, Hyer, Woods, and Boudewyns (1989) evaluated multiple measures of early memories in addition to further psychological testing. Results indicated that early recollections content of the patients reflected diminished social interest, a frequent pursuit of goals in a more "devious" social manner, an active instrumental style in life, a vigorous sense of being acted upon by others, and more negative outcomes and themes, including trauma. The authors concluded that it was unclear whether the perceptions and current problems of the patients were a direct result of Vietnam stressors or a reflection of preexisting functioning or both.

DISSOCIATIVE DISORDERS

Allers and Golson (1994) evaluated the early recollections of a group of clients with a diagnosis of dissociative identity disorder, which was formerly known as multiple personality disorder. The clients, from a perspective of various alters or discrete personality states, recalled different early memories. The recollections often manifested a pattern of behavior that was at variance from that of the host or original personality and other alters in the personality system. The authors also reported a history of trauma, in particular sexual abuse, among individuals with a dissociative identity disorder diagnosis. In a related investigation involving a case study, Allers and Snow (1999) discussed the therapeutic treatment of a young adult male with a diagnosis of dissociative identity disorder and a history of sexual abuse. The client, while demonstrating 17 fully separated identities, reported 31 distinct and unduplicated early recollections. The memories were related to each respective identity and were most distinguishable by positive and negative affect patterns and an active–passive interpersonal dimension. A passive orientation of particular identities involved more self-defeating and self-destructive behaviors and distorted attitudes toward self and others.

EATING DISORDERS

Williams and Manaster (1990) evaluated clinical samples of individuals diagnosed with specific types of eating disorders. Each of the female patients in the study recounted three early recollections in addition to completing another projective technique, the Thematic Apperception Test (Anastasi & Urbina, 1997). In comparison to a control group, the inpatient and outpatient subjects demonstrated greater external locus of control and negative affect through the projective techniques. Specifically, the restrictor anorexics group showed greater passivity and detachment from their own feelings and from others. Other individuals in the bulimic and bulimic anorexic groups produced projective responses revealing generally poor interpersonal relationships and defective relationships with their mothers. Providing a topical overview of eating disorders relative to anorexia nervosa, Barrett (1981) found common personality dynamics reflected in the early recollections of individuals diagnosed with the disorder. Frequently recognizable themes in multiple case presentations involved frustration of autonomy, preoccupations relating to food and weight in negative contexts, perceptions of malevolent maternal figures, and feelings of inferiority. A case example of an early recollection of a 22-year-old woman with a diagnosis of anorexia nervosa thematically illustrates a perceived lack of control and feelings of being trapped. The patient related:

> The first memory I had was when I was about three years old. It is the earliest thing I can remember in my life. I was inside our house in the basement. I saw a window or flash of light—a big pattern of light coming through the window, and I walked toward it because I wanted to be in that light. Anyway I was covered by a spider's web. I was completely caught in the web and I couldn't get away from it. (p. 9)

INFANCY, CHILDHOOD, OR ADOLESCENCE

In a study focusing on children and adolescents, 51 individuals were diagnosed by independent clinical teams for cases of psychoneurosis, conduct disturbance, and adjustment reactions (Hedvig, 1965). Experienced judges were then asked to determine the diagnoses of the subjects on the basis of early recollections without the benefit of additional background information. The judges were able to make accurate diagnoses to a limited extent. As a result, Hedvig felt that using early memories alone for diagnostic purposes had limitations in terms of accuracy, but she endorsed their use in a projective assessment battery or as an aid in formulating the lifestyle of individuals. Weiland and Steisel (1958) evaluated the early recollections of a group of 95 emotionally disturbed children and adolescents in outpatient and residential psychiatric treatment. Very few characteristics were found common to the generic emotionally disturbed group, and the authors thought that it might be more useful to classify the subjects into discrete units such as those represented in clinical diagnosis.

Another study focused on the relationship of children's early memories and four diagnostic types (Last & Bruhn, 1985). Diagnoses of the subjects from the ages of 8 through 12 were accurately identified by early memories data at a level far exceeding chance. In terms of diagnostic classifications, delinquent subjects typically perceived themselves as having minimal effective impact on those around them, and they generally viewed their environment as lacking support. Hyperactive subjects frequently recalled their mothers as present and generally perceived themselves as effective in a supportive environment. Schizoid subjects were relatively isolated from parental figures, yet they viewed themselves functioning in an environment that was generally seen as supportive. Subjects classified with somatic complaints tended to present a mixed picture with mid-range scores on all variables. In an earlier study, Last and Bruhn (1983) evaluated the early memories of 94 males between the ages of 8 and 12 and were able to discriminate at a significant level groupings of individuals on the basis of their memories into well-adjusted, mildly maladjusted, and severely maladjusted.

CONDUCT DISORDER

Exploring the nature of delinquency through early recollections has been a focus of several investigations. The violation of societal norms or rules in the pattern of behavior of the individuals evaluated suggests a diagnostic classification of conduct disorder of a child- or adolescent-onset type. Plottke (1949) assessed the written responses to papers on "My first childhood recollections" completed by 50 female adolescents in a normal day school near Paris and 50 papers provided by "delinquent" female adolescents residing in the region in an institution for reeducation. About one-third of the "normal" adolescents had pleasant early recollections, with the delinquent sample rarely reporting pleasant first memories. The most frequent theme found in the early recollections of the delinquent subjects was physical or verbal punishment. Researchers (Bruhn & Davidow, 1983) conducted another study evaluating four early memories of 15 male adolescents committing at least one property offense and 18 male students comprising a control group. Judges were able to discriminate between the two groups at a rate significantly greater than chance. The early memory content of the delinquent group generally involved serious rule breaking and personal injury, and a lack of trust, self-sufficiency, and impulse control.

In a study with implications for educational placement, Roth and Nicholson (1990) evaluated the earliest school recollections of violent and assaultive adolescents. Using a coding procedure, judges were able to successfully differentiate students who were successful or unsuccessful upon their reintegration into mainstreamed public school classes. Focusing on the early recollections and sexual fantasies of eight adolescent male sexual offenders, Dutton and Newlon (1988) found common thematic content expressed by the subjects. Prominent themes included in the adolescents' memory related to emotional detachment and objectification of others, control, victimization, isolation, and feelings of inadequacy. Finally, analyzing an early recollection in a case of juvenile delinquency, Thatcher (1944) discussed the therapeutic value of a single memory in positively influencing the behavior of an early adolescent.

PERSONALITY DISORDERS

In contrast to Axis I disorders, which tend to be acute and episodic, Axis II personality disorders represent chronic, habitual, and pervasive patterns of dysfunctional behavior (Sperry & Carlson, 1996). Primarily encompassing investigations involving criminal offenders, antisocial personality disorder has been a central research focus in regard to early recollections within Axis II of the *DSM–IV–TR* (2000). Diagnostic studies involving early memories also include borderline personality disorder and histrionic personality disorder.

ANTISOCIAL PERSONALITY DISORDER

Hankoff (1987) compared the early memories of 32 adult offenders with a history of serious crime and delinquency with 50 noncriminal control group members. Significant differences were found between the two groups pertaining to the content and feeling tone of the early memories. In contrast to the control group, content in the offenders' first remembrances was more dramatic and unpleasant, including a high proportion of disturbing or aggressive interactions. Hankoff observed that early recollections do not operate to reject or distort an offender's vision of an injurious world. In this regard, two early adulthood offenders respectively recounted the following early memories: "I played on the railroad tracks when I was a baby and got beat for it, before I started school, about 5." "I was chased by a chicken cock that is a fighting chicken, about 3 years old" (p. 200). In a related study, Elliot, Fakouri, and Hafner (1993) compared the early recollections of adult criminal offenders with a noncriminal control group. Fifty male prisoners incarcerated for felony offenses and 48 males in the control group provided early memories, which were scored systematically (Manaster & Perryman, 1974). The offender group recalled significantly more themes involving death, punishment, and misdeeds than did the noncriminal group. The offenders' early recollections also had significantly greater emphasis relating to concern with details, vigorous physical activity, and auditory detail involving volume and quality of sound.

In a comprehensive study designed to identify individuals at risk for dangerous acting out, Tobey and Bruhn (1992) compared the early memories of "dangerous" psychiatric patients with those of nondangerous control group members. The dangerous group consisted of 30 male patients in a maximum security forensic hospital, and 30 male psychiatric inpatients not convicted of felonies served as a control group. The subjects' scores were assessed through two systematic early memory scoring systems (Bruhn, 1990b). Results indicated that significantly more dangerous patients recalled aggressive early memories than the control group, and the nature of the aggression was more severe. Thematically, dangerous patients perceived their environment as hostile and other people as victimizers. Interestingly, the authors concluded that early memories data are more useful for identifying probable risk factors for acting out than as predictors of dangerousness. Grunberg (1989), who was also interested in predicting potential for criminal behavior, assessed the early memories of 30 mentally ill homeless males with criminal histories. The subjects, diagnosed as having clinical disorders, reported early recollections reflecting a high degree of victimization, alienation, and conflict.

An early case study involved an analysis of the earliest memory of a 24-year-old male referred to as a "delinquent" (Opedal, 1935). "Mr. B" was seen by the therapist upon his release from a federal prison, where he had been sentenced for a year and a day for counterfeiting. With a history of criminal activity, Mr. B related the following early memory:

> An aunt gave me a postman's uniform, and I remember going into the attic and taking a bundle of old letters, which the family had put away. Then I waited for the mailman, and when he came by I followed him down the street and distributed the letters I had taken from the attic. When the letters were gone, I was a long way from home, and I realized that I was lost. I started to cry, and two women who were passing stopped and asked me where I lived. I remember the more they asked, the harder I cried. Finally they took me to a police station, and the policeman brought me home. As soon as I got home my father gave me a good beating. (p. 54)

Mr. B. concluded in a mocking laugh, "There's one thing, though, the family never found out what happened to the letters in the attic" (p. 54). Mr. B's early recollection reflects qualities that are characteristic of memories of individuals with a diagnosis of antisocial personality disorder. His memory is dramatic and entails vigorous physical activity. He perceives other people as victims, and the situation involves misdeeds and aggressive interactions.

BORDERLINE PERSONALITY DISORDER

From a perspective of object relations theory, Arnow and Harrison (1991) evaluated the early memories of 45 adult outpatients representing three diagnostic groups: borderline personality disorder, neurotic character pathology, and paranoid schizophrenia. Each of the patients reported multiple memories, which included their feelings associated with each respective recollection. In comparison with the other groups, the authors found that individuals with a borderline personality diagnosis possess few sustaining or comforting images with respect to their representation of the self in relationship to others. In a related study, Nigg, Lohr, Westen, Gold, and Silk (1992) evaluated the object relations of a group of adult inpatients with a diagnosis of borderline personality disorder and another group with a major depression diagnosis. Assessing the individuals' early memories with a modified version of the Early Memory Test (EMT) (Mayman, 1968), Nigg et al.

(1992) found that the borderline group typically recalled memories attributing malevolent intentions to others and an expectation of insufficient care and support. Lacking a sense of protection, the persons feel even more anxious, enraged, and disappointed. In a study investigating the object representations of sexually abused inpatient adults with a borderline personality disorder diagnosis and another group with a diagnosis of major depressive disorder, Nigg, Silk, Westen, Lohr, Gold, Goodrich, and Ogata (1991) employed the EMT in evaluating the individuals' early memories. Nigg et al. (1991) reported an association between the borderline group and early memory portrayals of perceptions of injurious and malevolent object representations. The authors concluded that the study provides further support to the premise that a history of sexual abuse is linked to adult borderline personality disorder in terms of developmental aspects of pathology.

HISTRIONIC PERSONALITY DISORDER

Langs et al. (1960) evaluated the early memories of ten adult inpatients with a diagnosis of hysterical character disorder and 10 inpatients with a diagnosis of paranoid schizophrenia reaction. With respect to the patients with a diagnosis of histrionic (hysterical) personality disorder, they tended to express traumatic early memories relating to punishment, illness, rejection, and destruction. Other people were perceived as rejecting or hostile, and the memories were predominantly action-oriented. In their first memories, the patients made frequent reference to body parts, clothing and appearances, and moral issues. Representative of the histrionic diagnostic group, a patient related the following early memory: "Mother and father were fighting. I was 4. We were all eating at the table. Father got up and threw a dish of spaghetti against the wall" (p. 526).

SUMMARY

Attempts to evaluate the relationship between early recollections and various mental disorders have an extensive and lengthy history. Although a number of investigations predate the current diagnostic system, it is possible to categorize research findings in general accord with the *DSM–IV–TR* (2000). Research pertaining to studies consistent with Axis I clinical disorders include substance-related disorders, schizophrenia and other psychotic disorders, mood disorders, anxiety disorders, eating disorders, dissociative disorders, disorders relating to infancy, childhood, or adolescence, and conduct disorder. Research activity relative to Axis II personality disorders has been more limited and with a focus on antisocial, borderline, and histrionic personality disorders. Beyond reporting diagnostic impressions, a common research recommendation is that early recollections findings should be used in conjunction with other assessment methods such as clinical interviews, case records, and data from other appraisal devices in order to formulate comprehensive client or patient evaluations. Reference to the research on early recollections contributes to the interpretation of the memories in a contextual assessment approach. Table 4.1 provides a summary of early recollections research on clinical disorders and personality disorders.

TABLE 4.1: EARLY RECOLLECTIONS RESEARCH ON CLINICAL DISORDERS
AND PERSONALITY DISORDERS

CLINICAL DISORDERS
Substance-Related Disorders

1. Adult group in treatment for alcoholism reported memories characterized by fear, anxiety, threat, and an external locus of control. "Normal" group expressed higher frequency of theme of mutuality, which relates to feelings of acceptance, friendliness, and cooperation with others (Hafner et al., 1982).
2. Female adult group in treatment for alcoholism recalled significantly more memory themes involving fear and anxiety than control group (Hafner et al., 1988).
3. Adult males in treatment for alcoholism in comparison to a nontreatment group reported early recollections reflecting more negative affect, greater passivity, reduced self-concept, and an external locus of control (Chaplin & Orlofsky, 1991).
4. Adults in treatment for alcoholism were differentiated in regard to willingness or unwillingness to continue treatment on the basis of their early recollections (Chesney et al., 1986).
5. Adolescents in addictions treatment reported early memories reflecting feelings of inadequacy, isolation, and fear. Their memories also involved an expression of withdrawal or hostility and rule breaking in a perceived hostile environment (Laskowitz, 1961).
6. Young male group in addictions treatment expressed early recollections themes involving low social interest, dependence in learning, a perception of the world as hostile and dangerous, and a lack of goals and direction in life (Lombardi & Angers, 1967).
7. Adults in treatment for opiate abuse reported early recollections with a significantly reduced level of social interest in comparison to a control group (Colker & Slaymaker, 1984).

Schizophrenia and Others Psychotic Disorders

1. Adults with diagnosis of paranoid schizophrenia reported early memories with prominent expressions of fear and concerns with bodily harm. Adults with a diagnosis of psychotic depression frequently related memories emphasizing illness and good times lost (Friedman & Schiffman, 1962).
2. Female adults with a diagnosis of paranoid schizophrenia recalled memories that

tended to be relatively barren, isolated from others, and emotionally pleasant or neutral (Langs et al., 1960).

3. An adult male in a case study with a diagnosis of schizoaffective disorder related early memories emphasizing a self-boundedness and barrenness (Olson, 1979b).

4. In multiple cases, which include adults diagnosed with various types of schizophrenia, memories tended to reflect solitary and distressful experiences (Friedmann, 1950, 1952).

5. Experienced clinicians using early recollections were not able to make valid diagnoses between inpatients with a diagnosis of schizophrenia and outpatients with a diagnosis of neurosis. However, the clinicians were able to differentiate specific personality traits among the patients (Ferguson, 1964).

6. Among adult patients diagnosed with paranoid and undifferentiated schizophrenia and schizoaffective disorder, the only theme reaching significance involved the paranoid schizophrenia group mentioning "new situations" more frequently (Hafner et al., 1980).

7. A group of "normal" adults in comparison to adults with a diagnosis of paranoid schizophrenia reported significantly more memories involving illness and attention-getting behavior (Hafner et al., 1979).

8. Among adult patients with a diagnosis of various types of schizophrenia, they recalled a pronounced continuity from memories of the past and to present crises (Hafner & Fakouri, 1978).

Mood Disorders

1. In comparison with "normal" adults, patients diagnosed with neurotic depression reported significantly more early recollections involving anxiety, threat, and an external locus of control (Fakouri et al., 1985).

2. Persons in late adulthood with scores on a depression inventory in the depressed range related early recollections with negative affect, an external locus of control, and a passive versus active orientation (Allers et al., 1990).

3. Graduate level students with scores in the depressed range on a depression inventory reported significantly more early memories relating to passivity, an external locus of control, and negative affective tone (Allers et al., 1992).

4. College students with scores on a depression inventory in the depressed range related significantly more early recollections involving the following perceptions: self—passive, ineffectual, and damaged; others—need-frustrators; environment—threatening, unpredictable or unsafe; peer/sibling interactions—involving a higher frequency of defeat. Memories were also significantly more unpleasant in comparison to nondepressed individuals (Acklin et al., 1989).

5. A group of college students categorized as depressed or nondepressed on a depression inventory showed no difference in the recall of unpleasant early memories (Robbins & Tanck, 1994).

6. In a case study with an early adulthood client diagnosed with depression, a female patient reported an early recollection with themes involving anxiety, fear, and envy (Ilgenfritz, 1979).

7. Adult patients with a diagnostic impression of clinical depression expressed a

common theme of abandonment in their early recollections (Eisenstein & Ryerson, 1951).

8. A suicidal group of children and adolescents provided significantly more early memories than a control group. Individuals who talk about suicide reported more pleasant memories and described people as more caring and less often injured or ill than those who attempt suicide or persons in the control group (Monahan, 1983).

Anxiety Disorders

1. Adults with a diagnosis of neurosis demonstrated a low frequency of recalling early memories (Crook & Harden, 1931). No statistical relationship was found between relatively low reportings of early memories and degree of neuroticism (Child, 1940; Waldfogel, 1948).
2. In case studies of adults with assumed anxiety disorders diagnoses, patients reported early memories involving prominent themes involving fearful situations (Feichtinger, 1943).
3. Adult male patients diagnosed with obsessive-compulsive disorders related early memories involving passivity, voyeuristic content, a paucity of people, and a relative absence of people with active roles (Langs, 1965b).
4. Adult patients diagnosed with anxiety neurosis recalled early memories in which fear and threat are prominent, and others with gastrointestinal symptoms reported memories relating to gastrointestinal distress (Jackson & Sechrest, 1962).
5. Significant correlations were found between self-report inventories of college students and adults measuring obsessive-compulsive functioning and their early recollections (Warren, 1982).
6. Male Vietnam veterans diagnosed with posttraumatic stress disorder related early recollections content reflecting diminished social interest, a frequent pursuit of goals in a more "devious" social manner, an active instrumental style in life, a vigorous sense of being acted upon by others, and more negative outcomes and themes, including trauma (Hyer et al., 1989).

Dissociative Disorders

1. Clients with a diagnosis of dissociative identity disorder recalled different early memories from the perspective of various alters and the host personality. A history of trauma, particularly sexual abuse, was present in the experiences of the individuals (Allers & Golson, 1994).
2. A young adult male, with a diagnosis of dissociative identity disorder and a history of sexual abuse, demonstrated multiple identities with distinct early recollections. A passive orientation of particular identities involved dysfunctional behaviors and distorted attitudes toward self and others (Allers & Snow, 1999).

Eating Disorders

1. Female patients diagnosed with specific types of eating disorders demonstrated greater external locus of control and negative affect in comparison to a control group in projective technique content. Employing early recollections and another

projective technique, the restrictor anorexics group showed greater passivity and detachment from their own feelings and from others. Individuals in the bulimic and bulimic anorexia group revealed generally poor interpersonal relationships and defective relationships with their mothers (Williams & Manaster, 1990).

2. In case studies of individuals diagnosed with anorexia nervosa, patients reported early recollections with themes involving frustration of autonomy, preoccupations relating to food and weight in negative contexts, perceptions of malevolent maternal figures, and feelings of inferiority (Barrett, 1981).

Infancy, Childhood, or Adolescence

1. Children and adolescents diagnosed for cases of psychoneurosis, conduct disturbance, and adjustment reactions were independently evaluated based on early recollections alone. Judges were able to make a specific diagnosis only to a limited extent (Hedvig, 1965).

2. Children and adolescents designated emotionally disturbed in psychiatric treatment demonstrated common characteristics in their early recollections only to a very limited degree (Weiland & Steisel, 1958).

3. Diagnoses of children were statistically significant based on their early memories for four diagnostic types (delinquent, hyperactive, schizoid, and somatic complaints), and also for level of adjustment (Last & Bruhn, 1983, 1985).

Conduct Disorder

1. "Delinquent" females rarely reported pleasant early memories, and the most frequent theme found in the memories was physical or verbal punishment (Plottke, 1949).

2. A group of male adolescents designated as "delinquent" were differentiated from a control group based on their early recollections. The memory content of the delinquent group generally involved serious rule breaking and personal injury, and a lack of trust, self-sufficiency, and impulse control (Bruhn & Davidow, 1983).

3. Violent and assaultive adolescents were able to be differentiated in terms of success or failure upon their reintegration into mainstreamed public school classes (Roth & Nicholson, 1990).

4. Adolescent male sexual offenders expressed common themes in their early memories relating to emotional detachment and objectification of others, control, victimization, isolation, and feelings of inadequacy (Dutton & Newlon, 1988).

5. In a case study with an early adolescent involving juvenile delinquency, Thatcher (1944) discussed the therapeutic effect of employing a single early recollection.

PERSONALITY DISORDERS
Antisocial Personality Disorder

1. Adult offenders with a history of serious crime and delinquency were found to experience significant differences in their early memories in comparison to a control group. Memory content in the offender group was more dramatic and unpleasant, including a high proportion of disturbing or aggressive interactions (Hankoff, 1987).

2. Adult criminal offenders, in comparison to a control group, recalled significantly more themes involving death, punishment, misdeeds, concern with details, vigorous physical activity, and auditory detail (Elliot et al., 1993).
3. "Dangerous" adult males in a maximum security forensic hospital recalled significantly more aggressive early memories than a control group, and the nature of the aggression was more severe (Tobey & Bruhn, 1992).
4. Early memories of mentally ill homeless males with criminal histories reflected a high degree of victimization, alienation, and conflict (Grunberg, 1989).
5. In a case study, a "delinquent" young adult with a history of criminal activity recalled a dramatic memory emphasizing vigorous physical activity, victimization, misdeeds, and aggressive interactions (Opedal, 1935).

Borderline Personality Disorder

1. The early memories of adults diagnosed with borderline personality disorder reflected few sustaining or comforting images with respect to their representation of the self in relationship to others (Arnow & Harrison, 1991).
2. Adults with a diagnosis of borderline personality disorder typically recalled early memories attributing malevolent intentions to others and an expectation of insufficient care and support. The individuals' feelings related to anxiety, rage, and disappointment (Nigg et al., 1992).
3. An association was found between a group of adults with a diagnosis of borderline personality disorder and a history of sexual abuse, and early memory portrayals of perceptions of injurious and malevolent object representations (Nigg et al., 1991).

Histrionic Personality Disorder

Adult patients with a diagnosis of hysterical character disorder tended to recall early memories relating to punishment, illness, rejection, action-orientation, moral issues, and physical appearance (Langs et al., 1960).

11 EARLY RECOLLECTIONS
SCORING SYSTEMS, ADMINISTRATION, AND INTERPRETATION

5

Scoring Systems of Early Recollections

"I think, myself, that one's memories represent those moments which, insignificant as they may seem, nevertheless represent the inner self and oneself as most really oneself."
—Agatha Christie (1977, p. xiii)

INTRODUCTION

FOLLOWING AN EXAMINATION OF THEORETICAL PERSPECTIVES AND broad-based research up to this point, the next major section of the text focuses on specific aspects of the assessment function of early recollections. When practitioners employ first memories as a projective technique they customarily base their conclusions on their particular theoretical orientations and clinical and intuitive impressions. This subjective approach provides a variety and richness of client material and yields a virtually unlimited range and depth of idiosyncratic meanings (Sargent, 1945). At the same time, the possibility becomes remote for determining precise quantitative findings from evaluations subject to interpretation bias and a lack of normative data. Questionable psychometric properties have resulted in adverse reactions by a number of professionals on the use of early memories as a projective device, particularly by those individuals who prefer a more empirically based approach that is comparable to many other personality assessment procedures (Bishop, 1993; Malinoski et al., 1998). In response to this acknowledged preference or demand, researchers have attempted to devise more systematic methods for classifying and interpreting early recollections (Watkins & Schatman, 1986). Although numerous innovative approaches have been pursued to develop viable scoring procedures for early recollections, none of the methods have been widely used in counseling and psychotherapy. The various systems are most often based on the presence or absence of particular variables and the identification of relevant thematic content. Scoring does not actually involve normative data and statistical criteria, but instead focuses on the assignment of first memories inferential material to predetermined categories or designations (Olson, 1979d). The high number of potential scoring variables and diverse theoretical orientations have limited the development of more widely accepted assessment procedures for early recollections. Kal (1994) cautioned, however, that a single-minded pursuit of standardized psychometric properties may actually detract from the essential clinical message of early recollections and ultimately may be worse than relying on subjective and intuitive evaluation procedures.

SCORING SYSTEMS

In a biography of Alfred Adler, Orgler (1939/1965) wrote, "The realisation that first memories allow a deep insight into the human soul is one of Adler's greatest discoveries" (p. 29). Adler's original and routine use of early recollections as a projective technique involved an impressionistic and intuitive assessment approach. Although Adler did not establish an early recollections scoring system per se, he did suggest several key formulations that subsequently contributed to more systematic methods. In this regard, Munroe (1955) thought that "Adler's notion of comparing people on the basis of their spontaneous 'conscious' reaction to a fairly simple but dynamic question is the very core of contemporary projective techniques" (p. 429). Researchers after Adler largely followed the theoretical frameworks of Individual Psychology or the psychoanalytic schools of ego psychology and object relations in the assessment and therapeutic applications of early memories. Considering the divergent quality of Adlerian and Freudian viewpoints, it is understandable that theoretically related scoring approaches subsequently resulted in disparate models. In general, selected Adlerian theoretical factors have been augmented by the addition of other psychological dimensions, resulting in more lengthy and conceptually diverse appraisal procedures. The coding schemes of the psychoanalytic tradition typically reflect the complexities of the theory, and do so in a format that is often cumbersome and difficult to score (Kihlstrom & Harackiewicz, 1982). A unique theoretical method involves a cognitive-perceptual theory of personality for evaluating early memories and other memories over the course of the life span (Bruhn, 1990b, 1992a, 1992b). It is possible to identify significant features from the various theoretical approaches and procedures in order to formulate a practical, coherent, and comprehensive system. In this respect, a new contextural assessment approach integrates salient features from the work of previous researchers of early recollections with contemporary aspects of counseling and psychotherapy.

ADLER

When Adler wrote about the purpose and meaning of early recollections he was clear and descriptive. Adler (1931/1958) stated,

There are no "chance memories": out of the incalculable number of impressions which meet an individual, he chooses to remember only those which he feels, however darkly, to have a bearing on his situation. Thus, his memories represent his "Story of My Life"; a story he repeats to himself to warn him or comfort him, to keep him concentrated on his goal, to prepare him, by means of past experiences, to meet the future with an already tested style of action. (p. 73)

It is evident that Adler emphasized the instrumental function of early memories to justify or fortify an individual's goal structure and outlook on life (Bach, 1952). As eloquent as Adler could be in his commentary on early recollections, however, he was less clear in describing practical and systematic procedures for evaluating first memories. Most often, Adler provided a description or a verbatim account of a person's early recollections as a part of a broader discussion in the context of a detailed case study (Adler, 1929, 1929/1969, 1930/1982, 1931/1958). As an example, Adler (1930/1982) made reference to two brief early recollections of a rebellious boy whom he was treating: "He remembers his father chasing him around the table when he asked for a penny, and seeing his older sister fighting with another girl in the street" (p. 162).

In another case, Adler described the dysfunctional background of a 35-year-old male with a diagnosis of anxiety neurosis. The man experienced intense anxiety when he was away from home. On the relatively few occasions when he did attempt to leave home and go to work, the client cried during the day until he was able to go home to be with his mother. In this particular instance, Adler (1931/1958) provided a report of the man's early recollection: "I remember at four years of age staying at home close by the window, looking out on the street being interested to see the people working there" (p. 85). Adler thought that the client believed that the only way to live was to be supported by others in the secure setting of his home. As a treatment goal, Adler felt that it was necessary to change the individual's whole outlook on life. As therapy proceeded, over a period of time the client came to believe that he was capable of cooperating and becoming involved with others, and he eventually opened an art shop. In this capacity, the man maintained his observer status while making a socially useful vocational contribution (Ewen, 1998).

It is also possible to analyze Adler's various references to early recollections beyond his case material in order to identify particular points that are potentially relevant to comprehensive assessment procedures. Regarding the receptivity and cooperativeness of individuals in relating their early recollections, Adler (1931/1958) wrote: "In the main people are perfectly willing to discuss their first memories. They take them as mere facts, and do not realize the meaning hidden in them" (p. 75). In counseling, Adler (1929/1969) emphasized the importance of therapists being genuinely interested in the other person and employing a high degree of empathy in order to understand individuals, including their early recollections. With Adler's acknowledged assumption of holism and the unity of personality, he thought that childhood memories are inherently consistent and produce a coherent story when accurately interpreted (Slavik, 1991). In this regard it should be possible to formulate multiple early recollections of an individual into a cohesive whole that reflects unified personality characteristics. Employing the same line of reasoning, Adler did not distinguish between the interpretive importance of a person's first early memory report and the recall of subsequent early memories. Reflecting a holistic perspective, Adler (1929) pointed out that each early recollection, even though it may not be immediately apparent, involves a consistent expression of the lifestyle. Relatedly, with respect to the accuracy or inaccuracy of early recollections, Adler (1931/1958) felt that their veracity is immaterial because what is revealed reflects an individual's basic perception of life. Although Adler felt that early recollections were perhaps the single most important method for lifestyle assessment, he also recognized that the most trustworthy exploration of the personality should involve the consideration of multiple appraisals, including birth order, observations of childish errors, day and night dreams, and environmental factors (Adler, 1933/1964).

MANASTER–PERRYMAN

Originally developed for vocational guidance purposes, the Manaster–Perryman Manifest Content Early Recollection Scoring Manual (Manaster & Perryman, 1974, 1979) is one of the most frequently used early recollections scoring systems for research purposes (Fakouri & Hafner, 1994; Manaster, Berra, & Mays, 2001). The manual includes seven variables or categories representing diverse theoretical perspectives from the early recollections literature with an emphasis on Individual Psychology. Scores are evaluated on the basis of presence or absence of each particular category represented in an individual's early childhood memories. The following includes descriptions of each variable from the manual. *Characters* involve persons mentioned in the memory, such as mother, father, or siblings. *Themes* depict what the memory is about, such as illness or injury, punishment, or attention-getting. *Concern with Detail* relates to something seen, heard, or the description of vigorous physical movement. *Setting* concerns the place where the recalled incident took place. *Active–Passive* indicates the degree of initiation the individual demonstrates in regard to what happens in the memory. *Internal–External*

Control relates to whether the person assumes responsibility for what transpires in the memory. *Affect* signifies the pleasantness or unpleasantness of the early recollection.

LANGS AND ASSOCIATES

In a pilot study, Langs et al. (1960) developed a Manual for the Scoring of the Manifest Content of the Earliest Memory. The comprehensive manual contains four major sections with 43 items and is written primarily from an ego psychology perspective. Manaster and Perryman (1974) integrated several of the items from this manual into their system. Extending beyond Manaster and Perryman's selections, the following questions from Langs et al. (1960) also appear useful for scoring purposes with individuals: "Is the memory visualized in color or black and white?" "Other sensory modalities referred to?" "Patient's perception of the environment?" and "Patient's reactions to the environment?"

In an exhaustive study in terms of the scope of assessment, Langs (1965a) attempted to predict personality features from the early memories of 48 male professional actors. Hundreds of personality predictions are proposed, and specific findings are presented in 24 categories. Selected categories with applications potential for scoring purposes include the role of the subject (pawn of others, ineffectual, childish), the role of others (subservient to the subject), and the environment (unpredictable, both supportive and traumatic). Langs concluded that a significant relationship exists between first memories and an individual's personality when the context and roles of persons present in the memories are considered. In a related study, Langs (1965b) reported that early memories scores reflected characterologic diagnosis of the same groups of subjects evaluated in the predictive (1965a) investigation. Mosak (1969) summarized and evaluated the research of Langs and his associates from an Adlerian perspective.

LEVY

From an ego psychology point of view, Levy (1965) devised an intricate system for evaluating early memories. The complex procedure conceptualizes two continuums of active–passive and negative–positive dimensions. This creates a hybrid of four basic "modes" or typical ways of approaching emotional situations. The characteristic psychological functioning of an individual is assessed by combining the modes of a number of early memories in order to construct a "type." In scoring an early memory, the modes are evaluated as they relate to the emotional areas of "givingness," "mastery," and "mutuality." Finally, the four modes cut across the emotional areas and result in 12 units of scoring early memories. The dimensions of active–passive and positive–negative are prominent in the history of evaluating early memories and in the analysis of recollections in scoring systems. Finally, the particular emotional areas suggest prospective themes to consider for scoring purposes in a comprehensive assessment system.

In an earlier study, Levy and Grigg (1962) devised three thematic scales consistent with ego psychology and object relations orientations. The themes include dependency–independency, destructive–constructive aggression, and sexuality. Themes are functionally viewed as capturing an essential emotional state of an individual. The study involved thematically matching early recollections of 21 outpatients evaluated by the authors with assessment data provided by therapists on the same patients. Levy and Grigg found that central to an early memory is one focal theme or a configuration of themes. The significance of themes and the integration of thematic material for analysis purposes becomes primary. Additionally, the integral relationship of themes in conjunction with an individual's emotional state is emphasized for evaluating early recollections.

MAYMAN

Writing primarily from an object relations orientation, Mayman (1968) cited case illustrations involving the narrations of adolescents in the thematic analysis of early memories. Mayman also outlined a classification of prototypical interpersonal themes in first memories in relationship to psychosexual stages. In Mayman's view, the systematic scrutiny of themes in early recollections provides a rich source of data relating to how individuals define enduring perceptions of themselves and relationship predispositions toward other people. When assessing representations of self and others through early memories, Mayman emphasized the importance of determining the affective tone of an individual at the point of memory recall.

In a brief case example, Mayman presented two early memories of a female adolescent. Thematically, both recollections depict object relationships as empty, predatory, and cold-blooded. The following is one of the adolescent's early memories:

> I had a little white kitten that I had found and was taking care of. Mother wouldn't let me keep the cat in at night. I remember this very cold night, it was snowy and icy outside. I begged her to let the cat stay in but she didn't even listen to me. The next morning when I woke up and looked out the window, the cat's guts and blood were all over the street. It had been run over during the night. (Mayman, 1968, p. 308)

In a chilling conclusion to the case, Mayman reported that the girl had murdered her mother. She fed her mother poison and laughed at her as she writhed in pain and died. Following Mayman's object relations approach for assessing early memories, other researchers reported empirical and treatment utility support for correlating the qualitative aspects of human relationships and psychopathology (Acklin, Bibb, Boyer, & Jain, 1991; Fowler, Hilsenroth, & Handler, 2000), basic personality factors (Caruso & Spirrison, 1994), ambitious–narcissistic character style (Harder, 1979), dependency (Fowler, Hilsenroth, & Handler, 1996a), and a memory probe for identifying transitional phenomena (Fowler, Hilsenroth, & Handler, 1998).

In an innovative direction, Mayman routinely asks for specific types of early memories in addition to the earliest one. Inquiries are made in regard to the first memories of mother and father, happiest and unhappiest, and when time permits, the "most special" and "most striking." Finally, memories relating to a variety of feelings are explored. In an earlier study, Mayman and Faris (1960) demonstrated the use of specific or directed types of early memories in a case presentation of an early adulthood male in the course of an outpatient diagnostic evaluation. The patient's mother and father were also separately asked to provide a number of specific early memories in regard to their son. The authors concluded that the sets of memories from the perspectives of three persons contributed significantly to facilitating the total diagnostic process and for clarifying relational themes. More recently, Fowler, Hilsenroth, and Handler (1995) and Karlinger, Westrich, Shedler, and Mayman (1996) provided empirical support for eliciting specific types of early memories. From an opposite point of view, although specific or directed first memories may potentially engender diagnostic material, the extensive time required for elicitation from one person or multiple individuals and interpretation complexity may simply be prohibitive for many practitioners.

BRUHN AND ASSOCIATES

The Early Memories Scoring System–Revised is a comprehensive and carefully researched procedure that is theoretically grounded in a cognitive–perceptual theory of personality (Bruhn, 1981, 1984, 1985, 1990a, 1990b, 1992a, 1992b, 1995a, 1995b, 1998; Bruhn & Last, 1982; Bruhn & Schiffman, 1982a, 1982b; Last, 1997; Last & Bruhn, 1985; Tobey & Bruhn, 1992). Cognitive–perceptual theory holds that individuals tend to recall from long-term autobiographical memory what has utility and relevance in the present. Current perceptions also have continuity with the past in terms of major conclusions or axioms established early in life. The function of memory is to evoke constructions or fantasies from the past that have an immediate bearing on a person's present situation (Singer & Salovey, 1993). In this regard, Bruhn (1990b) believed that an individual's first memory has a special importance, as it tends to stimulate a series of early memories. For most persons, subsequent early memories elaborate thematic material introduced in the initial memory. In terms of procedures, the system involves requesting individuals to provide 6 spontaneous and 15 directed or specific memories. The directed memories include a variety of particular inquiries (e.g., school, punishment, happiest, most traumatic) that extend from early childhood across the life span. A person is requested by a therapist to complete the early memories assessment at home, which will take approximately three to four hours to finish.

Bruhn's elicitation of early memories and follow-up questions exclusively involve a written procedure. He makes the point that individuals are likely to be more comfortable in privately writing memories at home, rather than orally reporting them to a therapist. This approach also avoids the potential embarrassment that may occur with an in-depth inquiry into the memories on a face-to-face basis. In order to evaluate possible differences between the content of early memories elicited through a written procedure or through an interpersonal exchange, Fowler, Hilsenroth, and Handler (1996b), conducted a study with clinical groups at a university-based outpatient training center and with groups of undergraduate student volunteers. The authors reported that the early recollections written method appears to have given the clinical respondents a perception of a healthier adjustment, while the student group assumed an appearance of a poorer adjustment. Fowler et. al (1996b) attributed their findings to the presence of an examiner as a crucial interpersonal variable for prompting transference and defensive reactions of the individuals, which became manifest in the oral reporting of early memories. In contrast, the formal and impersonal written procedure tended to engender minimal stimulation and ego involvement when eliciting early recollections. The authors concluded that the use of an early memories written method could lead to erroneous and misguided interpretations, and that the interview procedure was superior for differentiating clinical from nonclinical subjects.

In a related study with female college students, Allers, Katrin, and White (1997) investigated possible content differences with respect to written and tape-recorded early recollections. Using an early recollections scoring system (Manaster and Perryman, 1974), the authors reported that tape-recorded memories contained significantly more words and self-references than handwritten memories. At the same time, Allers et al. (1997) concluded that the content of the early memories was not significantly affected by the method used to communicate the recollections. In this regard, approximately the same projective material was produced by tape-recording and handwriting of early recollections.

OTHER SYSTEMS

Rather than use a more common dichotomous procedure to evaluate the presence or absence of various early recollections variables, Altman (1973) devised a bipolar seven-point scale, referred to as the Early Recollections Rating Scale, with a thematic focus on social interest. The factors were then divided into two groups reflective of an individual's behavior toward the environment and perception of the environment (Zarski, 1981). As an example, a person's behavior toward the environment is evaluated on a continuum from aggressive and hostile to benevolent and kind. Using another organizational format, Rule (1972) devised early recollections content scales relating to the internal frame of reference of a subject, the behavior of the subject, and the behavior of others. In one specific scoring example, the level of curiosity (eagerness or openness to learning) pertains to the internal frame of reference of an individual.

In a preliminary investigation, Acklin et al. (1991) outlined the development of an early memory relationship scale scoring system focusing on particular variables. Employing clinical and nonclinical samples, Acklin et al. (1991) evaluated early memory relationship expressions of instrumental mastery, caregiver interactions, and peer–sibling interactions. The authors reported that relationship episodes or transactions may reliably be coded from early memories. It is apparent that organizing responses of early recollections by particular classifications allows for a more manageable assessment of data findings for scoring purposes. In a unique approach, Powers and Griffith (1987) employed a system in which two therapists collaborate in scoring and interpreting early recollections. The therapists discuss possible meanings of each memory in the presence of a client in order to immediately assess nonverbal and verbal reactions. A follow-up session involving only the two practitioners allows for a review and discussion of client early recollections in order to further clarify meanings in terms of particular categories. Finally, Wynne and Schaffzin (1965) devised a procedure that exclusively focuses on the emotional content of early memories. The approach involves evaluating the number and intensity of subjective feelings in the early memories of individuals.

CONTEXTURAL ASSESSMENT

After reviewing the various systems for scoring early recollections, several prominent directions emerge making it possible to distinguish viable features for use in a contextural system that integrates data from multiple sources. In this regard, more comprehensive procedures allow for evaluations that encompass broad representations of personality functioning. At the same time, individual assessments that provide an ease of administration within a relatively brief period of time are clearly more appealing to practitioners. Relatedly, specific scoring methods that do not consume an excessive amount of interpretive appraisal time are another practical feature. As indicated in research findings, an interpersonal procedure that elicits oral rather than written early memories appears to produce more accurate clinical results. In regard to scoring, themes are a prominent focus in almost all identified systems, and a thematic analysis of early recollections seems to be a sound assessment direction. Further, a system that evaluates details in early memories provides specificity to focal themes. Most procedures adopt a dichotomous approach to assessing early recollections, and this format appears compact and manageable for classification purposes. A scoring system that is able to make applications from the vast theoretical and empirical data in the literature relating to early recollections will also likely be more useful to practitioners. Beyond scoring procedures, an assessment model that may be integrated into the therapeutic process and offers potential for treatment utility would also be beneficial in counseling and psychotherapy.

An overview of a contextural scoring system involves two primary areas: administration of early recollections and the interpretation of memories. The next chapter of the text provides specifics on administering early memories, and chapters 7 and 8 focus on the interpretation process.

ADMINISTRATION

For most clients, a practitioner's elicitation of a small number of early recollections, perhaps three, provides sufficient information for viable interpretation purposes. Requesting a reasonable number of first memories also tends to maintain client focus and interest. Specific directions for administering early memories and follow-up inquires allow for a standardized format, and transcribing verbatim accounts of reminiscences enables therapists to refer back to protocols representing original client data. Several selected examiner questions ensure comprehensive client responses with respect to detail inclusion, thematic focus, and affective tone. Empathic and receptive counselor interactions enhance individuals' sense of support and understanding as they recall their early memories. Although early recollections can provide an overarching framework for organizing appraisal client material, the specific procedure represents one part of a systematic and comprehensive assessment process.

INTERPRETATION

After a client has fully responded to an early recollections appraisal, the therapist is in a position to develop particular hypotheses. Upon concluding a

subjective and intuitive analysis of a client's initial early recollection, a counselor begins to scrutinize the memory for thematic content from an interpersonal perspective. As a guide for clarifying themes, reference can be made to
22 dichotomous variables (e.g., significant–insignificant, secure–insecure,
constructive–destructive), which are to be found in Table 7.1 later in this
text. Next, details receive interpretive attention in terms of sensory modalities, colors, locations, and physical objects. Beyond an analysis of subjective
and interpersonal perspectives, practitioners may assume an objective stance
by considering the vast investigative research data available on diverse populations relating to early recollections. A counselor follows this same procedure in evaluating each early recollection within a set. Through this multiple
perspective process, the therapist develops working hypotheses that are integral to a comprehensive assessment effort involving the consideration of
client data from additional sources. By synthesizing varying facets of information on an individual, it is possible to complete a lifestyle syllogism or a
formulation of a model of a person.

TABLE 5.1: EARLY RECOLLECTIONS INTERPRETATION SYSTEMS

RESEARCHER	PRIMARY THEORETICAL ORIENTATION	INTERPRETIVE FOCUS	SIGNIFICANT FEATURE
1. Adler	Individual Psychology	Intuitive and impressionistic	Holistic and functional
2. Manaster–Perryman	Individual Psychology	Categorical	Scoring variables
3. Langs and Associates	Ego Psychology	Categorical	Personality predictions
4. Levy	Ego Psychology	Multiple levels	Thematic emphasis
5. Mayman	Object Relations	Thematic analysis	Directed memories
6. Bruhn and Associates	Cognitive–perceptual	Functional and comprehensive	Directed memories
7. Altman	Individual Psychology	Social interest	Bipolar scale
8. Rule	Individual Psychology	Self–others evaluation	Content scales
9. Powers and Griffith	Individual Psychology	Categorical	Collaborative interpretation
10. Clark	Individual Psychology	Multiple perspectives	Treatment utility

SUMMARY

Beyond the Adlerian orientation of Individual Psychology, various scoring systems present material drawn from ego psychology, object relations, and cognitive–perceptual theory. The degree of complexity varies considerably among the individual systems in regard to the explication of theoretical factors, scoring classifications, and data interpretation. Table 5.1 briefly outlines early recollections interpretation systems. Most often thematic content is a primary evaluative emphasis, and the presence or absence of particular personality variables becomes a focus for scoring purposes. An in-depth evaluation of the numerous published sources on the appraisal of early memories allows for the introduction of selected elements into a comprehensive system that offers viable and practical scoring and interpretive dimensions. A contextural assessment system emphasizes a multifaceted analysis of early recollections that can serve as an overarching framework for organizing client appraisal data from diverse sources.

6

ADMINISTRATION OF EARLY RECOLLECTIONS

"When we desire to recall what befell us in the earliest period of youth, it often happens that we confound what we have heard from others with that which we really possess from our own direct experience."
—J. W. Goethe (1811/1872, p. 1)

INTRODUCTION

THE ELICITATION OF EARLY RECOLLECTIONS AS A PART OF A CLIENT appraisal involves specific methods that are relatively easy for practitioners to complete in a reasonably brief period of time. When the assessment is an integral part of the counseling process, inquiry about early memories appears to be an appropriate and appealing activity to most clients. Typically, early recollections are a component of a multi-instrument assessment approach, which may include both objective and projective evaluation measures. When administering early recollections, certain general procedures apply to all clients, such as the requirement that memories be visualized and occur before eight years of age. In other instances, as in the infrequent cases when individuals are unable or unwilling to recall early memories, specific administration guidelines relate to particular interactive contexts.

GENERAL ADMINISTRATION PROCEDURES

As with any psychological appraisal process, the therapist should attempt to establish a nonjudgmental and supportive climate in which clients feel emotionally receptive to relating their early recollections. Directions for eliciting early memories must be clear and specific, and their transcription conform to a particular written format. The utilization of certain questions relating to early recollections responses is imperative; alternative or nonstandard queries may be potentially misleading and obscure the interpretation process. It is also necessary to designate an age ceiling for the attribution of memories within the chronological span of the early childhood period. Early recollections representing specific events must also be distinguished from reports of experiences that have been told to a person or those occurring over an extended period of time. Finally, a decision needs to be made regarding the particular number of early recollections to be elicited from individuals.

ESTABLISHING RAPPORT

After discussing immediate concerns and interests and employing other strategies that engender involvement, a counselor may begin the process of eliciting early recollections in one of the initial counseling sessions with a client. Clarifying the purpose and procedures of the evaluation, including early recollections and other appraisal approaches, should be done prior to initiating the transcription process. During assessment interactions, a therapist is in a position to empathize with a client and acknowledge feelings and perceptions that are evoked through the exchange of evaluating early recollections and the administration of other appraisals. A practitioner's expression of genuine and sensitive observations of an individual's perspectives enhances the counseling relationship in terms of the development of trust and rapport (Borden, 1982). Empathic attunement to a client's experiencing is also crucial for maximizing the accuracy of early recollections interpretation at a later point in the appraisal process. As is the case with any assessment procedure, the therapist should ensure that clients are not distracted or agitated to a degree where it affects their ability to attend to and report early recollections. Most individuals become quickly absorbed in relating their early memories and usually find the transaction appealing and stimulating. Although practitioners have individual preferences in the selection of various assessment instruments, early recollections may be particularly compatible with other such projective devices as human figure drawings and sentence completion tasks (Clark, 1995c, 1998a).

DIRECTIONS

The counselor or therapist may begin eliciting early recollections by saying to a client, "Think back to a long time ago when you were little, and try to recall one of your earliest memories, one of the first things that you can remember." If an individual responds with a question like, "What do you want me to say?" a general ambiguous response, such as, "Whatever one of your first memories that comes to your mind," or "Try to remember one of your earliest memories." In other instances, it may be helpful to repeat a part of the original directions, or encourage a person to take the time necessary to think about an early memory. When it appears that the client has completed stating his or her early memory report, immediately ask three follow-up questions:

1. "Is there anything else that you can recall in the memory?"
2. "What part do you remember most in the memory?"
3. "How are you feeling at that point?" or "What feelings do you remember having then?"

Responses to the first question often provide essential details that affect the meaning of the recollection or clarify vague narrative material. Olson (1979c) suggested that the second question, identifying the memory's most vivid aspect, usually pinpoints or highlights the central or focal theme of the recollection. The third and final question in the format elicits a person's affect in response to what is most salient in the memory. Understanding a client's feelings at this point clarifies the meaning of the most vivid part of the recollection and is crucial for interpretation purposes. Asking directed or specific questions beyond these three may bias an individual's responses with respect to an open-ended quality. For example, "Is your father present in the memory?" or "Who else is in the memory with you?" may distort or confound perceptions in a person's early recollection and clearly affect its interpretation. When requesting additional early memories beyond the initial memory elicited, a question like, "What is another early memory that you remember or recall?" generally prompts an individual to continue.

TRANSCRIBING

It is essential to record a client's early recollections and to write down what is said verbatim in order to create a protocol for subsequent scoring and interpretation purposes. Often very subtle changes may occur when an early recollection is restated at a later time (Terner & Pew, 1978). Most early memories tend to be relatively brief, and the responses to follow-up questions typically involve only several words. At the same time, it may be helpful for a therapist to abbreviate words or use a personal shorthand to try to keep pace with what an individual reports. Using an initial for commonly stated words, such as "m" for mother, "f" for father, "s" for sister, or "b" for brother may facilitate the recording effort. The transcribing process also reflects the value and respect that the counselor attributes to narrations that have a special meaning to a client. This position may be emphasized by explaining to a client, "I need to write down what you are saying in order for me to remember it." At times, individuals will make tangential or extraneous comments that are only indirectly related to the immediate context of the early recollections. As an example, a client may say, "I remember we moved into the house when my father got a new job. I was playing with a ball on the floor. . . ." The details provided in this material, however, may be significant for interpretation purposes and should be written down.

After concluding the report of an early recollection, occasionally an individual will express spontaneous comments relating to the content of the memory, and a practitioner should make a notation of these statements. Referring to such remarks as "afterthoughts," Bruhn and Bellow (1987) observed that the verbalizations typically suggest the meaning of the experience to an individual and how the person subsequently is affected by the memory. Consider, for example, the last part of an early recollection recounted by Brian, a certified public accountant with an inquisitive cognitive style. "I remember asking my mother how the fish could swim in the towers." The most vivid part of the memory for Brian was, "How confused I was about how it was possible that fish could swim in glass towers." His feelings at this point were, "Curious. I wanted to know how the thing worked." A moment after reporting the early recollection, Brian expressed this afterthought, "I always wanted to know how things work, and this is why I became an engineer early in my career. An outgrowth of this is that I always want to know why; as in putting a puzzle together." McCabe et al. (1991) referred to this type of early memory elaboration as "the voice of experience," as an individual narrates the event from a wider temporal perspective. Upon concluding the transcription of an early recollection, any further discussion of the memory should be avoided. Inquiring about the content of the memory or expressing exploratory verbal reactions may prompt a client to begin prematurely processing its meaning.

AGE

For a memory to represent a period from early childhood, it must occur before an individual is eight years of age (Mosak, 1958). It is rare for a person to report what is perceived as an early memory after this designated age. If, however, a counselor is uncertain about the age of a client in relationship to an early recollection and deems this information necessary, an appropriate question is, "How old do you think you were in the memory?" At times, persons spontaneously state their ages in their memories. Some practitioners prefer to ask clients about their approximate age in reference to each memory (Sweeney, 1998). This practice enables the therapist to evaluate the recollection in the context of significant events that occurred in the client's family, such as a birth, death, or relocation. From a contrasting point of view, information on an individual's age relating to a specific memory is not an interpretive factor in most early recollections scoring systems. Unless a therapist is uncertain about the ceiling age of a person or the age relating to a particular event seems to be important, it is not necessary to routinely elicit a client's perceived age in his or her early recollections.

In regard to age of a client and ability to produce early recollections, Kopp and Dinkmeyer (1975) stated that children eight years and older can usually recall early recollections that are of interpretive value. Bruhn (1981) found that children from five to eight years of age vary markedly in their ability to produce early memories that are useful in terms of interpretation. In a children's discussion group, Borden (1982) reported the effective use of early recollections as an adjunct diagnostic tool with primary age children five through eight years old. In a study involving children from six to eight years of age, Lord (1982) related that early memories reveal clinically useful information. In my experience, most children age eight and older express early recollections that are of therapeutic value, whereas individuals seven and younger are inconsistent in their ability to formulate and report early recollections.

RECOLLECTIONS VERSUS REPORTS

For scoring and interpretation purposes, it is essential to distinguish between an early recollection, which has projective value, and a report of repeated events that occurred in the experience of an individual's early childhood (Mosak, 1958). As evident by the quotation introducing the chapter, Goethe reflected on the clarification of this point in the nineteenth century. Occasionally, persons will relate generally positive remembrances of activities that took place over a period of time in childhood (Hanawalt & Gebhardt, 1965). For example, a client states, "I remember going for drives on Sunday afternoon with my family, and we would always stop for ice cream. It was something that I enjoyed a lot." This report of a recurrent incident differs from a recollection that involves a distinct episodic experience. Further, an early recollection is usually clearly visualized, whereas a report is often remembered in terms of a vague or blurry image. It is also possible to understand the difference between a recollection and a report in terms of a remember–know distinction (Bruce, Dolan, & Phillips-Grant, 2000; Tulving, 1985). To *remember* an event entails an awareness of the experience within one's personal history. To *know* an event involves knowledge from outside one's self-awareness. If clients persist in relating reports, asking a person to close his or her eyes and visualize a memory scene may prompt the expression of an early recollection (Verger & Camp, 1970).

In a study with college students, Hanawalt and Gebhardt (1965) reported that individuals recalled single incident early childhood memories significantly more frequently than recurrent incidents. A report may also reflect a single "dramatic" occurrence that has been repeatedly discussed by or among family members, even though a person has no personal memory of the event (Munroe, 1955). As an example of a report, I remember my mother telling me about an incident that occurred with my family when I was just under three years of age. We were at the seashore in the summertime and I almost drowned. My older sister ran up on the beach and told my mother that I was floating. Frantically, my mother ran and jumped in the water and pulled me out. Mosak (1958) suggested that the more dramatic the incident, such as an accident or a disaster, the less significance should be given to its interpretation. These experiences may be partially dictated externally through verbal reminders. This is in contrast with more innocuous incidents that for idiosyncratic reasons assume a special significance to an individual (Olson, 1979c). Although reports possibly have value for understanding a person, they do not meet the critical criteria for serving as a source of projective data.

NUMBER

The number of early recollections elicited from a client largely depends on the judgment and discretion of a therapist, although certain factors need to be considered in making this assessment decision (Watkins, 1985). In the literature, the number of first memories requested by counselors ranges from one to ten. In practical terms, a determination of the retrieval number of early recollections may likely be influenced by time constraints placed on practitioners and interpretive complexities once memories are gathered. Some individuals readily report three or four early memories in a relatively brief period of time, whereas others have difficulty and struggle to recall two or three recollections. Urging clients to provide additional early memories when the effort becomes demanding and laborious can have a negative effect on the counseling relationship. This pursuit may also extend the assessment period for eliciting early recollections beyond a prohibitive point with respect to prudent time economy. As the requested number of first memories increases, the subsequent task of interpretation also becomes more intricate and lengthy. In my experience with a diverse range of clients, eliciting three early recollections provides sufficient interpretive data, and allows for a reasonable allocation of appraisal and evaluation time.

SITUATIONAL ADMINISTRATION PROCEDURES

Situations occasionally arise during the administration of early recollections that will require particular strategic responses. Although it is seldom that it occurs, at times clients may state that they do not have any early memories or they are reluctant to report their remembrances. In other infrequent instances, individuals may express an inability or unwillingness to recall spontaneous early recollections, but be willing to make one up. Occasionally a person does not provide a feeling response to the follow-up question relating to the most vivid part of an early memory. Finally, although it may be a rare occurrence in the course of reporting early recollections, it is possible that a client may disclose an abuse experience. In the event of a disclosure of abuse, a practitioner must be prepared to respond effectively.

UNCERTAINTY ABOUT FEELINGS

Sometimes a client may experience difficulty expressing or determining feelings in response to the follow-up question about the most vivid part of an early recollection. It may be advantageous in these situations to repeat the request for feelings or to encourage the person to take the time necessary to provide a response. When it appears that an individual remains uncertain about responding, but is experiencing an affective reaction, the employment of reflection as a counseling technique may serve to clarify his or her feelings. As an example, consider the following early recollection of Joe, a late adulthood male, who is highly successful in a business career. "I was living in East Boston and that had to be before the age of five. There was a dirigible flying over my head and right close to that I was looking down from the window of a third floor tenement. I could see a policeman running after some kids pushing a Model T." In response to my question about feelings in relation to the most vivid part of the memory, Joe stated, "I can't say any feelings." At this point, Joe appeared to be captivated by emotionally reacting to his memory report. After a few moments, I responded with, "You seem fascinated by it all." Joe then said, "Yes, I am amazed by everything that was going on." Finally, if a client, even after being encouraged, is not able or chooses not to express feelings in regard to an early recollection, it is judicious to note this occurrence and immediately conclude the inquiry phase about the particular memory.

ABSENCE OR RELUCTANCE

Although it seems implausible that a client cannot recall a single incident from the first seven years of his or her life, therapeutically it is more productive to acknowledge this claim than to intrusively probe for a recollection. It may be helpful to say to a person something like, "Take your time and perhaps a memory may come to your mind" or "Some people take longer than others to recall a memory." Attempting to direct or prompt recall at this point (i.e., "Perhaps you could start with your first memory of school") negates the possibility of evaluating the recollection as projective material in an open-ended respect. At other times, an individual may be reluctant to report early memories. In these instances, an empathic response may possibly be effective. For instance, a counselor states to a client who appears hesitant and anxious, "You feel uncertain about what this is all about," or "This is not easy for you." This type of intervention may prompt an expression of client feelings and a reconsideration of the task at hand. If efforts by the therapist to encourage the client fail to produce a positive reaction in terms of memory reporting, it is a sound practice to shift away from early recollections and proceed with other appraisal procedures, and subsequently consider why a client was unable or unwilling to comply.

CREATED VERSUS ACTUAL

In the literature it is well-established that an individual's report of an early recollection may constitute a construction process rather than a more precise recording of actual facts (Adler, 1933/1964, 1937b; Papanek, 1972; Schrecker, 1973). In this regard, the historical accuracy of an early memory is immaterial, and it is not germane to its interpretation because the selected report of the incident reflects a person's characteristic outlook on life (Mosak, 1958). Taking this view a step further, what are the interpretive implications if a therapist asks a client who professes an inability or hesitancy to provide an early recollection to make one up? Does the content of the early memory reflect an individual's personality dynamics in both actual and created memories? Buchanan, Kern, and Bell-Dumas (1991) explored these questions in a study involving clinical and graduate student populations. The authors appraised three variables, themes, affect, and an active/passive dimension in the subjects' actual and created early recollections. In evaluating the results, themes was the only variable that was statistically significant in regard to persistence between the respective sets of early memories. The authors concluded that the findings provide some preliminary evidence that when clients are unable to recall early recollections, created memories may provide a useful therapeutic alternative.

In a related study, Barker and Bitter (1992) utilized the expression of social interest as a variable in evaluating created versus actual early recollections among a group of graduate students. The results indicated that created memories of the students reflected significantly higher social interest than actual memories. In this instance, the students appeared to express created early memories that placed them in a more favorable or positive light. From the authors' perspective, the assumption that fabricated memories are consistent with actual recollections may not prove to be valid. In terms of assessment practice, Barker and Bitter expressed caution when substituting created memories in those instances where clients do not generate spontaneous early recollections. In my experience, I have had limited success with fabricated memories, and presently rarely pursue this appraisal direction.

ABUSE DISCLOSURE

Although the situation may emerge infrequently, a practitioner should be prepared to respond strategically if clients disclose instances of physical or emotional abuse during an early recollections assessment. A memory of abuse may represent current or past conditions that place an individual in peril. As mandated reporters, counselors and therapists are required to promptly notify child protective services when suspicion of abuse of a child is present (Berliner & Briere, 1999). As discussed in chapter 2 of the text, when employing early recollections as a projective technique, trauma and abuse memories rarely occur because the approach typically prompts remembrances that are consistent with an individual's life perspectives. Unless a person specifically maintains a trauma-related outlook on life, traumatic or abusive memories are likely to be relatively uncommon. At the same time, it is also possible that the supportive and nonthreatening conditions intrinsic to a sound psychological evaluation may provide sufficient security to enable a client to disclose instances of abuse not directly related to the collection of early recollections. Another possibility is that a young person may recall an early recollection, such as one involving the sexual misconduct of an adult, without being aware of its abuse implications.

In the event of suspicion of abuse, it is vital that a therapist refrain from conducting a detailed and possibly invasive inquiry that may subsequently raise issues of influence and suggestibility by an adult authority figure (Berliner & Briere, 1999; Goodman & Clarke-Stewart, 1991; Horton & Cruise, 1997). In this regard, avoid asking leading or suggestive questions and do not persist in repeating questions (Alessi & Ballard, 2001). The treatment context should also not involve demands to remember or the encouragement of memory construction (Hyman & Pentland, 1996). Instead, the assessment process and counseling should continue in a supportive way, while the therapist proceeds to make an immediate protective service referral. In those instances where adults disclose incidents of abuse from their childhood, unlike children they are not likely to be in potential or immediate peril, however they still require support and treatment that sensitively addresses perceived trauma.

SUMMARY

Administering early recollections as a projective technique involves both general and situational procedures. General guidelines are pertinent to all individuals in the course of providing early memories. The counselor or therapist initiates the procedure by asking a client for a set of early recollections and additional responses to follow-up questions in a supportive and empathic context. Directions and questions should be stated in a standard format and sequence. It is also essential to transcribe early memories verbatim and to ensure that each recollection took place before the client was eight years of age.

Another imperative is to differentiate discrete recollections from reports of an event or a series of events.

Situational guidelines are relevant in particular circumstances that occasionally arise in the administration of the early memories procedure. At times, individuals profess that they are unable to remember early recollections or they are uncertain about their feelings in regard to reported memories. In other instances, clients are reluctant to participate in the interactive task. A therapist's empathic stance may prompt such individuals to recall early recollections or feel more inclined to become involved in the assessment process. The validity of created versus actual memories is open to debate, but the possibility of requesting a client to fabricate an early recollection is a therapeutic option. Practitioners must also be alert to the possibility of abuse disclosure when eliciting early recollections, and to follow professional standards of practice when providing support to children and adults in the event of suspicion of abuse. The administration of early recollections comprises one phase of a contextural assessment process involving a client. Table 6.1 provides a summary of procedural guidelines for the administration of early recollections.

TABLE 6.1: ADMINISTRATION OF EARLY RECOLLECTIONS: PROCEDURAL GUIDELINES

1. Consider integrating early recollections in the counseling process.
2. Establish a receptive and supportive appraisal climate.
3. Provide specific directions and follow-up questions.
4. Transcribe early memories verbatim.
5. Ensure recollections are within ceiling limit of eight years of age.
6. Differentiate between a recollection and a report.
7. Encourage clients who profess an inability or reluctance to express early recollections.
8. Evaluate the use of created versus actual first memories.
9. Follow professional standards of practice in instances of disclosure of abuse.
10. Employ early recollections in the context of a comprehensive assessment process.

INTERPRETATION OF EARLY RECOLLECTIONS

"How we remember, what we remember, and why we remember forms the most personal map of our individuality."
—Christina Baldwin (1977, p. 68)

INTRODUCTION

AFTER ADMINISTERING EARLY RECOLLECTIONS AS A COMPONENT OF THE
assessment process, a practitioner is in a position to evaluate the meaning of
the memories through a framework involving multiple perspectives from
three ways of knowing. Initially, a therapist subjectively appraises his or her
frame of reference in response to a client's disclosure of early memories and
strives to vicariously experience the internal state of an individual through an
empathic interaction. The next step in the interpretive procedure emphasizes
an interpersonal perspective, as the focus shifts to understanding the phenomenological experiencing of a person. This effort primarily entails scrutinizing the early recollections reports of an individual for discernable themes
and details. Through an objective perspective, the interpretation sequence
concludes by evaluating a client's early recollections in relationship to broad-
ranging reference groups appearing in the research literature. As apparent in
the first section of the text, there is a substantial body of investigative material available on early recollections relating to developmental, personality,
and diagnostic variables. Synthesizing inferences from each of the ways of
knowing enables the counselor to formulate a model of a person or a client.

SUBJECTIVE, INTERPERSONAL,
AND OBJECTIVE PERSPECTIVES

SUBJECTIVE PERSPECTIVES

When practitioners evaluate early recollections outside of a formal scoring
and interpretive system, they typically do so by reacting to client memories
on a subjective or intuitive basis. Although this impressionistic approach
lacks objectivity, it does provide a unique way of knowing that is essential
when considering first memories from multiple perspectives. From an imagi-

native posture, a counselor attempts to psychologically "merge" with clients and empathically relate to their experience involving each early recollection disclosure (Finn & Tonsager, 1997). This interaction occurs in the immediate context of listening to and transcribing early recollections and, at a later point when the therapist further evaluates client memories, in a structured interpretation procedure. Essentially, this response involves an open-minded search for the "big picture" by assessing early recollections holistically. As an exploratory appraisal process, it is possible to rapidly draw inferences and recognize overall patterns of the recollections (Eisengart & Faiver, 1996). A therapist typically experiences visual images and an emotional reaction to client memory reports, which provide a vital data source. Through a deep interest in an individual's feelings and meanings, the counselor idiosyncratically begins the interpretation process, and the development of subjective inferences serves as a foundation for understanding early recollections in a broader framework.

A counselor's empathic capacity allows for the possibility of momentarily imagining what it is like to be a client in the temporal context of a report of his or her early recollections. Through a subjective reaction, the therapist vicariously experiences the frame of reference of another individual (Watson, Goldman, & Vanaerschot, 1998). In a "bodily-felt" encounter, a client's internal state briefly resonates within the counselor, and this feeling in itself can be diagnostic (Ivey, 1991). The interaction involves a counselor or therapist's sensitive attunement to a client's functioning, but also relates to an awareness of the practitioner's own response to empathically processing early memories (Bohart & Greenburg, 1997). From this private identification with a client, the counselor begins to develop inferences or clues about an individual's belief system or convictions about life. As an example, a young adult recalls a fearful memory as a young child in which she is lost on a beach, and people present seem indifferent to her panic. A therapist can imagine the individual's terrified feelings and recognize the implications of the remembrance with respect to her ingrained perspectives. The therapist is able to utilize this subjective knowledge at a later time when systematically interpreting the client's early recollections. In relatively rare instances, a practitioner may experience a situation in which a client resists reporting his or her early recollections. A therapist must then subjectively determine if the resistance represents an unwillingness to disclose personal information, uncertainty about being helped, or a lack of cooperation (Nikelly & Verger, 1971).

In order to be more specific about the nature of subjective perspectives and their function in the evaluation process, it may be instructive to present the client's complete early memory from the cited example in addition to a counselor's intuitive reactions. Ann, a 30-year-old client states, "I was about four or five, and I was at the seashore with my family. I must have wandered off because I couldn't find my mother or father and I was very scared. I looked at a lot of different people, but they didn't seem to care that I was lost or so afraid." The only detail that Ann recalled was that the sand felt hot and coarse beneath her feet. The most vivid part of the memory involves the frustration she experienced when no one seemed to care about her plight. At this point, she felt even more scared and frightened. Several immediate impressions occurred to the counselor as she listened to Ann's early recollection. The counselor shared Ann's sense of anxiety and bewilderment in the memory. At the same time, she experienced doubt about the perceived accuracy of the recollection. It is certainly possible for Ann as a young child to wander away from her parents at a beach, but responsible individuals would likely recognize her fear and attempt to bring Ann back to her family. The counselor also empathizes with Ann's sense of desperation and confusion when she attempts to get help and nobody is there to assist or comfort her. The environment seems harsh; even the sand is hot and rough. After concluding the meeting with Ann, the counselor writes down her personal impressions and reactions, as she begins the initial phase of the early recollections interpretation process.

While recognizing the value of appraising early memories from a subjective perspective, a practitioner must also be aware that resultant intuitive findings may involve biases emanating from his or her own frame of reference. In particular, confirmatory bias entails a tendency to attend to those factors that substantiate a therapist's initial judgments and be close-minded to new or alternative data. Safran and Segal (1990) cautioned that therapists should be aware of being blinded by their preconceptions of clients' internal working model, and the formulation must be continually open to refinement. A related form of convictional bias involves relying primarily on a counselor's personal belief system when evaluating the functioning or needs of a client. In order to minimize susceptibility to biased and constricted views, it is essential for practitioners to seek knowledge sources beyond a purely subjective stance. With these more expansive considerations in mind, emphasizing interpersonal perspectives as a way of knowing becomes a focus for evaluating an individual's early recollections.

INTERPERSONAL PERSPECTIVES

After initially employing intuition and personal impressions to discern familiar patterns of early recollections from a subjective perspective, it becomes therapeutically productive to examine the memories from another vantage point. In this regard, a distinction needs to be made between subjective processes internal to the therapist or counselor and the more observable interactions that represent exclusively a client's frame of reference (Watson et al. 1998). An interpersonal way of knowing manifests a practitioner's capacity to express empathy toward the phenomenological experiencing of individuals (LaFountain & Bartos, 2002). With this understanding, a counselor is in a position to analyze discrete parts of memories in order to understand their nature and function (Eisengart & Faiver, 1996). Subjective and interpersonal perspective-taking are distinct yet complementary aspects of early recollections assessment, and in combination contribute to a more comprehensive evaluation of the memories of an individual. Using the model of a person or lifestyle syllogism as an organizing framework, interpersonal knowledge emphasizes the formulation of a client's fundamental perceptions of life. This pursuit is primarily accomplished by gleaning particular themes and details that emerge from early recollections. A thematic and detailed analysis of the first memories of life is a prominent aspect of the interpretive process, and the interpretive method will receive extensive focus in the pages ahead.

THEMATIC ANALYSIS.   Since Adler first emphasized the functional value of understanding dominant themes in an individual's early recollections, interpreting first memories thematically has been a primary focus among researchers and practitioners. Among others, Mayman (1968) thought that individuals retrospectively build convincing views of life around essential themes. As a source of information, thematic material from early memories reveals data on self-representations and relationship predispositions in regard to others. A thematic analysis of early recollections enables counselors or therapists to recognize prominent subjects and patterns in the human experience of clients (Ackerknecht, 1976; Schwartz, 1984–1985). Although a particular early recollection may reveal one or more central themes, it is also possible to identify recurring or repetitive themes among multiple first memories reported by an individual. In terms of critical themes, consider the example presented earlier in the chapter of the early recollection of the young child lost on the beach. The memory evokes feelings of terror and bewilderment in the client and suggests possible themes of insignificance, helplessness, and abandonment. Within an early memory, as is the case of the young girl at the seashore with her family, situations may begin well on a thematic basis and then deteriorate (Bruhn, 1985). In other instances, conditions may start off poorly but improve through the course of the narration of the memory.

The potential range of early recollections themes is vast and rich; therefore, a means for organizing thematic data should prove to be useful for interpretation purposes. One viable way to organize wide-ranging themes represented in a person's early memories is through the lifestyle syllogism or model of a person. This rubric organizes an individual's core beliefs or private logic in reference to oneself, the world (others and events), and life. Details mentioned and objective perspectives are also significant in the development of inferences, and these areas will be addressed later in the chapter. In the continuing example of the young child lost at the seashore, the following suggests thematic perceptions relating to Ann: "I am . . . insignificant because nobody cares about me." "Others are . . . indifferent to me or are rejecting." "Events are . . . tormenting and bewildering in spite of my efforts." The syllogism concludes with deductions about life: "Therefore, life is . . . a burden." The perspectives relating to life may be finalized with multifaceted material from the complete set of early recollections of an individual.

To further assist in the evaluation of particular themes, thematic content variables structured around the lifestyle syllogism provide topic alternatives. Table 7.1 presents the thematic variables organized in a tripartite rubric of self, others, and events, and practitioners may make reference to this chart when interpreting early recollections. The binary variables in the chart represent topics commonly found in the literature in relationship to early recollections. The terms are suggestive of prominent thematic material, but it is also

---

TABLE 7.1: THEMATIC VARIABLES

"*I am . . .*"	Acceptable–Unacceptable
	Significant–Insignificant
	Competent–Incompetent
	Active–Passive
	Independent–Dependent
	Secure–Insecure
	Cooperative–Defiant
	Internally–Externally Controlled
"*Others are . . .*"	Nurturing–Neglectful
	Friendly–Hostile
	Worthy–Unworthy
	Tolerant–Intolerant
	Encouraging–Discouraging
	Trustworthy–Untrustworthy
"*Events are . . .*"	Bountiful–Disappointing
	Constructive–Destructive
	Gratifying–Distressful
	Harmonious–Disagreeable
	Invigorating–Debilitative
	Manageable–Overwhelming
	Stimulating–Dull
	Safe–Fearful

possible for a counselor to recognize particular themes in an individual's early recollections beyond those presented in the rubric. In the following sections, major components of the lifestyle syllogism or model of a person will include clarifying information on the thematic variables.

SELF.   As a hypothetical construct, the self relates to an individual's perceptions or phenomenological stance toward himself or herself (Kopp & Der, 1979). In the context of a unique belief system, a person maintains enduring convictions or conclusions about the self that manifest in evaluative and motivational schemas. In an evaluative or critical mode, an individual typically maintains a general conception of his or her abilities and personal characteristics. These qualities may involve such particular areas as competency, independence, and feelings of significance. With respect to motivation, a person commonly acts in ways that are consistent with perceptions of selfhood. For instance, an individual who holds a self-perception of insignificance may function in a manner that reflects a sense of being devalued and ineffectual. As a unitary and coherent conceptualization, the self as a frame of reference assumes a constancy over an extended period of time and circumstances (Lachman, 1996). In this regard, a person's early recollections representing the self should reflect a reasonable degree of distinction and coherence.

For the purposes of thematic analysis, a focus will be given at this point to particular variables that are pertinent to the self model. This material should be helpful to practitioners for the purpose of clarifying early recollections relating to the self. The topical data outlines an individual's self representation in regard to each thematic binary variable. Each variable also includes a brief definition in a first person account. An example requesting a response about the most vivid part of a person's first memories emphasizes its thematic focus. A follow-up response, which is also asked in the form of a question, includes the person's feelings relating to the part of the memory that stands out the most. After becoming familiar with this material, it is possible to refer to the topical listing of Thematic Variables in Table 7.1 in order to develop thematic inferences. As a component of the lifestyle syllogism, each of the binaries should be proceeded with: "I am . . ."

ACCEPTABLE–UNACCEPTABLE

Acceptable. I have a sense of worth and a certainty about being favorably received by other people. I feel like I am a part of things and that I am approved of by others.

"What part do you remember the most in the memory?" (This question relates to the most vivid part of the memory and is designated with "Vivid").

"When I was in the middle and jumping rope between my two friends."

"How are you feeling at that point?" or "What feelings do you remember having then?" (These questions clarify feelings relating to the
most vivid part of the memory and are designated with "Feelings").
"Happy and included."

Unacceptable. I do not feel worthy, and I am uncertain about being favorably
received by other people. I usually feel like I am not a part of things, and I
am not approved of or welcomed by others.

Vivid: "When the girl said that I wasn't invited to her birthday party."
Feelings: "Hurt and not good enough."

SIGNIFICANT–INSIGNIFICANT

Significant. I am important and a person of some consequence. I feel like I
matter and make a difference in life.

Vivid: "When my dad let me push the lawnmower."
Feelings: "Proud and helpful."

Insignificant. I am unimportant and a person of little consequence. I feel like
I don't matter that much and that I hardly make a difference in life.

Vivid: "When the two kids looked away from me when they were
choosing sides for the game."
Feelings: "Sad and diminished."

COMPETENT–INCOMPETENT

Competent. I feel capable in most situations. I am generally aware of performing effectively and "measuring up."

Vivid: "The part when I am pulling on the rope to raise the flag."
Feelings: "Strong and able to do things."

Incompetent. I feel less capable and insufficient in most situations. I am
acutely aware of performing ineffectively and "coming up short."

Vivid: "When it was my turn, and I couldn't remember my part of the
ABCs."
Feelings: "Dumb and stupid."

ACTIVE–PASSIVE

Active. I tend to be energetic and like to take the initiative to get things done.
I don't particularly like to waste time.

Vivid: "Putting my paddle in the water and seeing the boat move."
Feelings: "Intrigued and full of energy."

Passive. I tend to be apathetic and rarely show initiative in getting things
done. I often find myself wasting time.

Vivid: "Watching the other kids play."
Feelings: "Like a neutral feeling; not bad or good."

INDEPENDENT–DEPENDENT

Independent. I like to set the direction of my life and make decisions. I feel restricted in situations when I'm controlled by other people.

> Vivid: "The moment when my mother let go of the bicycle, and I rode it by myself."
> Feelings: "Free and on my own."

Dependent. I prefer to let other people set the direction of my life, and I don't like to make decisions. I feel comfortable in situations when I'm told what to do.

> Vivid: "My mother buttoning my shirt."
> Feelings: "Good, because I didn't have to do it myself."

SECURE–INSECURE

Secure. Most of the time, I feel free from doubts and fears. I believe in myself and trust in my abilities.

> Vivid: "As my aunt was softly singing to me."
> Feelings: "Warm and nice."

Insecure. Most of the time, I feel burdened with uncertainties and fears. I constantly question myself and my abilities.

> Vivid: "As my teacher was yelling at me and the other kids."
> Feelings: "Frightened."

COOPERATIVE–DEFIANT

Cooperative. I like to get along with people and to contribute my share. Most often, I make an effort to make things work out.

> Vivid: "Putting the clothes on my dolls with my friend."
> Feelings: "Content."

Defiant. I provoke people, and I resist being told what to do. Most often, I thwart things from working out.

> Vivid: "Refusing to pick up the toys."
> Feelings: "Angry."

INTERNALLY–EXTERNALLY CONTROLLED

Internally controlled. Positive and negative events that occur in my life are largely under my control. I typically take responsibility for my actions and the consequences of my behavior.

> Vivid: "Holding my head up out of the water and paddling as I was swimming for the first time."
> Feelings: "Knowing that I could do it, but ready to try again if I didn't. Determined."

Externally controlled. Positive and negative events that occur in my life are largely out of my control. I typically avoid taking responsibility for my actions and the consequences of my behavior.

Vivid: "When the dog bit my hand as I was patting it."

Feelings: "Startled and mad at the dog."

OTHERS. As another essential hypothetical construct, "others" relates to an individual's social perceptions or expectations about other people (Fakouri & Zucker, 1987). Within a personal belief system, a person maintains predispositions toward the behavior of others. In this regard, an unchallenged assumption of an individual is that people will tend to act in accordance with static expectations in social interactions. As an example, a client assumes that people are largely untrustworthy and upon meeting the therapist believes or anticipates that the individual cannot be trusted. From an object relations perspective, this perception reflects an internalized mental image and representation of others in the world (Last, 1997; St. Claire, 2000). For interpretation purposes, persons perceived in the early recollections of individuals may generally serve as prototypes for classes of people (Mosak, 1958; Wolman, 1970). As an example, a parent or a teacher may represent an authority figure. In a more specific direction, perceived social interactions with a particular person or persons in an early memory may also reflect long-standing relationship perspectives. For instance, encouragement from a parent in a memory suggests that the individual characteristically is recognized as encouraging.

Using a format similar to the previous section on the self, the following presents particular binary variables relevant to the others model. Examples include individuals' responses to a practitioner's questions relating to their early recollections. As a component of the lifestyle syllogism or model of a person, each of the binaries should be proceeded with: "Others are . . ."

NURTURING–NEGLECTFUL

Nurturing. I generally feel that people give me attention and respect. Typically, the way they treat me ranges from appropriate care to uncompromising support.

Vivid: "My mother putting a new bandage on my cut."

Feelings: "Comforted."

Neglectful. I generally feel that people fail to give me attention or respect. The way they treat me ranges from indifference to total disregard.

Vivid: "My mother telling me that she was too busy to take care of my cut."

Feelings: "Resentful."

FRIENDLY–HOSTILE

Friendly. I usually find people to be kind and agreeable. Generally, they can be comforting and thoughtful.
　　Vivid: "Seeing the man fix the broken wing on my toy airplane."
　　Feelings: "Grateful."
Hostile. I usually find people to be malevolent and disagreeable. Generally, they can be punishing and thoughtless.
　　Vivid: "Running with my older brother and the big kids yelling and
　　　　chasing us."
　　Feelings: "Very scared."

WORTHY–UNWORTHY

Worthy. Most people are deserving of respect and recognition. It is possible to find merit and value in others.
　　Vivid: "Combing my grandmother's hair."
　　Feelings: "I felt good because she seemed to really enjoy it."
Unworthy. Few people are deserving of respect and recognition. It is rarely possible to find merit and value in others.
　　Vivid: "Taking the kid's toy."
　　Feelings: "The kid was a jerk, and I wanted the toy."

TOLERANT–INTOLERANT

Tolerant. I find that most people allow me to be myself. They usually back me up even when they don't agree with me.
　　Vivid: "My teacher waiting for me to finish my song."
　　Feelings: "Appreciative."
Intolerant. I find that most people prevent me from being myself. They rarely back me up or seem to agree with me.
　　Vivid: "My teacher telling me to stop singing, even though I hadn't fin-
　　　　ished my song."
　　Feelings: "Upset and angry."

ENCOURAGING–DISCOURAGING

Encouraging. People frequently give me hope by believing in me. They bolster my confidence and promote my development.
　　Vivid: "My dad telling me to try again after I fell off of my bicycle."
　　Feelings: "Relief and hope."
Discouraging. People frequently deprive me of hope by not believing in me. They destroy my confidence and hinder my development.
　　Vivid: "When my father told me to put my bicycle away, after I fell off
　　　　of it."
　　Feelings: "Crushed."

TRUSTWORTHY–UNTRUSTWORTHY

Trustworthy. In general, people can be trusted and relied upon. I often put my confidence in others, and they come through for me.

Vivid: "When my mother held me when I was scared."

Feelings: "I felt that I could depend on her."

Untrustworthy. In general, people cannot be trusted or relied upon. I rarely put my confidence in others because they don't come through for me.

Vivid: "When I fell after my brother said that I wouldn't get hurt."

Feelings: "Disbelieving and angry."

EVENTS.   Virtually all of the first memories of life involve an event. In a study representing 799 cases with college students, only one person did not report an event (Howes et al. 1993). The one exception related to a memory in which an individual recalled a green stool or chair that she owned when she was three years old. With respect to particular historical events, they may or may not be verifiable in the early childhood experiences of a person. At the same time, basic conclusions about occurrences can be influential in the construction of how an individual construes the world. As a component of a personal belief system, convictions about impressionable events form a hypothetical construct. In this regard, individuals maintain an anticipatory stance toward what takes place in environmental situations. As an example, a person assumes that, in general, events tend to be stimulating. Consequently, the individual approaches experiences with an expectation that they will provide variety and interest. Conversely, another person maintains a conviction that, generally speaking, events tend to be dull. In this case, the individual anticipates that pending experiences will be dreary and uninteresting.

Using the same format of the other components on the self and others, a focus will be given to binary variables pertinent to the events model. Examples include individuals' responses to questions relating to their early recollections. As a segment of the lifestyle syllogism, each of the binaries should be proceeded with: "Events are . . ."

BOUNTIFUL–DISAPPOINTING

Bountiful. There are a multitude of experiences that I find fulfilling. Most of the time, I feel uplifted by things, and they seem rich to me.

Vivid: "I was with my family sitting on comfortable metal chairs on the porch of our home. The porch was painted a pretty green color."

Feelings: "Delighted. It was such a pleasure to be with my loving family."

Disappointing. There are few experiences that I find fulfilling. Most of the time, I feel let down by things, and they seem deficient to me.

Vivid: "Looking under the Christmas tree to see if there were any more
   gifts for me and not finding any."
Feelings: "Empty."

CONSTRUCTIVE–DESTRUCTIVE

Constructive. Many situations seem to offer possibilities for productivity and
development. These experiences engender a sense of purpose and creativity
in me.
   Vivid: "Helping my father and brothers dig a big rock out of the
      ground."
   Feelings: "Useful and content."
Destructive. Many situations seem to be either noxious or injurious. These
experiences engender a sense of recklessness and devastation in me.
   Vivid: "Throwing the rocks through the windows and hearing them
      smash."
   Feelings: "Excited and wanting to destroy more of the old house."

GRATIFYING–DISTRESSFUL

Gratifying. Most often, events entail pleasure and satisfaction. I find delight
and fulfillment in many things.
   Vivid: "Seeing the sun's rays strike the wall in the kitchen."
   Feelings: "Enjoying the moment."
Distressful. Most often events entail pain and misery. I find a sense of tor-
ment and anguish in many things.
   Vivid: "Sleeping on the ground in a tent, and it was cold and miserable."
   Feelings: "As I said, miserable."

HARMONIOUS–DISAGREEABLE

Harmonious. I often find experiences to be pleasing and agreeable. My aware-
ness of most events is one of accord.
   Vivid: "Looking out of my bedroom window and seeing the twinkling
      lights of the city."
   Feelings: "Delight."
Disagreeable. I often find experiences to be displeasing and harsh. My aware-
ness of most events is one of repugnance.
   Vivid: "Having to clean the putrid mess up off of the floor."
   Feelings: "Irritated and put upon."

INVIGORATING–DEBILITATIVE

Invigorating. I often find myself in stimulating and uplifting situations. Frequently, I feel fortified by events in my life.

Vivid: "Seeing my baby sister's face for the first time."

Feelings: "Joyful."

Debilitative. I often find myself in enfeebling and despairing situations. Frequently, I feel diminished by events in my life.

Vivid: "Feeling really sick to my stomach."

Feelings: "Sick and trapped."

MANAGEABLE–OVERWHELMING

Manageable. Most situations can be handled with skillful action. However, it is necessary to plan in order to influence events.

Vivid: "Putting the last pieces together from my erector set to make a box."

Feelings: "I knew that I could do it, and I felt proud."

Overwhelming. Most situations are too much to handle. It is futile to try to plan because events are uncontrollable.

Vivid: "Looking out the window wishing that my father would stop drinking."

Feelings: "Scared and powerless."

STIMULATING–DULL

Stimulating. There are so many things that I find exciting and interesting. Countless events invigorate me and provoke my spirit.

Vivid: "Seeing the different flowers in the garden."

Feelings: "Excited and wanting to see more."

Dull. Most often, I find things rather dreary and uninteresting. Various events typically furnish me little delight and leave me feeling listless.

Vivid: "Leafing through the pages of a boring book."

Feelings: "Sluggish."

SAFE–FEARFUL

Safe. Most of the time, I experience a sense of stability and security in regard to the events in my life. I rarely anticipate harm or danger in my surroundings.

Vivid: "Standing near the water, fishing."

Feelings: "Peaceful."

Fearful. Most of the time, I experience instability and a lack of security in regard to the events in my life. I frequently anticipate harm or danger in my surroundings.

Vivid: "My father yelling really loud when the car wouldn't start."

Feelings: "Terrified."

When appraising the thematic variables in regard to an individual's early recollections, other themes may spontaneously emerge beyond those represented in the lifestyle rubric. Particular themes that augment the variables may become recognizable and provide a more precise and comprehensive view of a person. After notation of the material from the thematic variables and spontaneous recognition, the early memories interpretation focus of a practitioner shifts to scrutinizing details.

DETAIL ANALYSIS

The details expressed in the early recollections of individuals are of utmost importance in the interpretation process because they influence the significance and meaning of the memories (Dreikurs, 1967). When interpreting first recollections, details coalesce with themes to begin to form a coherent model of an individual's perception of self, others, and events (Watkins, 1984). Details include the dynamic implications of a person's report of sensory impressions, color, location, and physical objects. In regard to sense details, the preponderance of individuals experience their early recollections through their visual modality, and to a far lesser extent report memories involving other sensory functions (Dudycha & Dudycha, 1933a; Kihlstrom & Harackiewicz, 1982; Saunders & Norcross, 1988; Winthrop, 1958). Most early recollections are nonverbal, but occasionally individuals reporting a memory recall verbally communicating with other persons (Westman & Wautier, 1994a). First recollections associated with the detail of the expression of color occur among a minority of persons (Howes et al.; Smith, 1952). The location or setting and the depiction of particular objects vary considerably among prominent details in the first memories of individuals.

SENSES.   Because individuals typically experience their early recollections through a visual channel, when other senses are mentioned, they take on added significance for interpretive purposes. Most often people visualize or picture themselves engaging in some type of activity in their memories. The dominance of the *visual* modality in early recollections indicates the profound influence of the sensory perception in conveying convictions of life. The following example is typical of an early recollection as it manifests a visual impression of events: "I remember seeing my mother carrying my baby brother through the front door, and I felt jealous." Considering that visual imagery prevails among individuals, particular inferences rest in the qualitative analysis of early recollections. Many persons, as in the cited example, experience generalized visual memories depicting various interactions. In other instances, however, the visual aspect of the recollections are acute and poignant. Consider the following early memory in terms of interpretation implications: "My father took off the back of his pocket watch and let me look at it. Inside, I could see two large springs and three or four gears that were connected. It was fascinating to see how the pieces all worked together." It is obvious that the prominent and distinct quality of the individual's visual imagery in the memory presents significant inferential material.

Early recollections associated with an *auditory* sensation occur far less frequently than visual memories. More than 100 years ago, Potwin (1901) pointed out the curious quality of this fact given the vast number of stories and lullabies that most young children hear and the generally pleasant associations of these experiences. At the same time, recollections with an acoustic emphasis provide interpretive data that is potentially useful for understanding individuals. As an example, a middle adulthood male relates the following early memory: "I recall my Aunt Mary singing to me when I was in my crib. I can see her face and hear her lovely voice singing, 'Merry doce, doce, doce'." In the case of this individual, music has been a life-enhancing avocation. It is, however, important to keep in mind that the absence of a conspicuous auditory aspect in one's early recollections does not imply that a person lacks an appreciation or sensitivity to listening activities. What appears to be the case is that prominent auditory perceptions are relatively rare in early recollections, and consequently, manifest sensory content has a special meaning in terms of inferential significance.

The *tactile* sense is another modality that infrequently appears in the accounts of the early recollections of individuals. As a kinesthetic experience, persons emphasize physical contact in their first memories. Like other sensory details, for interpretation purposes, the tactile expression must be understood in the broader context of the thematic quality of early recollections. In this regard, consider the qualitative differences of the following two early memories with a prominent tactile aspect. "I remember running up the lawn of my grandfather's house. I could feel the cool, soft grass under my feet." "I recall walking to school in the wet, cold slush. I could feel my frozen socks stuck to my shoes." It is evident in these examples that the meaning of a tactile experience in an early recollection relates to an individual's unique sensory image of the event in terms of it being positive or negative.

Early recollections with an association pertaining to an *olfactory* sense are rare. Of the 83 college students surveyed by Westman and Westman (1993), only one reported an early memory involving an odor. Like other sensations, a pleasant or unpleasant impression of a smell depends on the thematic context of the memory. As an example, consider the following contrasting first memories featuring salient olfactory aspects. One individual recalls: "I remember playing in the garden behind my house and smelling the beautiful fragrance of all the different flowers." Another person reports: "I was not feeling well and my mother put some kind of ointment on my chest. The smell was putrid." An inferential question relates to how individuals perceive and find expression in regard to the olfactory faculty in their lives. Could it be that the sense of smell is clearly life-enhancing for some persons, and for others a prominent aspect of life that more often is offensive?

The *gustatory* function is another sensory modality that is uncommon in the early recollections of individuals. It is interesting that although interactions involving food and eating are universally prevalent in the early childhood period, this behavioral pattern rarely becomes manifest in the first memories involving conspicuous gustatory activity. The following is an example of an early recollection involving a prominent experience relating to the sense of taste: "I recall being in my grandmother's kitchen a long time ago. She had just baked an apple pie, and it was still warm. Nana gave me the first piece, and my mouth was watering. I distinctly remember the taste of the sweet apples and the flaky crust." The associations with food and eating are apparent in this example, and the counselor must integrate the meaning of this observation with other details and themes in formulating a coherent view of the person.

A final consideration is that combinations of sensory expressions may also appear in the early recollections of particular persons. As an example of a multisensory early recollection, consider the dramatic first memory of Tom, who is a college professor of English. "I was put down to take a nap by my mother in my bedroom. I wasn't at all sleepy. I got up and ripped a tag off of a wire connected to an iron. I decided to stick the wire into the socket. There was a giant explosion with a big bright globe of huge sparks flying all over the room."

Details: "A blinding flash of light and a whole series of loud pops."

Vivid: "The loud popping and seeing flashes of lights."

Feelings: "Dazzled."

Ivey and Ivey (1999) made reference to how individuals perceive the world through sensory verbal styles. This perceptual system or orientation may be reflected in a person's choice of language. As an example, a client with a visual orientation states, "I see what is happening," and another client who is kinesthetically inclined says, "I need to feel out the situation." Counselors may note the words that individuals employ that relate to particular visual, auditory, or tactile verbal expressions. Expanding beyond Ivey and Ivey's sensory verbalizations, it may also be possible to include an individual's orientation to olfactory and gustatory sensory functions. This may be a stretch, but people do use the expressions, "It is possible to smell it out," and "It is so close that I can taste it." In a more certain direction, the assessment of early memories augments the observation of client verbal styles by clarifying their sensory orientation at the core level. In this regard, Friedmann (1935) observed that many childhood recollections reveal an individual's method of perception or preferred habitual sensory realm. In combination, evaluating the clients' sensory verbal styles and preferred sensory realms contributes to a more comprehensive understanding of their perceptual systems.

COLOR. As a visual experience of individuals, the mention of color typically occurs in a minority of first memories. Howes et al. (1993) surveyed college students about their early recollections, and they asked a specific question, "Was color a part of your memory?" The authors reported that about one-third of the respondents responded in the affirmative. This figure would likely be lower without being influenced by a directed inquiry. In my experience, about one out of six persons spontaneously mentions or refers to color as a part of his or her early memories. The following is an early recollection of an art teacher, Spring, that clearly conveys a sensual and color emphasis:

> I was about three years old. My mother took me to visit a long-time friend of the family who lived in a farmhouse. There was a big long wooden table. In the center of the table was a wooden bowl filled with bright red apples. My mother and Mrs. Lacey were talking. I grabbed the apples, lining them up in a row, and took a bite out of each. Mrs. Lacey said, "What are you doing?" I said that I was taking a bite out of each apple to see which one tastes best. They laughed and smiled and thought it was funny.

Details: "I remember how the kitchen smelled like old papers and cinnamon."
Vivid: "I was most intent on the big bowl of red apples."
Feelings: "Content; not trying to cause trouble. They are happy and talking, and it smelled good in the kitchen."

The mention of color in an early recollection is generally an indication of an aesthetic interest or an artistic inclination (Mosak & Kopp, 1973; Sweeney & Myers, 1986). This does not mean, however, that an absence of color in early memories indicates a lack of interest or appreciation of aesthetics or art. What seems to be the case is that for individuals with a color emphasis in their early recollections, color is a compelling influence in their lives. For these persons, color as a prominent orientation typically finds expression in home décor, clothing, and avocational or vocational interests (Clark, 2001; Sweeney, 1990).

LOCATION. Virtually every early recollection involves a location or situation in which the memory takes place. At the same time, the perceived site of the memory may or may not be significant in terms of inferential meaning. At times, the circumstances of the recollection highlight or give prominence to the location, and in other instances, the memory locale takes on an incidental quality (Brodsky, 1962; Francis, 1995; Sobel, 1990). As an example, in the following early recollection, the location conveys a place of special importance: "I recall being in my bedroom in the old house where I grew up. From where I was sitting in my bed, I could see all around my room and look down the hall to my parent's room. I felt really calm and peaceful." In a contrasting example, the particular site appears to be secondary to other aspects of the early memory: "I remember seeing my best friend get in a car with his parents and leave for camp for the whole summer, I was so sad." Sobel (1990) evaluated adults' memories of special places that they recalled from their middle childhood. Finding and making special places appears to be a common experience for children in various cultures as they pursue such constructions as "forts," sculptured tunnels in hedgerows, and playhouses built from discarded scrap materials. Sobel (1990) stated that "Almost all verbal recollections by adults of special places have a kind of breathless, twinkle-in-the-eye animation" (p. 10) and convey that they hold a particular meaning to some persons in shaping of the self.

Generally, it is possible to determine if an early recollection setting takes place indoors or outdoors. Again, it is necessary to assess the thematic quality of the memory in order to clarify its meaning in terms of inference. In this regard, consider the following first recollection of Alex, which takes place outside: "I was very young. My mother and I were outside in our yard. It was a beautiful day, sunny and warm. I had no shoes on and I remember the feel of the grass on my feet. We had two biggish turtles that mom had brought outside. I remember being fascinated with them, and following them as they walked around."

Details: "Having an Oreo cookie in my hand and I was slowly gnawing on it."
Vivid: "The vivid blue of the sky and the green of the grass."
Feelings: "Wonder at the whole experience; warm and comfortable."
The importance of the outdoor life to Alex is apparent in regard to the locale of the early memory. His favorite activities include hiking, running, and skiing.

In a related context, the season of the year may be detectable in the report of early recollections of individuals. More often this seasonal location memory takes place out-of-doors and suggests a person's perception of the season or climate. As an example, Karen reported the following early recollection involving a time of year: "I was three or four. It was wintertime, and my father made a huge slide out of snow. He built it up so there were 10 or

12 steps made out of snow. He even made handles so you could hold on to something when you were climbing up. My father helped me and my brother climb, and we played on the slide."

> Details: "I was little, but I felt like part of the family, and I could build part of the slide."
> Vivid: "Having fun with my family."
> Feelings: "Happy and content."

Karen says that she loves the winter. She has mixed feelings about the weather at other times of year, but she enjoys all of the seasons. In Karen's case, an understanding of her feelings about the winter season is not difficult to ascertain. Other persons may have similar views about particular seasons or they may be quite different depending on the emotional tone expressed in each memory.

Individuals may make tangential remarks about the location or other details of an early recollection that appear only indirectly related to the context of the memory. As an example, a client states, "I was out in the back of our house with my parents. We moved into the house when I was about four years old. It was the first time that my family had moved. My mother had a flower in her hand, and she gave it to me. I felt so special." The client's comments about moving appear to be extraneous, but this type of remark may serve an orienting function as the memory is recalled. When such comments are excessive or irrelevant, however, they suggest a more obsessive or a distracted quality with regard to a client's early recollections.

OBJECTS.   Physical objects are perceptible in most early recollections, but their significance depends on a particular focus of attention attributed to items by an individual. Like other details, tangible materials take on an importance in relation to the thematic content of a particular memory. It is interesting to observe that in early childhood, young persons often encounter the same pieces of furniture, toys, and books on countless occasions. Yet, if the objects are remembered at all in early recollections, they are typically recalled only as components or elements in a memory event (Howes et al. 1993). At the same time, individuals may report an early childhood memory involving a transitional object, such as a rocking horse, stuffed animal, or blanket, which may have a special meaning. In a study eliciting the specific recall of transitional objects with adolescents, Lundy and Potts (1987) reported that the presence of the objects related to the need for affection as a personality characteristic. In a related study with college students, Cohen and Clark (1984) also directly elicited early memories involving transitional objects. Evaluating personality functioning with the Sixteen Personality Factor Questionnaire (16PF) (Hood & Johnson, 2002), the authors found the presence of a transitional object related to the Tense factor of the 16PF, and the absence of a transitional object related to the Reserved factor of the 16PF.

The variety and potential meanings of objects is vast, and first memories must be scrutinized for conspicuous items that appear to play an influential role in a memory. The following is one of my early recollections, which involves a prominent object: "I was about six years old. I was trying to ride a bicycle for the first time. My mother and father were with me on the street in front of our house. My father was holding me and he let go, and I rode the bike."

Details: "The open sky and road."
Vivid: "Riding the bicycle by myself."
Feelings: "Exhilaration and delight."

After putting away my bicycle for the winter, I yearn for the first day in the spring when I can once again experience the joy of riding my bike. In contrast to my memory, objects may also assume a negative connotation, as in the following early recollection of a person involving a swimming pool and water: "I remember being at my uncle's house, and he had a swimming pool. He was holding me up, and I was pretending to swim. Then he let me go, and I couldn't breathe, and I was swallowing the water."

Details: "The water in my nose and throat."
Vivid: "Gasping and not being able to breathe because of the water."
Feelings: "Fear and helplessness."

As an object, a possession that evokes emotion may assume a distinct significance that has enduring implications in the life of an individual. My father's early recollection provides an example of a special possession that he received from his father: "My father gave me a rabbit as a present. I held it in my arms."

Details: "The rabbit's eyes and ears."
Vivid: "Me holding the rabbit."
Feelings: "I felt responsible to take care of the rabbit."

My father raised rabbits all the years that I was growing up and well into the latter years of his life. The memory of the rabbit gift assumes an even more compelling quality given the fact that my grandfather died when my father was only 10 years old.

Finally, it is possible that an object or a possession may be lost in an early recollection, and this perceived event may be influential in regard to convictions about life for a person. The following is an example of an early memory involving the loss of a significant transitional object: "I was staying at my aunt's house overnight. In the morning, I couldn't find my dear teddy bear named "Princess." I always took Princess everywhere that I went. My aunt told me that because Princess was very dirty, she tried washing her, but she fell all apart. She had to throw her away."

Details: "Seeing my aunt's mouth move when she told me Princess was gone."

Vivid: "Realizing that I would never see her again."

Feelings: "A deep hurt and heartache."

OBJECTIVE PERSPECTIVES

Evaluating early recollections from an interpersonal perspective involves the most extensive phase of the three-part interpretation process. In the third and final assessment phase, emphasis shifts to analyzing first memories from an objective perspective by making reference to relevant research data. As an immediate information source, practitioners may refer to chapters 3 and 4 in this volume on various taxonomic, personality, and diagnostic topics. For example, consider the illustration presented earlier in the chapter of the individual with an early recollection of being lost on a beach. Ann found other people to be either insensitive or uncaring despite her efforts to communicate with them. Events for her seem harsh and punitive. Clearly social issues are conflicted for Ann, and her outlook on life takes on the qualities of an affect disorder. Considering the diagnostic impression information on depression or mood disorders with respect to early recollections may provide relevant findings. In terms of personality dimensions, referring to pertinent research on interpersonal style and explanatory style in regard to first memories may also prove to be useful. With other persons beyond Ann, evaluating objective data may contribute to a more complete understanding of their early recollections. Research material on early childhood memories continues to expand (Watkins, 1992b), and counselors and therapists can develop comprehensive resources and reference material from the professional literature that is relevant to their particular clientele. When evaluating early recollections research, it is important to keep in mind the psychometric limitations of the material, such as a lack of normative data and the frequent use of college students as subjects (Malinoski et al. 1998).

ORGANIZING AND SYNTHESIZING
EARLY RECOLLECTIONS PERSPECTIVES

Upon concluding a multiperspective analysis of a client's early memories, it is necessary to draw the data together in an orderly way. A practitioner's subjective perceptions typically include several impressionistic statements that should be written down. It is helpful to organize interpersonal perspectives in a manner based on the tripartite conception of self, others, and events. The analysis of themes and details readily accommodates this framework. After examining the information yield from subjective and interpersonal perspectives, reference may then be made to objective perspectives that access the published material in the research literature. This procedure should then be followed in the evaluation of each respective early recollection. The process concludes by reconciling any differences in findings among the early recollections and constructing a lifestyle syllogism. The completion of this model, "I am . . . ," "Others are . . . ," "Events are . . . ," "Therefore, life is . . ." synthesizes all perspectives. This model of a person or a client is open to change as further pertinent information becomes available from corroborative sources. The rubric also serves as a guiding principle for organizing further material in a contextural assessment, and as an overarching framework for subsequent client development in counseling and psychotherapy. The next chapter includes more specific information and numerous examples relating to the organization and interpretation of early memories.

SUMMARY

The interpretation of early recollections involves a three-step procedure employing multiple perspectives. Initially, from a subjective stance, analysis of first memories entails an impressionistic and intuitive process on the part of a practitioner. An interpersonal perspective focuses on discerning prominent themes and details. Reference to a table of thematic variables contributes to this effort. The rubric of the self, others, and events provides a framework for organizing pertinent data. Detail analysis emphasizes the scrutiny of early recollections for sensory modalities, colors, locations, and physical objects. An objective perspective relates prominent aspects of an individual's first memories to relevant topics in the research literature. The synthesis of information from each of the three perspectives contributes to the formulation of a model of a person or a client. Table 7.2 provides a summary of procedural guidelines for the interpretation of early recollections.

TABLE 7.2: INTERPRETATION OF EARLY RECOLLECTIONS: PROCEDURAL GUIDELINES

1. Complete a subjective analysis through an intuitive and impressionistic process.
2. Conduct a thematic analysis to identify prominent patterns and subjects.
3. Examine the thematic variables in reference to the constructs of self, others, and events.
4. Explore additional themes that emerge beyond the thematic variables.
5. Consider sensory details: visual, auditory, tactile, olfactory, and gustatory.
6. Scrutinize details pertaining to color, location, and objects.
7. Complete an objective analysis by relating early recollection data to pertinent research.
8. Follow the proceeding guidelines for interpreting each respective early recollection.
9. Reconcile any differences in interpretive findings among the set of early recollections.
10. Synthesize perspectives through the model of a person.

TRAINING AND PRACTICE OF EARLY RECOLLECTIONS

"The important things are what we remember after we have
forgotten everything else."
—Virginia Axline (1964, p. 216)

INTRODUCTION

APPROPRIATE TRAINING IS AN ESSENTIAL FIRST STEP FOR DEVELOPING
proficiency in the utilization of early recollections as an assessment tool in
the counseling experience. Unfortunately only limited instructional opportunities exist at this time for human service students and professionals to develop the necessary knowledge and skills for effectively employing early
memories with clients. Training in projective techniques is infrequent or inconsistent in most counseling and psychology programs, and instruction and
practice activity is even less common for early recollections. A general lack of
awareness and experience in first memories among faculty members and
practitioners further contributes to the constraints on the use of early memories for psychological appraisal. It is reasonable to assume that the lack of a
contemporary book-length publication focusing on the theory and practice
of early recollections in counseling and psychotherapy has been a significant
factor in further limiting the professional use of the instrument. Hopefully,
the present volume will adequately address this particular need and serve to
expand treatment applications of first memories in the counseling process.

The second and most extensive section of this chapter introduces a broad
range of sample exercises for scoring and interpreting first memories. Two
other publications (Mosak, Schneider, & Mosak, 1980; Shulman & Mosak,
1988) present further pertinent practice material for evaluating early recollections as an integral component of a comprehensive lifestyle assessment.
Olson's (1979a) edited work on early recollections provides an instructive
chapter for reader practice. Bruhn's (1990b) text emphasizes a cognitive–perceptual system for analyzing early memories and includes relevant examples.
Unfortunately, a second planned volume on early childhood memories emphasizing research and clinical applications was never published.

TRAINING IN EARLY RECOLLECTIONS

In training situations, counselors and therapists should first examine their theoretical orientation and conceptual assumptions in the practice of early recollections. Practitioners must also be alert to the potential influence of personal bias relating to early memory assessment. With these initial considerations in mind, the development of competency in understanding and evaluating first memories is possible through various instructional pursuits involving classroom instruction and self-study.

TRAINING IMPLICATIONS

The contextural assessment model rests on certain assumptions for practitioners to consider in the therapeutic use of early recollections. When interpreting first memories, it is advantageous to evaluate data from multiple levels of analysis. In this regard, a therapist's early memory appraisal involves an evaluation orientation from subjective, interpersonal, and objective perspectives. Another key assumption is that the conceptualization of a model of a person or client is viable, and provides a practical rubric for individual assessment through perceptions of self, others, and events. With respect to these central constructs, an assumption is that they are relatively stable and enduring, yet also potentially modifiable through the counseling process. Finally, erroneous counselor judgments may occur when employing a model of a person in assessment and counseling, and it is possible to minimize misconceptions through an awareness of particular types of bias.

THEORETICAL AND CONCEPTUAL ASSUMPTIONS.   The use of multiple levels of analysis through three ways of knowing provides a comprehensive framework for the assessment of early recollections. In the most recent revision of the *Standards for Educational and Psychological Testing*, a recommendation is for practitioners to go beyond exclusively relying on intuitive impressions with projective instruments.

> When the professional uses tests that employ an unstructured response format, such as some projective techniques and informal behavioral ratings, the professional should follow objective scoring criteria, where available and appropriate, that are clear and minimize the need for the scorer to rely only on individual judgment. (American Educational Research Association, American Psychological Association, & National Council on Measurement in Education, 1999, p. 133)

The value of gaining a broad understanding of clients through diverse perspective-taking and multiple methods of appraisal maintains a prominent position in contemporary and multi-cultural assessment literature (Dana, 1995, 2000; Hood & Johnson, 2002; Paniagua, 1994). Through an evolving process, the counselor keeps an open mind in order to be receptive to additional factors and information that contribute to a sound conceptualization of a client.

It is possible to formulate a theoretical model of a person through the framework of the lifestyle syllogism. The constructs of the self, others, and events are essential for interpreting early recollections and for providing an overarching guide for determining interventions within the counseling process. Although the lifestyle is a central Adlerian concept, the schema components of the syllogism or rubric find broad representation and acceptance among practitioners beyond Individual Psychology. The schema as a psychological entity is integral to the practice of diverse psychotherapies, including psychodynamic, humanistic–existential, and cognitive–behavioral. Such dynamic constructs as the self (object relations), self-concept (person-centered), and cognitive distortions (cognitive psychotherapy) rely on schema conceptualizations for explanatory power. Almost 50 years ago, Pepinsky & Pepinsky (1954) made the point that counselors tend to construct a hypothetical client who will proceed or function according to certain assumptions held by the individual therapist. In this regard, the lifestyle rubric makes a practitioner's client model explicit and more amenable to therapeutic intervention.

As a fluid formulation, perspectives gained from early recollections suggest tenable hypotheses or possibilities about characteristic client functioning. The construction of a model of a person should be tentative and open to change as further information accrues through the assessment process. Only after submitting the early recollections material to additional levels of analysis beyond impressionistic findings can a viable conceptualization emerge. This schema framework (of the self, others, and events) provides a structure to organize client data from a variety of sources. However, the rubric is subject to change in response to appraisal perspectives beyond those engendered by the evaluation of early memories. As an example, a client's outlook based exclusively on his or her early recollections toward others suggests perceptions of suspicion and doubt. In contrast to this perspective, however, behavioral observations, verbal accounts from third parties, and objective personality testing indicate that the individual more often tends to trust and rely on others. It then becomes necessary to reconcile disparities in the assessment material and make appropriate adjustments in the client's hypothesized perception of others. In regard to potential schema adjustments during counseling, life perspectives of an individual may change with respect to his or her model of a person. This interaction reflects a second-order change (Lyddon, 1990; Lyddon & Satterfield, 1994), and is consistent with the goals of particular theories of counseling and psychotherapy that emphasize structural personality change.

POTENTIAL PRACTITIONER BIAS.   In a shift from a focus on client functioning, counselors and therapists must be aware of their own biases that may negatively influence the accuracy of the assessment process relating to early recollections and other appraisal information. In particular, practitioners should attempt to avoid errors in judgment resulting from the construction of a static model of a client. Confirmatory bias involves a tendency to continue to substantiate a counselor's initial hypotheses, rather than engage in an active search or exploration of alternative explanations (Spengler et al. 1995). In this regard, the therapist often fails to elicit or be open-minded about discrepant information and pays attention only to data supporting one's first impressions (Hood & Johnson, 2002). For example, a client's early recollections suggest perceptions associated with hostile tendencies. Rather than openly evaluate other appraisal material, the counselor easily follows the path of least resistance and prematurely adopts a client model assuming the operation of hostility. Subsequently, the counselor becomes receptive only to additional information that confirms this initial perspective.

In order to minimize confirmatory bias, practitioners should be open to search for new or even disconfirmatory data with the potential to modify a conceptualization of a client. Further, the utilization of multidimensional and multimethods of assessment often precludes a tendency to primarily attend to factors that confirm the preconception of an individual. As another type of bias, practitioners may hold ingrained convictions that contribute to inferential errors in assessment and counseling. As an example, a counselor's outlook on life is that it is fulfilling depending on a willingness to take risks. In working with clients, the counselor applies subtle pressure for individuals to engage in behaviors that involve increasing levels of risk, even when lacking a readiness to perform effectively. In order to limit this type of convictional bias, it is helpful for counselors and therapists to reflect on their fundamental belief system through a personal appraisal of early recollections and other available sources. With an awareness of this possible judgment error, practitioners may avoid unduly influencing clients with positions based on their long-held assumptions about life.

TRAINING OPPORTUNITIES

Although formal instruction in early recollections occurs only infrequently in counseling and psychology training programs, there is a clear potential for expanding learning activity on the topic due to the increasing availability of literature and resources on first memories (Warren, 1987). Currently, instructional opportunities are available for advanced students and practitioners on a limited scale in higher education settings and in professional development institutes. Self-study as an independent training direction is also possible, and there are a variety of innovative ways to pursue this option.

CLASSROOM INSTRUCTION.   In advanced courses devoted to evaluation and appraisal techniques and techniques of counseling, training in the theory and practice of early recollections is particularly relevant. In the context of understanding personality dynamics and treatment interventions, an emphasis on early memories provides a practical focus that is applicable to a diverse range of clients. Most often, an introduction of early recollections occurs as a part of a general discussion of projective techniques from a theoretical perspective and consideration of the devices as therapeutic tools. As a creative endeavor, students tend to be particularly interested in this topic and in developing skills for integrating early memories in counseling and psychotherapy. In graduate counseling classes and professional training programs, Eckstein (1999) and Kern and Eckstein (1997) have made numerous presentations on early recollections as a projective technique. After the introduction of theoretical aspects of early memories, participants gain practical experience in interpreting instructor-generated memories. As an instructional strategy, early recollections are written on note cards, and individuals in groups attempt to analyze each of the memories. One exercise, with implications for the counseling relationship, focuses on clarifying the potential resistance and receptivity to counseling of clients based on illustrations of their early recollections. Another activity emphasizes interpreting the early memories of Freud, Adler, and Jung in terms of how the recollections possibly reflect their personality functioning and psychological theories. Finally, in classroom exercises introducing Adlerian theory, Parrott (1992) has encouraged undergraduate and graduate students to explore and evaluate their earliest recollections and birth order.

SELF-STUDY.   Examining one's own early recollections is a sound way for students and professionals in the human services field to begin the study of first memories. This may be done independently through an introspective process or in conjunction with a formal class. Evaluating early recollections in an analytic sense expands self-understanding while developing proficiency in order to ultimately employ the technique (Myer & James, 1991). On an independent basis, it is helpful to discuss personal impressions of early memories with a trusted person who also has an understanding of their meaning.

From a personal perspective, beyond evaluating my own early recollections, I have found it helpful to gather childhood memories from my parents, brothers and sisters, my wife and children, and some of my friends. The extent of this endeavor has broadened my self-knowledge, in addition to increasing my understanding of those individuals who are significant in my life. As practitioners evaluate their own early recollections, this awareness should enhance their ability to recognize convictional bias that may tend to inadvertently influence their work with clients.

As with other psychological assessment procedures, training and supervision should be completed prior to using early recollections with clients independently. At the point when a practitioner is sufficiently proficient in the use of early recollections as a projective technique, it is then appropriate to administer the instrument to clients and begin the process of acquiring a stock of impressions of persons (Brown, 1972). The broadening experience for counselors and therapists in evaluating early memories obtained from their clientele enables them to more effectively conceptualize personality dynamics of people in general (Craddick, 1972). As experience accrues in the administration and interpretation of early recollections, a practitioner's skill level with the instrument deepens with each new assessment. The next section provides extensive practice examples for individuals beginning the study of early recollections and for professionals with an interest in expanding their skills with the instrument.

PRACTICE EXERCISES IN EARLY RECOLLECTIONS

For the intent of training, this section includes early recollection reports from 18 individuals. For organizational purposes, the practice exercises include an equal number of examples within each of the three sets. With some exceptions the examples represent composite first memories from persons with diverse backgrounds. The first memories emphasize content that practitioners will frequently hear from a range of clients in their therapeutic practice. The early recollections also reflect memories of individuals who have an outlook on life that suggests more adaptive psychological characteristics. In order to allow for practice in interpreting multiple early memories, each person relates three of his or her recollections. It is helpful to organize inferences from each early memory into a coherent format. In order to assist in this effort, Table 8.1 provides an Early Recollections Interpretation Worksheet. The organization of the worksheet follows the format of evaluating early recollections in a sequence in terms of subjective, interpersonal, and objective perspectives. Each of these assessment areas was discussed in detail in the previous chapter. Initially, a subjective perspective evaluation involves

TABLE 8.1: EARLY RECOLLECTIONS INTERPRETATION WORKSHEET

NAME: DATE:

I. Subjective Perspectives
   A. Early recollection #1 (ER1)
   B. Early recollection #2 (ER2)
   C. Early recollection #3 (ER3)
II. Interpersonal Perspectives
   A. Thematic Analysis
      1. "I am . . ."
         a. ER1:
         b. ER2:
         c. ER3:
      2. "Others are . . ."
         a. ER1:
         b. ER2:
         c. ER3:
      3. "Events are . . ."
         a. ER1:
         b. ER2:
         c. ER3:
   B. Detail Analysis
      1. Senses (visual, auditory, tactile, olfactory, and gustatory)
         a. ER1:
         b. ER2:
         c. ER3:
      2. Color
         a. ER1:
         b. ER2:
         c. ER3:
      3. Location
         a. ER1:
         b. ER2:
         c. ER3:
      4. Objects
         a. ER1:
         b. ER2:
         c. ER3:
III. Objective Perspectives
   A. ER1:
   B. ER2:
   C. ER3:
IV. Lifestyle Syllogism
   "I am . . ."
   "Others are . . ."
   "Events are . . ."
   "Therefore, life is . . ."

a practitioner notating his or her immediate reactions and impressions for each individual memory.

From an interpersonal perspective, evaluation emphasis relates to a thematic and detailed analysis of the early recollections. It is helpful to refer to Table 7.1, Thematic Variables, in chapter 7 in order to complete the thematic analysis section. Detail analysis requires the scrutiny of each memory to determine representation of sensory modalities, colors, locations, and objects. Evaluation from an objective perspective focuses on identifying pertinent material relating to each memory with respect to diagnostic and personality impressions found in chapters 3 and 4 of the text or from other pertinent published sources. Finally, completion of the lifestyle syllogism involves the synthesis of subjective, interpersonal, and objective perspectives from the three early recollections of a person.

EARLY RECOLLECTIONS: SET ONE

In a therapeutic setting, extensive biographical information relating to the background of an individual is generally available to counselors and therapists. In order to avoid biasing early recollections practice responses, identification data is limited to only the first name of a person in this practice section. After individuals report three early recollections, three follow-up questions are asked relating to relevant details, vivid aspects, and pertinent feelings. Following the information provided by various individuals relating to their early recollections, I provide my evaluation of the respective memories through the format of the Early Recollections Interpretation Worksheet (Table 8.1). This material reflects my independent analysis of the early memories and serves as an instructional appraisal guide. The responses represent interpretations of the early recollections and are subject to differing opinions, as is the case of any inference. In particular, the subjective perspectives include my personal impressions, and other individuals may determine alternative views from their own intuitive stance.

JASON   Early Recollections 1 [ER1]: "I had some matches and I went outside to set a fire. I found some old newspapers and wood behind my house and started a fire. It got really going with a lot of smoke. My father came running out of the house and smacked me in the face."
Details: "Seeing the newspaper turn black."
Vivid: "The huge size of the fire."
Feelings: "Excitement."
ER2: "I was playing soldiers with one of my friends in a field. I belted him over the head with the butt of my rifle. The kid started crying and ran into his house. His mother came out and chased me with a broom."

Details: "We dug fox holes and they were pretty good."

Vivid: "Hitting him on the head with my rifle. I think some blood came out."

Feelings: "Kind of thrilling; like real war."

ER3: "I was down the cellar in our house. I kept turning the power saw on and off. I cut up a few broom handles and other stuff. All of a sudden my father appeared and grabbed me. He shook me hard and yelled."

Details: "Seeing the white sawdust on the metal plate of the saw."

Vivid: "The really loud noise of the saw and my father grabbing me."

Feelings: "It was a lot of fun. Exciting."

I. Subjective Perspectives
    A. ER1: Father's punishment is not adversive. Thrill-seeker. Acting out with fire setting.
    B. ER2: Low level of moral development. Lack of feelings for others.
    C. ER3: Destructive. Seeks excitement. Punishment is not adversive.

II. Interpersonal Perspectives
    A. Thematic Analysis
        1. "I am . . ."
           a. ER1: defiant
           b. ER2: defiant
           c. ER3: defiant
        2. "Others are . . ."
           a. ER1: hostile
           b. ER2: unworthy
           c. ER3: hostile
        3. "Events are . . ."
           a. ER1: destructive
           b. ER2: destructive
           c. ER3: destructive
    B. Detail Analysis
        1. Senses
           a. ER1: visual
           b. ER2: visual
           c. ER3: visual and auditory
        2. Color
           a. ER1:—(no representation)
           b. ER2:—
           c. ER3: white—saw dust
        3. Location
           a. ER1: outside, behind his house
           b. ER2: outside in a field

      c. ER3: home
    4. Objects
      a. ER1: fire
      b. ER2: rifle
      c. ER3: sawdust

III. Objective Perspectives
    A. ER1: Dramatic, misdeeds, punishment, aggression (Antisocial personality disorder).
    B. ER2: Dramatic, misdeeds, aggression (Antisocial personality disorder).
    C. ER3: Misdeeds, aggression (Antisocial personality disorder).

IV. Lifestyle Syllogism
    "I am . . . defiant."
    "Others are . . . unworthy or hostile."
    "Events are . . . destructive."
    "Therefore, life is . . . combat."

ALICE   "I was swimming in my neighbor's pool. She pushed me under the water and held my head under. I couldn't breathe."
    Details: "Seeing how gross she looked in a bathing suit."
    Vivid: "Seeing the bluish water and trying to lift my head."
    Feelings: "Very scared."
ER2: "Playing with my friend's pet hamster. It was fun. All of a sudden the thing bit me on my finger. It really hurt."
    Details: "Feeling how soft the hamster's fur was."
    Vivid: "The hamster nipping my finger."
    Feelings: "It was painful and unexpected."
ER3: "It was a rainy day and I was carrying a twisted branch. I was on the side of my house where there were a lot of green trees. I started to climb a tree with the branch in my hand, and I fell. I really hurt my arm and my side when I hit the ground. I yelled but nobody came to help me."
    Details: "Seeing how twisted the branch was."
    Vivid: "Hitting the ground."
    Feelings: "It hurt and I cried."

I. Subjective Perspectives
    A. ER1: Pain can occur unexpectedly. Others are threatening and hurtful.
    B. ER2: Things are enjoyable, but can quickly go wrong. Vulnerable.
    C. ER3: Enjoys physical activity. Something painful will happen. Nobody helps.

II. Interpersonal Perspectives
    A. Thematic Analysis

1. "I am . . .
    a. ER1: insecure
    b. ER2: insecure
    c. ER3: insecure
2. "Others are . . ."
    a. ER1: untrustworthy and hostile
    b. ER2: hostile
    c. ER3: neglectful
3. "Events are . . ."
    a. ER1: destructive and fearful
    b. ER2: unpredictable and fearful
    c. ER3: gratifying and fearful
B. Detail Analysis
    1. Senses
        a. ER1: visual
        b. ER2: visual and tactile
        c. ER3: visual and tactile
    2. Color
        a. ER1: bluish water
        b. ER2:—
        c. ER3: green trees
    3. Location
        a. ER1: outside, swimming pool
        b. ER2: inside?
        c. ER3: outside
    4. Objects
        a. ER1: gross quality of the woman neighbor
        b. ER2: hamster
        c. ER3: twisted branch
III. Objective Perspectives
    A. ER1: Fearful and threatening (Anxiety disorder).
    B. ER2: Fearful and painful (Anxiety disorder).
    C. ER3: Fearful and isolated (Anxiety disorder).
IV. Lifestyle syllogism
    "I am . . . insecure."
    "Others are . . . fearful or neglectful."
    "Events are . . . distressful."
    "Therefore, life is . . . ultimately fearful."

HAROLD   ER1: "I remember making funny faces and burping noises on the playground. A few kids were looking at me and laughing. So I kept doing it. But then they walked away and ignored me."

Details: "Seeing the backs of the kids as they are walking away."

Vivid: "Kids walking away."

Feelings: "Feeling foolish. Empty. A painful hurt."

ER2: "I must have been about six or seven. We were trying to name our new kitten. I suggested the name 'Midnight.' No one in my family said anything. A few minutes later, my little sister said to name the cat 'Midnight.' My parents said that was a good idea and gave my sister credit for naming the kitty."

Details: "Not much."

Vivid: "My parents saying it was a good idea."

Feelings: "Sad and overlooked."

ER3: "I woke up late at night and called for my mother. She didn't come, and I pulled the blankets over my head. My room felt cold."

Details: "It was cold and dark."

Vivid: "Yelling for my mother."

Feelings: "Scared, alone."

I. Subjective Perspectives

    A. ER1: Desperate for attention. Rejected. Makes a fool of himself. Feels used by others.

    B. ER2: Feels overlooked. Younger sibling gets parents' attention.

    C. ER3: Scared. Nobody cares. Lack of support and protection. Vulnerable.

II. Interpersonal Perspectives

    A. Thematic Analysis

        1. "I am . . ."

            a. ER1: unacceptable

            b. ER2: insignificant

            c. ER3: insecure

        2. "Others are . . ."

            a. ER1: neglectful

            b. ER2: neglectful

            c. ER3: neglectful

        3. "Events are . . ."

            a. ER1: debilitative

            b. ER2: disappointing

            c. ER3: fearful

    B. Detail Analysis

        1. Senses

            a. ER1: visual

            b. ER2: visual

            c. ER3: visual

2. Color
   a. ER1:—
   b. ER2:—
   c. ER3:—
3. Location
   a. ER1: playground
   b. ER2: home?
   c. ER3: bedroom
4. Objects
   a. ER1: backs of children
   b. ER2:—
   c. ER3:—

III. Objective Perspectives
   A. ER1: Negative affect. Ineffectual. Unpredictable environment (Mood disorder).
   B. ER2: Negative affect. Ineffectual. Passive orientation. Negative affective tone (Mood disorder).
   C. ER3: Unsafe environment (Mood disorder).

IV. Lifestyle Syllogism
   "I am . . . insignificant."
   "Others are . . . neglectful."
   "Events are . . . debilitative."
   "Therefore, life is . . . tormenting."

HANNAH   ER1: "I was fishing with my father. He asked me to put the lure on the fishing line. I pretended that I didn't know how to do it so that he would put it on."
   Details: "Seeing all the different colored lures in the tackle box."
   Vivid: "When my dad said that he would put the lure on the line."
   Feelings: "Relieved. I didn't feel like doing it."
ER2: "My mother was teaching me how to swim, and she was holding me up in the water. Every time she let go I would stand up in the water. I was afraid. She got angry at me because she wanted me to try to swim."
   Details: "Seeing all the people around me."
   Vivid: "My mother holding me."
   Feelings: "Good until she let me go."
ER3: "I was with my parents, and we were walking in the woods. I got tired and made a fuss. My father then carried me on his shoulders."
   Details: "Seeing so many trees and plants."
   Vivid: "Getting carried."
   Feelings: "It felt good because I didn't have to walk."

I. Subjective Perspectives
   A. ER1: Dependent. Manipulative. Avoids challenges.
   B. ER2: Fearful. Avoids risks.
   C. ER3: Dependent. Passive. Avoids pain.
II. Interpersonal Perspectives
   A. Thematic Analysis
      1. "I am . . ."
         a. ER1: incompetent
         b. ER2: incompetent
         c. ER3: passive
      2. "Others are . . ."
         a. ER1: nurturing
         b. ER2: intolerant
         c. ER3: nuturing
      3. "Events are . . ."
         a. ER1: overwhelming
         b. ER2: overwhelming
         c. ER3: disagreeable
   B. Detail Analysis
      1. Senses
         a. ER1: visual
         b. ER2: visual
         c. ER3: visual
      2. Color
         a. ER1: mention of colors
         b. ER2:—
         c. ER3:—
      3. Location
         a. ER1: outdoors
         b. ER2: outdoors
         c. ER3: outdoors
      4. Objects
         a. ER1: fishing lures
         b. ER2:—
         c. ER3:—
III. Objective Perspectives
   A. ER1: External locus of control. Anxiety. (Interpersonal functioning).
   B. ER2: External locus of control. Anxiety. (Interpersonal functioning).
   C. ER3: External locus of control. (Interpersonal functioning).
IV. Lifestyle Syllogism
   "I am . . . dependent."

"Others are . . . nurturing."

"Events are . . . overwhelming."

"Therefore, life is . . . manageable when I can rely on others."

ROSE   ER1: "My older sister said that I could have her radio if I could sleep in a chair in her room all night. I really wanted the radio. During the night she pushed me off of the chair and kicked me out of her room."

Details: "Seeing the big brown radio."

Vivid: "Sitting in the chair knowing that I could do it."

Feelings: "Determined to get the radio."

ER2: "My mother wanted me to wear a blue dress, but I wanted to wear a green one. She kept insisting that I wear the blue dress, but I refused to do so."

Details: "Sort of different things in my room."

Vivid: "Seeing the green dress."

Feelings: "I was angry and knew that I was right."

ER3: "I was riding my bike, and I skidded and fell on the street. A couple of neighbors ran up to me and asked me if I was OK. I said that I was even though I really hurt my elbow and hands. They were bleeding a little. I just didn't want to say anything."

Details: "Riding the bike before I fell."

Vivid: "Telling the people that I was alright."

Feelings: "I knew that I could take care of myself."

I. Subjective Perspectives

    A. ER1: Goal-oriented. Determined. Others break promises.

    B. ER2: Self-certain. Determined. Confrontational.

    C. ER3: Self-reliant. Determined.

II. Interpersonal Perspectives

    A. Thematic Analysis

        1. "I am . . ."

           a. ER1: internally controlled

           b. ER2: internally controlled

           c. ER3: internally controlled

        2. "Others are . . ."

           a. ER1: untrustworthy

           b. ER2: intolerant

           c. ER3: friendly

        3. "Events are . . ."

           a. ER1: disagreeable

           b. ER2: disagreeable

           c. ER3: manageable

    B. Detail Analysis

1. Senses
   a. ER1: visual, tactile (pushed, kicked)
   b. ER2: visual
   c. ER3: visual
2. Color
   a. ER1: brown radio
   b. ER2: green and blue dress
   c. ER3:—
3. Location
   a. ER1: sister's room
   b. ER2: home?
   c. ER3: outside on street
4. Objects
   a. ER1: radio
   b. ER2: dresses
   c. ER3: bicycle

III. Objective Perspectives
   A. ER1: Internal locus of control. Active. (Interpersonal functioning).
   B. ER2: Internal locus of control. Active. (Interpersonal functioning).
   C. ER3: Internal locus of control. Active. (Interpersonal functioning).

IV. Lifestyle Syllogism
   "I am . . . determined."
   "Other are . . . discouraging."
   "Events are . . . disagreeable."
   "Therefore, life is . . . manageable when I can direct myself."

MARIA ER1: "I remember working down in the basement with my dad. We were both doing woodworking projects together. I felt so proud."
   Details: "Seeing the basement door area where it curved in."
   Vivid: "Nailing a piece of wood."
   Feelings: "Proud and happy."
ER2: "I was sitting on a changing table, and my two sisters were dressing me up."
   Details: "Sitting and my feet dangling."
   Vivid: "My sisters pulling up my hair and putting it in pigtails."
   Feelings: "Like a doll. I knew that I was loved at that moment."
ER3: I was playing with a toy cash register with my younger sister and making believe that I was a cash register girl."
   Details: "Seeing the different keys on the cash register with numbers on them."

Vivid: "Pretending, like acting."
Feelings: "Almost like a dream; very pleasant."
I. Subjective Perspectives
   A. Active. Constructive. Purposeful.
   B. Secure. Pleasant experience.
   C. Active. Harmonious situation. Idyllic.
II. Interpersonal Perspectives
   A. Thematic Analysis
      1. "I am . . ."
         a. ER1: significant
         b. ER2: significant
         c. ER3: significant
      2. "Others are . . ."
         a. ER1: encouraging
         b. ER2: nurturing and friendly
         c. ER3: friendly
      3. "Events are . . ."
         a. ER1: constructive
         b. ER2: gratifying
         c. ER3: bountiful
   B. Detail Analysis
      1. Senses
         a. ER1: visual
         b. ER2: visual, tactile
         c. ER3: visual
      2. Color
         a. ER1:—
         b. ER2:—
         c. ER3:—
      3. Location
         a. ER1: home
         b. ER2: home
         c. ER3: home
      4. Objects
         a. ER1: wood
         b. ER2: hair
         c. ER3: cash register
III. Objective Perspectives
   A. ER1: Secure. Competent. (Interpersonal functioning).
   B. ER2: Secure. Competent. (Interpersonal functioning).

C. ER3: Secure. Competent. (Interpersonal functioning).
IV. Lifestyle Perspectives
"I am . . . significant."
"Others are . . . nurturing."
"Events are . . . invigorating."
"Therefore, life is . . . abundant."

EARLY RECOLLECTIONS: SET TWO

The next set of early recollections will follow the same organization as the initial collection of practice exercises. Six individuals report their early memories, and evaluations are entered on the Early Recollections Interpretation Worksheet. For interpretation training purposes, it may be helpful to score each recollection and then check my analysis for comparison of findings. The concluding set of early recollections include three of my first memories. Of the dozen or so early childhood recollections that I can recall, three reflect a particular theme that has been prominent in the pattern of my life.

BOB ER1: "I remember taking a long time to put up a tent. When I was done, I went inside and looked out the window. I saw the boy down the street rip the tent and knock it down,"
Details: "Seeing the look of delight on the kid's face."
Vivid: "Seeing him rip the tent down."
Feelings: "Stunned and helpless."
ER2: "We moved to a new neighborhood when I was about six. I went out on the street to play. A boy out there looked at me with a mean look on his face. It was scary, and I went back into my house."
Details: "Seeing the kids out on the street."
Vivid: "The boy's angry face."
Feelings: "Scared."
ER3: "I had just got a vaccination shot in my arm. A neighborhood kid was sitting on my chest and was punching me on the arm where I had gotten the shot."
Details: "Seeing the grass on the hill when the kid is punching me."
Vivid: "Getting hit on the arm."
Feelings: "It hurt. Knowing how serious it was because it would leave a scar."
I. Subjective Perspectives
  A. Makes an effort that gets destroyed. Helpless to stop destruction—observes it.
  B. Others are threatening, menacing. Withdraws.
  C. Situation makes no sense. Serious consequences. Destructive.

II. Interpersonal Perspectives
   A. Thematic Analysis
      1. "I am . . ."
         a. ER1: insignificant and passive
         b. ER2: insecure
         c. ER3: unacceptable
      2. "Others are . . ."
         a. ER1: hostile
         b. ER2: hostile
         c. ER3: hostile
      3. "Events are . . ."
         a. ER1: destructive
         b. ER2: distressful
         c. ER3: destructive
   B. Detail Analysis
      1. Senses
         a. ER1: visual
         b. ER2: visual
         c. ER3: visual
      2. Color
         a. ER1:—
         b. ER2:—
         c. ER3:—
      3. Location
         a. ER1: inside home (looking outside)
         b. ER2: outside
         c. ER3: outside
      4. Objects
         a. ER1: tent
         b. ER2:—
         c. ER3:—
III. Objective Perspectives
   A. ER1: External locus of control. Insecure. (Interpersonal functioning).
   B. ER2: Insecure. External locus of control. Fearful. (Anxiety disorder).
   C. ER3: Insecure. External locus of control. Fearful. (Anxiety disorder).
IV. Lifestyle Syllogism
   "I am . . . vulnerable."
   "Others are . . . hostile."
   "Events are . . . destructive."
   "Therefore, life is . . . threatening."

ELAINE   ER1: "I was walking in the May Day parade, and I had to wear an old hat. All the other girls had on a brand new bonnet with ribbons and flowers."

    Details: "People looking at me."

    Vivid: "Wearing an old white bonnet."

    Feelings: "Really embarrassed."

ER2: "I was the flower girl at my uncle's wedding. I wore a beautiful white dress. Right before the ceremony I spilled a glass of grape juice on the front of my dress."

    Details: "Looking down at the red rug."

    Vivid: "Seeing the grape juice spill on my dress."

    Feelings: "Total disgust at myself."

ER3: "I was invited to a girl's birthday party in my class. When she opened the presents, she liked all of her gifts until she got to mine. I gave her a box of red, white, and blue pencils. All of the kids laughed at me for giving her pencils."

    Details: "The box of pencils with different colors. I thought it was nice."

    Vivid: "Seeing the kids laughing."

    Feelings: "Embarrassed and stupid."

I. Subjective Perspectives

    A. Concerned about appearance. Other people have more. Inferior to others.

    B. Self-contempt. Aesthetic emphasis. Situation starts well, but ends in calamity.

    C. Ridiculed by others. Self-loathing.

II. Interpersonal Perspectives

    A. Thematic Analysis

        1. "I am . . ."

            a. ER1: unacceptable

            b. ER2: incompetent and loathsome

            c. ER3: unacceptable

        2. "Others are . . ."

            a. ER1: intolerant

            b. ER2:—

            c. ER3: intolerent

        3. "Events are . . ."

            a. ER1: debilitative

            b. ER2: distressful

            c. ER3: distressful

    B. Detail Analysis

        1. Senses

    a. ER1: visual
    b. ER2: visual
    c. ER3: visual
2. Color
    a. ER1: white
    b. ER2: red
    c. ER3: red, white, and blue
3. Location
    a. ER1: outside
    b. ER2: inside
    c. ER3: inside
4. Objects
    a. ER1: bonnet
    b. ER2: grape juice
    c. ER3: box of colored pencils

III. Objective Perspectives

  A. ER1: Insecure. Aesthetic emphasis. Need for approval. Negative affective tone. (Affect disorder).

  B. ER2: Ineffectual. Negative affective tone. Aesthetic emphasis. (Affect disorder).

  C. ER3: Ineffectual. Negative affective tone. Aesthetic emphasis. (Affect disorder).

IV. Lifestyle Syllogism

"I am . . . inadequate."

"Others are . . . intolerant."

"Events are . . . distressful."

"Therefore, life is . . . full of anguish."

JUSTIN   ER1: "When I was in the second grade, I remember picking on a nerdy kid with real thick glasses. I grabbed his glasses and stepped on them and laughed."

Details: "Knowing the teacher was not around."

Vivid: "Hearing the glasses crunch as I twisted my shoe."

Feelings: "Pure fun."

ER2: "I must have been about seven years old. I was holding a frog that I caught near the railroad tracks. I found a big rock near the track, and I smashed the frog. Blood and guts came out."

Details: "Seeing broken beer bottles near the track."

Vivid: "Hearing the frog squish."

Feelings: "I don't know. Fun, I guess."

ER3: "When I was little, my father took me and my sister to visit a farm. We walked around a chicken coop. All of a sudden my dad started kicking and chasing the chickens. I did the same thing. It was a lot of fun. We laughed like crazy."

Details: "Seeing so many chickens."

Vivid: "Kicking the chickens and hearing them squawk."

Feelings: "It was really great. I felt kind of powerful."

I. Subjective Perspectives
   A. ER1: Hurts others. Delights in destruction. No remorse.
   B. ER2: Aggression. No remorse.
   C. ER3: Delights in taunting animals. Models parent's aggression.

II. Interpersonal Perspectives
   A. Thematic Analysis
      1. "I am . . ."
         a. ER1: defiant
         b. ER2: defiant
         c. ER3: defiant
      2. "Others are . . ."
         a. ER1: unworthy
         b. ER2: unworthy
         c. ER3: unworthy
      3. "Events are . . ."
         a. ER1: destructive
         b. ER2: destructive
         c. ER3: invigorating
   B. Detail Analysis
      1. Senses
         a. ER1: auditory (hearing glasses crunch)
         b. ER2: auditory (hearing frog squish)
         c. ER3: visual
      2. Color
         a. ER1:—
         b. ER2:—
         c. ER3:—
      3. Location
         a. ER1: outside
         b. ER2: outside
         c. ER3: outside
      4. Objects
         a. ER1: glasses
         b. ER2: frog
         c. ER3: chickens

III. Objective Perspectives
   A. Misdeed. Aggression. Lack of social interest. (Antisocial personality disorder).
   B. Dramatic. Misdeed. Aggression. Lack of social interest. (Antisocial personality disorder).
   C. Dramatic. Misdeed. Aggression. Lack of social interest. (Antisocial personality disorder).
IV. Lifestyle Syllogism
   "I am . . . defiant."
   "Others are . . . unworthy."
   "Events are . . . destructive."
   "Therefore, life is . . . a ruinous pursuit."

NANCY   ER1: "I remember getting into my Aunt Mary's new car. It was a gleaming black color. We were going to visit my Aunt Ann."
   Details: "Seeing the brown color of the seats as I got in the car."
   Vivid: "Getting into the car."
   Feelings: "Excited to be going for a ride."
ER2: "Sitting in during recess time. We were supposed to go outside, but it was raining. We couldn't go out on the playground."
   Details: "Seeing the rain hit the windows in the classroom."
   Vivid: "Looking out the window and thinking about running on the playground."
   Feelings: "Unhappy."
ER3: "Riding on the street in a red wagon. My friend and I were taking turns pushing each other."
   Details: "We had painted the wagon red and it was really pretty."
   Vivid: "Riding in the wagon."
   Feelings: "Having fun and enjoying it."
I. Subjective Perspectives
   A. Enjoys traveling. Colors are prominent. Impressed by the new car.
   B. Feels restricted in having to stay inside.
   C. Cooperative experience. Color prominent.
II. Interpersonal Perspectives
   A. Thematic Analysis
      1. "I am . . ."
         a. ER1: active
         b. ER2: active
         c. ER3: competent and active
      2. "Others are . . ."
         a. ER1: friendly

      b. ER2:—
      c. ER3: friendly
    3. "Events are . . ."
      a. ER1: invigorating
      b. ER2: restrictive
      c. ER3: invigorating
  B. Detail Analysis
    1. Senses
      a. ER1: visual
      b. ER2: visual
      c. ER3: visual
    2. Color
      a. ER1: black and brown
      b. ER2:—
      c. ER3: red
    3. Location
      a. ER1: outside
      b. ER2: inside
      c. ER3: outside
    4. Objects
      a. ER1: car
      b. ER2: playground
      c. ER3: wagon
III. Objective Perspectives
  A. ER1: Active. Internal locus of control. Aesthetic interest. Involves movement.
  B. ER2: Involves restriction of movement. Active intellectually.
  C. ER3: Aesthetic interest. Involves movement. Social interest (cooperative activity).
IV. Lifestyle Syllogism
  "I am . . . active."
  "Others are . . . friendly."
  "Events are . . . bountiful."
  "Therefore, life is . . . enriching when I can be active."

PAUL   ER1: "My parents gave me a toy horn. I was playing on it and making nice sounds. They were listening to me and looked happy."
    Details: "The big size of the brass horn."
    Vivid: "Seeing my parents and their sense of delight."
    Feelings: "Just happy and sort of proud."
ER2: "I was about four years old. I was in the back of my house with my

mother and father. I saw a yellow buttercup growing on the side of the grass. I picked it and gave it to my mother. She lifted me up and hugged me."

Details: "Seeing all the beautiful flowers. I especially remember the yellow and blue ones."

Vivid: "Looking at my mother's happy face when I gave her the buttercup."

Feelings: "Delight and satisfaction."

ER3: "I was in my backyard again. There was a rock that I was trying to dig out of the dirt. I kept digging, but it was too big to lift out of the ground."

Details: "Seeing how big the rock was as I was digging."

Vivid: "Realizing that I couldn't get the rock out of the ground. It was too big."

Feelings: "Kind of frustrated."

I. Subjective Perspectives

    A. Idyllic experience. Receives rapt attention. Natural setting.

    B. Aesthetic emphasis. Cooperative.

    C: Alone. Persistent. Frustrated in not completing task.

II. Interpersonal Perspectives

    A. Thematic Analysis

        1. "I am . . ."

            a. ER1: significant

            b. ER2: secure

            c. ER3: active

        2. "Others are . . ."

            a. ER1: nurturing

            b. ER2: friendly and encouraging

            c. ER3:—

        3. "Events are . . ."

            a. ER1: gratifying

            b. ER2: harmonious

            c. ER3: distressful

    B. Detail Analysis

        1. Senses

            a. ER1: visual and auditory ("making nice sounds")

            b. ER2: visual and tactile ("hugged me")

            c. ER3: visual

        2. Color

            a. ER1: brass

            b. ER2: yellow

            c. ER3:—

        3. Location

        a. ER1: inside?

        b. ER2: outside

        c. ER3: outside

    4. Objects

        a. ER1: horn

        b. ER2: flowers

        c. ER3: rock

III. Objective Perspectives

    A. ER1: Secure. Social interest.

    B. ER2: Secure. Social interest.

    C. ER3: Cause of problem outside oneself (Explanatory style).

IV. Lifestyle Syllogism

    "I am . . . secure."

    "Others are . . . nurturing."

    "Events are . . . gratifying."

    "Therefore, life is . . . gratifying when I'm with other people."

ART   ER1: "It was the day of my First Communion. I still had my white suit on after going to church. My younger brother and I were playing outside of the apartment building where my aunt and uncle lived. All of a sudden, I realized that I had lost all of the money that my relatives had given me for my First Communion."

    Details: "Standing near the brick buildings where we were playing."

    Vivid: "Looking through all of my pockets and realizing that all of the
        money was gone."

    Feelings: "Shocked."

ER2: "It was breakfast time and my mother and my older sister said that there was only enough oatmeal for one person. Since it was my first day of school, they decided to give it to me."

    Details: "Seeing the pan on the kitchen stove."

    Vivid: "Being told that I could have the oatmeal."

    Feelings. "That it wasn't a good thing that there was only enough oat-
        meal for me."

ER3: "I remember asking my father for ten cents for a postcard that I needed for school. He got irritated at me, and said that he didn't have the money."

    Details: "Standing on the front lawn with my father and it was nice and
        sunny out."

    Vivid: "My father saying that he didn't have the money."

    Feelings: "Perplexed and concerned with the seriousness of my father not
        having an extra ten cents."

I. Subjective Perspectives

A. ER1: Makes irretrievable mistake. Self-reproach. Inept. Serious economic situation.
B. ER2: Taken care of by family. Not enough food for the rest of the family. Serious economic situation.
C. ER3: Lack of money for necessary things. Serious economic situation.
II. Interpersonal Perspectives
  A. Thematic Analysis
    1. "I am . . ."
      a. ER1: incompetent
      b. ER2: worthy
      c. ER3: insecure
    2. "Others are . . ."
      a. ER1: not able to help
      b. ER2: nurturing
      c. ER3: needy
    3. "Events are . . ."
      a. ER1: debilitative
      b. ER2: meager
      c. ER3: deficient
  B. Detail Analysis
    1. Senses
      a. ER1: visual
      b. ER2: visual
      c. ER3: visual
    2. Color
      a. ER1: white suit
      b. ER2:—
      c. ER3:—
    3. Location
      a. ER1: outside
      b. ER2: inside home
      c. ER3: outside
    4. Objects
      a. ER1: money
      b. ER2: oatmeal
      c. ER3: money
III. Objective Perspectives
  A. ER1: Insecure. Blame oneself (Explanatory style).
  B. ER2: Social interest.
  C. ER3: Insecure. Social interest.
IV. Lifestyle Syllogism

"I am . . . vulnerable."
"Others are . . . impoverished."
"Events are . . . debilitative."
"Therefore, life is . . . unprotected."

EARLY RECOLLECTIONS: SET THREE

In the concluding set of early recollections, in terms of an inference relating to my belief system, it may be apparent that money, or my perceived lack of it, has played a prominent role in my life. Some people say that I am so cheap that I still have the gifts of money that I received for my First Communion. They are wrong about that but are totally right about my being frugal. There have been numerous times over many years when my actions to save money have been excessive and self-defeating. At the same time, an insight into my "problem" enables me to gain some measure of control on what can be an extreme and largely unnecessary pursuit. In this instance for me, and more broadly speaking for practitioners in general, evaluating one's own early memories offers potential for enhancing self-understanding and clarifying issues that may contribute to convictional bias with clients. In the final set of early recollections, six individuals report their memories, and the interpretive format remains the same as in the previous exercises. As in some of the other early recollections examples, it may be necessary to reconcile thematic differences among a person's memories in order to determine a coherent model of a person.

ANDREA   ER1: "I was very excited to go to the carnival, as my father had promised. I got dressed up and waited on the couch. It got real dark, and I realized that my father wasn't coming."
  Details: "Looking at the pattern of the couch and how tight my hands were folded."
  Vivid: "Getting so dark and knowing that he wasn't coming."
  Feelings: "It felt like a knife in my gut."
ER2: "I was waiting my turn to go to the blackboard. I was next in line. The teacher said the game was over, and we all had to return to our seats."
  Details: "Seeing the kids writing on the blackboard."
  Vivid: "Hearing the teacher saying that we had to stop."
  Feelings: "Very disappointed and let down."
ER3: "All of the kids in my class were invited to a girl's birthday party at the end of the school year in the second grade. My mother said that I should go, but I wasn't sure if I wanted to because I wasn't one of the popular kids. I decided to stay home, but then I regretted that I did."
  Details: "Playing with my doll after I decided not to go."

Vivid: "Realizing that it was too late to go to the party."

Feelings: "Regret and kind of sad."

I. Subjective Perspectives

    A. ER1: Profound disappointment. Breaking of trust. Dark.

    B. ER2: Disappointment. Things quickly turn bad. Other people hurt.

    C. ER3: Uncertain. Regret. Alone.

II. Interpersonal Perspectives

    A. Thematic Analysis

        1. "I am . . ."

            a. ER1: unacceptable

            b. ER2: insignificant

            c. ER3: incompetent

        2. "Others are . . ."

            a. ER1: untrustworthy

            b. ER2: discouraging

            c. ER3:—

        3. "Events are . . ."

            a. ER1: debilitative

            b. ER2: disagreeable

            c. ER3: distressful

    B. Detail Analysis

        1. Senses

            a. ER1: visual

            b. ER2: visual

            c. ER3: visual

        2. Color

            a. ER1:—

            b. ER2:—

            c. ER3:—

        3. Location

            a. ER1: home

            b. ER2: school

            c. ER3: home

        4. Objects

            a. ER1:—

            b. ER2: blackboard

            c. ER3:—

III. Objective Perspectives

    A. ER1: Others are need frustraters. Unpredictable environment. Negative affective tone. Hopelessness. (Affect disorder).

    B. ER2: Others are need frustraters. Unpredictable environment.

Negative affective tone. (Affect disorder).

   C. ER3: Ineffectual. Passive orientation. Negative affective tone. (Affect disorder).

IV. Lifestyle Syllogism

   "I am . . . unacceptable."

   "Others are . . . neglectful."

   "Events are. . . debilitative."

   "Therefore, life is . . . agonizing."

HOWARD   ER1: "I had been playing with matches in a shed attached to the back of our house. I went into the house, and my mother asked me if I had taken matches from the kitchen. I said 'no.' She then said nothing would happen if I told the truth. So I told her that I had taken the matches. Immediately, she whacked me in the face."

   Details: "Seeing my mother's face as she was talking to me."

   Vivid: "Getting hit in the face."

   Feelings: "It hurt and I didn't expect it."

ER2: "It was time to go to school, and I didn't want to go. I ran down the hall, and my father ran after me. He grabbed me by the neck and dragged me to the front door."

   Details: "Running down the hall thinking that I could get out of going to school."

   Vivid: "My father grabbing me by the neck."

   Feelings: "It hurt, but I still thought that I could avoid going to school."

ER3: "I broke into an old house with a few of my buddies. Nobody was living in the house. We found paint in the cellar. Then we went upstairs and poured the paint all over the floors and splattered it against the walls. It was a lot of fun."

   Details: "Seeing the paint cans."

   Vivid: "Getting the paint all over everything."

   Feelings: "Great. Exciting."

I. Subjective Perspectives

   A. ER1: Impulsive. Breaking of trust.

   B. ER2: Resists authority. Manipulative. Willing to pay the price to get own way.

   C. ER3: Impulsive. Destructive.

II. Interpersonal Perspectives

   A. Thematic Analysis

   1. "I am . . ."

      a. ER1: defiant

      b. ER2: defiant

    c. ER3: destructive
2. "Others are . . ."
    a. ER1: untrustworthy
    b. ER2: hostile
    c. ER3: agreeable (peers)
3. "Events are . . ."
    a. ER1: disagreeable
    b. ER2: manageable
    c. ER3: destructive
B. Detail Analysis
  1. Senses
    a. ER1: tactile (struck by mother)
    b. ER2: tactile (grabbed and dragged)
    c. ER3:—
  2. Color
    a. ER1:—
    b. ER2:—
    c. ER3:—
  3. Location
    a. ER1: home
    b. ER2: home
    c. ER3: house
  4. Objects
    a. ER1: face
    b. ER2: neck
    c. ER3: paint
III. Objective Perspectives
  A. ER1: Physical punishment. Lack of trust. (Juvenile delinquency).
  B. ER2: Lack of impulse control. Physical punishment. Emotional detachment. (Juvenile delinquency).
  C. ER3: Serious rule breaking. Lack of impulse control. Emotional detachment. (Juvenile delinquency).
IV. Lifestyle Syllogism
"I am . . . defiant."
"Others are . . . unworthy."
"Events are . . . destructive."
"Therefore, life is . . . getting away with anything that I feel like doing."

ALLISON   ER1: "I remember I was in a room somewhere. I am by myself, and I'm looking out a window. There's a big chair near me and I'm sitting on the floor."

Details: "The cold floor."

Vivid: "Nothing."

Feelings: "Nothing really. I was just there."

ER2: "I was on a beach and there were jelly fish in the water with me. I heard somebody say that they bite, and at that moment, one of them bit me."

Details: "Seeing the jelly fish."

Vivid: "Feeling the bite."

Feelings: "It hurt and I felt scared."

ER3: "I was outside sitting in a sandbox. That's about it."

Details: "Not that much."

Vivid: "I'm not sure. The sand, I guess."

Feelings: "Nothing. It was quiet."

I. Subjective Perspectives
   A. ER1: Lack of stimulation. Alone.
   B. ER2: Painful experience. Nobody to help out. No mention of initially enjoying the water.
   C. ER3: Lack of stimulation. Alone. Lack of feeling.
II. Interpersonal Perspectives
   A. Thematic Analysis
      1. "I am . . ."
         a. ER1: passive
         b. ER2: insecure
         c. ER3: passive
      2. "Others are . . ."
         a. ER1:—
         b. ER2: incidental
         c. ER3:—
      3. "Events are . . ."
         a. ER1: dull
         b. ER2: fearful and distressful
         c. ER3: dull
   B. Detail Analysis
      1. Senses
         a. ER1: visual
         b. ER2: tactile (bite)
         c. ER3: visual
      2. Color
         a. ER1:—
         b. ER2:—
         c. ER3:—
      3. Location

       a. ER1: inside
       b. ER2: outside
       c. ER3: outside
   4. Objects
       a. ER1: –
       b. ER2: jelly fish
       c. ER3: –
III. Objective Perspectives
   A. ER1: Relatively barren situation. Isolated. Passive (Schizophrenia disorder).
   B. ER2: Lack of interaction with others. Fearful experience (Schizophrenia disorder).
   C. ER3: Alone. Passive. Barren (Schizophrenia disorder).
IV. Lifestyle Syllogism
   "I am . . . passive."
   "Others are . . . largely nonexistent."
   "Events are . . . barren or fearful."
   "Therefore, life is . . . empty and threatening."

VICTORIA ER1: "I remember going up an escalator in an old train station with my mother. I must have been about four or five. The stairs were huge and kind of dark. Then my mother told me that you can get your foot caught in the moving stairs. I was really scared."
   Details: "Seeing the stairs moving and making a clattering noise."
   Vivid: "Looking down where my feet could get caught in the escalator."
   Feelings: "Scared."
ER2: "I was in bed sick. It was my birthday, and they had to call off my party. So I ate a small piece of cake alone."
   Details: "Seeing the frosting on the cake."
   Vivid: "Knowing that I wasn't going to have a birthday party."
   Feelings: "Let down, disappointment."
ER3: "I was walking on the street with my father. All of a sudden, he started yelling at a man who walked by. Then both of them started shouting at each other. It was very scary."
   Details: "A few cars slowly driving by."
   Vivid: "My father yelling."
   Feelings: "Shock and fear."
I. Subjective Perspectives
   A. ER1: Fearful situation. Warning to be vigilant.
   B. ER2: Missing out. Alone.
   C. ER3: Fearful situation. Chaotic. Threatening.

II. Interpersonal Perspectives
  A. Thematic Analysis
    1. "I am . . ."
      a. ER1: insecure
      b. ER2: passive
      c. ER3: insecure
    2. "Others are . . ."
      a. ER1: discouraging
      b. ER2:—
      c. ER3: hostile
    3. "Events are . . ."
      a. ER1: overwhelming and fearful
      b. ER2: debilitative
      c. ER3: fearful
  B. Detail Analysis
    1. Senses
      a. ER1: visual
      b. ER2: visual
      c. ER3: visual
    2. Color
      a. ER1:—
      b. ER2:—
      c. ER3:—
    3. Location
      a. ER1: inside (train station)
      b. ER2: home
      c. ER3: outside
    4. Objects
      a. ER1: escalator stairs
      b. ER2: birthday cake
      c. ER3:—
III. Objective Perspectives
  A. ER1: Fearful event. (Anxiety disorder).
  B. ER2: Passive. Isolated.
  C. ER3: Fearful event. Unpredictable environment. (Anxiety disorder).
IV. Lifestyle Syllogism
  "I am . . . insecure."
  "Others are . . . threatening."
  "Events are . . . fearful."
  "Therefore, life is . . . tormenting."

KATHERINE   ER1: "I was sitting on the sun porch of our house. The golden rays of the sun are coming in and hitting the different shades of brown in the wood on the walls."

Details: "The room was warm and pleasant."

Vivid: "Seeing the golden rays of the sun in the room."

Feelings: "Comfortable, almost serene."

ER2: "I was in the backyard of my house with my grandfather. I was sitting in a brown highchair, and I was looking down at the green grass."

Details: "The colors of the yard. The sky was a beautiful blue."

Vivid: "Seeing the green grass and knowing my grandfather was with me."

Feelings: "Very pleasant feelings."

ER3: "One night, after my mother read to me, she gave me one of her rings as a way of saying that she was still with me while I was sleeping. She tied it on a thin rope and then tied it to my bedpost. The stone in the ring was like a cat's eye. It was gray and black."

Details: "My dolls in my room."

Vivid: "Looking at the ring with the two shades that seemed to blend into one another."

Feelings: "Intrigued by the ring on the rope."

I. Subjective Perspectives
   A. ER1: Aesthetic quality. Self-directed.
   B. ER2: Active intellectually. Self-directed. Color emphasis.
   C. ER3: Positive interpersonal experience. Curious. Mention of color.
II. Interpersonal Perspectives
   A. Thematic Analysis
      1. "I am . . ."
         a. ER1: internally controlled
         b. ER2: internally controlled
         c. ER3: secure
      2. "Others are . . ."
         a. ER1: –
         b. ER2: nurturing
         c. ER3: nurturing and friendly
      3. "Events are . . ."
         a. ER1: invigorating
         b. ER2: harmonious
         c. ER3: invigorating
   B. Detail Analysis
      1. Senses
         a. ER1: visual

      b. ER2: visual

      c. ER3: visual

    2. Color

      a. ER1: golden rays

      b. ER2: multiple colors

      c. ER3: gray and black stone in ring

    3. Location

      a. ER1: home

      b. ER2: outside (backyard of home)

      c. ER3: home

    4. Objects

      a. ER1: golden rays of sun

      b. ER2: grass and sky

      c. ER3: ring

III. Objective Perspectives

    A. ER1: Aesthetic orientation. Internal locus of control. (Interpersonal functioning).

    B. ER2: Aesthetic orientation. Internal locus of control.

    C. ER3: Secure. (Security).

IV. Lifestyle Syllogism

    "I am . . . significant."

    "Others are . . . encouraging."

    "Events are . . . bountiful."

    "Therefore, life is . . . an opportunity."

TOM   ER1: "I had a gun and a holster, and I was playing cowboys. The belt on the holster kept slipping because it was too big. I stuffed newspapers around the top of my pants to hold the belt up."

    Details: "Seeing how big the belt was."

    Vivid: "Realizing the newspapers would work."

    Feelings: "Good. Satisfied."

ER2: "I remember putting a coin on the railroad track to see what would happen when the train ran over it."

    Details: "Seeing the length of the shiny track."

    Vivid: "Touching the flattened penny after the train ran over it."

    Feelings: "Fascinated."

ER3: "I was playing baseball in the backyard of my house. I hit the ball and it broke a window in the back of the house. My father came out and he didn't look happy. He said that I could help him fix it later."

    Details: "The bat and the ball."

    Vivid: "My father saying that it was OK."

Feelings: "Relief and kind of gratitude."

I. Subjective Perspectives
  A. ER1: Resourceful. Making the best of a situation. Self-directed. Problem-solving orientation.
  B. ER2: Self-directed. Inquisitive. Problem-solving orientation.
  C. ER3: Support from others. Physical orientation.
II. Interpersonal Perspectives
  A. Thematic Analysis
    1. "I am . . ."
      a. ER1: competent
      b. ER2: curious
      c. ER3: acceptable
    2. "Others are . . ."
      a. ER1:—
      b. ER2:—
      c. ER3: encouraging
    3. "Events are . . ."
      a. ER1: manageable and stimulating
      b. ER2: stimulating
      c. ER3: gratifying
  B. Detail Anlaysis
    1. Senses
      a. ER1: tactile (stuff newspapers)
      b. ER2: tactile (touching)
      c. ER3: visual
    2. Color
      a. ER1:—
      b. ER2:—
      c. ER3:—
    3. Location
      a. ER1: home?
      b. ER2: outside
      c. ER3: outside
    4. Objects
      a. ER1: holster belt
      b. ER2: coin
      c. ER3: baseball
III. Objective Perspectives
  A. ER1: Secure. Internal locus of control. Active.
  B. ER2: Secure. Internal locus of control. Active.
  C. ER3: Secure. Active.

IV. Lifestyle Syllogism
   "I am . . . resourceful."
   "Others are . . . encouraging."
   "Events are . . . stimulating."
   "Therefore, life is . . . what I make of it."

SUMMARY

Appropriate training for counselors and therapists in early recollections appraisal contributes to competency development in the use of the memories as a therapeutic tool. Although instructional opportunities are limited, it is possible to pursue learning activities through various forms of formal instruction and self-study. A contextural assessment process enables practitioners to conduct an evaluation from multiple perspectives in the construction of a model of a person or a client. This tripartite conceptualization consists of an individual's perception of self, others, and events, and concludes with convictions about life. While evaluating early recollections, it is necessary for practitioners to be aware of the potential for confirmatory and convictional bias. An extensive series of early memories exercises allows for practice in scoring and interpreting responses. Particular examples include early recollections reports, which suggest diagnostic disorders, in addition to memories reflecting more adaptive psychological functioning.

III EARLY RECOLLECTIONS

APPLICATIONS IN COUNSELING
AND PSYCHOTHERAPY

9

EARLY RECOLLECTIONS IN THE COUNSELING PROCESS

"In memory each of us is an artist: each of us creates."
—Patricia Hampl (1981, p. 5)

INTRODUCTION

UP TO THIS POINT IN THE TEXT, THE PRIMARY EMPHASIS HAS BEEN ON understanding assessment practices relating to early recollections. Expanding beyond this central focus, discussion now extends to the integration of first memories into the counseling process. Consideration of the theoretical issues of a model of a client and the nature of desirable therapeutic change provide conceptual formulations for setting and pursuing goals in counseling and psychotherapy. Clarification of a stage sequence in the therapy process enables practitioners to employ early recollections data in an overarching framework for utilizing particular counseling interventions. An examination of specific counseling concerns, such as predicting the relationship of a client with a therapist or counselor, contributes to a broader context for effectively applying early recollections in diverse ways.

THEORETICAL CONSIDERATIONS

Almost 50 years ago, Pepinsky and Pepinsky (1954) urged counselors to organize the data developed in the early stages of counseling by constructing a model of a person or a client. This conceptualization would function as a theoretical framework for understanding client behavior and serve as a foundational guide to explain complex phenomena in the counseling process. From a contemporary perspective, Watkins (2000) also felt that a client model informs and facilitates counseling practice by identifying process and outcome variables. Additionally, a conceptual structure constitutes a means for organizing client information from various and often disparate sources. In spite of these heedful recommendations, the model of a client largely remains a vague concept in its composition and therapeutic application. As one possible response, the formulation of a model of a person, which encompasses the self, others, and events, serves to provide a reasonably clear scheme of qualitative features. In addition, the resulting rubric is sufficiently broad to serve as an overarching framework for integrating data from multiple sources, and to function as a point of reference for promoting developmental change in counseling. The tripartite model also assists in evaluating the nature or type of desired client change in therapy, which is an essential consideration in treatment planning and goal setting. In this regard, first-order change tends to emphasize symptom relief and the stabilization of a client's experience within a generally sound perceptual system relating to the self and the world (Lyddon & Satterfield, 1994). In contrast, second-order change focuses on challenging maladaptive perceptions of the self and the world through structural alteration of a client's belief system.

CLIENT CONCEPTUALIZATION

As a working hypothesis, an evolving model of a client is always subject to modification in light of new information that becomes available in reference to an individual. Initially, the conceptualization provides a tenable framework in the early stages of therapy for guiding counseling practice. As knowledge about a person accrues, the rubric evolves, but continues as a stabilizing dynamic for assessing progress in counseling. Additional data beyond early recollections from multiple sources, such as behavioral observations and objective appraisals, serve to both refine and extend the client model. With the integration of further data from a broad spectrum of factors, the formulation assumes a comprehensive and multidimensional quality (Cates, 1999; Morran et al., 1994). In this capacity, the client model serves a synthesizing function that becomes amenable to change through selected interventions in the counseling experience (Karoly, 1993). As an example, an in-depth conceptualization of a client confirmed by multiple indicators suggests that a person maintains a fearful and threatening outlook on life. In response, the therapist emphasizes relationship-building transactions that evoke trust and support. Attunement to the fear that the individual is experiencing is crucial for conveying an empathic understanding. In time, the therapist begins to challenge the client's perceptions in an effort to develop more secure and functional life convictions. Finally, as the client increases cognitive control, the individual assumes a readiness to pursue more adaptive actions. Throughout the counseling process, a client conceptualization provides a schematic map, which reflects both present functioning and a goal direction for personal development (Watkins, 2000).

FIRST- AND SECOND-ORDER CHANGE

As a model of a client emerges through the early period of counseling, it subsequently becomes necessary to determine appropriate interventions and goal formulations that are consistent with the individual's therapeutic needs (Seligman, 1996). The distinction between first- and second-order change facilitates such treatment planning by signifying when alterations in a client's belief system seem appropriate. Essentially, first-order change does not alter the structure of an individual's outlook on life (Lyddon, 1990). Instead, counseling treatment addresses the resolution of problems and treatment issues that may enable a client to regain a sense of equilibrium within his or her relatively adaptive meaning structure (Lyddon & Satterfield, 1994). In this regard, therapy goals attend to immediate situations that are producing adverse reactions in a person's functioning. As an example, a client may be experiencing coping difficulties in an academic subject or with adjusting to a new school. In both situations, the work of counseling emphasizes active problem solving instead of pursuing change in the structural integrity of an individual's cognitive organization. Although first-order change directly stresses the pursuit of adaptive behavior rather than system change, evaluating a model of a client contributes to sound treatment planning. Consider the utility of understanding that a young adult client's outlook of life involves a physically active orientation and an aesthetic emphasis. In counseling, the individual reports that her current career position requires that she sit in an office cubicle for most of the day. It is apparent that the person's work environment is incompatible with her basic life convictions, and this situational problem assumes a prominent focus in counseling.

Second-order change emphasizes altering the fundamental structure of an individual's belief system (Lyddon, 1990). Therapeutic focus attends to maladaptive schemas in an attempt to transform personal meanings in a more constructive direction. At times, challenge to a client's basic and unshakable convictions about life can be intense and evoke threat by disrupting his or her psychological equilibrium (Lyddon & Satterfield, 1994). In the context of a supportive and stabilizing counseling relationship, a treatment goal entails the construction of new meanings that can translate into more adaptive behavior. This pursuit involves the evolving recognition of a person's untenable core assumptions or private logic relating to the self and the world. As an example, a client maintains the enduring conviction that he is deeply flawed in a world that is indifferent to his pain. Encouraging full expression of these maladaptive beliefs, the therapist then works with the client to create alternative cognitions that are credible and more purposeful. Only after progress is made toward the development of more advantageous meaning structures does attention turn more fully to pursuing instrumental actions as a goal in counseling.

THE COUNSELING PROCESS

In order to understand the broader therapeutic context in which client conceptualization and first- and second-order change function, it is necessary to clarify the functional role of early recollections across the counseling process. A generic three-stage model provides a comprehensive and coherent framework for fostering client development and for recognizing the clinical utility of early memories (Clark, 1998a; Patterson & Welfel, 2000). In the initial or relationship stage, humanistic and psychodynamic orientations are prominent in the fostering of a supportive climate and for understanding clients. In this period, early recollections illuminate ingrained convictions of individuals and contribute to the construction of an overarching scheme for organizing multiple sources of data. The middle or integration stage builds upon the theoretical foundation of the early phase of counseling while introducing cognitive-behavioral interventions. Early recollections maintain a central focus in the form of client conceptualizations, which serve as a guide for escalating strategic challenge during this phase. The final or accomplishment stage features action-oriented procedures to effect adaptive client change. The sustaining influence of early memories continues through the evolving model of a client, and this structure assists in silently informing therapeutic interventions (Singer & Salovey, 1993).

RELATIONSHIP STAGE

Establishing a therapeutic alliance in which a client gains a sense of trust and understanding is a process goal in the first stage of counseling (Doyle, 1998; Hackney & Cormier, 2001). The intrinsically interesting and engrossing function of reporting early recollections has the potential to engage individuals and can contribute to the development of a sound counseling relationship. Efforts to expand open communication and supportive conditions, however, must extend beyond the early memories procedure and find expression in various counseling interventions within the initial and subsequent treatment periods. This becomes particularly important when the therapist begins to challenge ingrained core convictions of clients in the pursuit of second-order change. Client resistance is predictable at this point in order to ward off perceived threat and protect the individual's psychic equilibrium. For many persons, this stage of the counseling experience is destabilizing, and clients frequently employ various defensive and evasive behavioral patterns in order to ward off conflict and protect self-esteem. The task of the counselor in this initial period is to develop sufficient rapport within the therapeutic relationship in order to reduce an individual's guardedness and feelings of threat. Generating a model of a person or a client through the assessment phase enables practitioners to detect long-held convictions that may contribute to resistance in therapy. Beyond the appraisal procedures, various other interventions are available that enhance the counseling relationship and promote client development. In particular, reflection, encouragement, and counselor self-disclosure engender a potential for involving clients in the counseling process.

REFLECTION.   As a counseling technique, reflection functions to empathically acknowledge the explicit and implicit feelings and meanings of individuals (Ivey & Ivey, 1999; Young, 2001). Clarifying client verbalizations and experiences often involves communication that may only be partially understood or articulated by a person. Through a pattern of interactions involving reflection, a practitioner also begins to develop a conceptualization of a client that assumes a structural clarity with the subsequent appraisal of early recollections. As an aspect of an attitudinal expression of empathy or a counseling intervention, reflection contributes to a mutually receptive and trust-inducing therapeutic relationship (Bohart & Greenburg 1997; Noonan, 1981). Consider the example of a client mandated to attend counseling due to alleged abuse of her children. In the initial counseling session, the counselor reflects the person's feelings of irritation and anger for being subjected to an investigation. Subsequently, another reflection evokes an expression of her implicit sense of shame for being perceived as a "bad mother" and a "loathsome person." In both exchanges the client experiences a keen sense of being understood, and a supportive tone is set for introducing early recollections as a component of the assessment process.

ASSESSMENT.   Beginning the assessment process by introducing projective techniques generally promotes a positive interaction between client and therapist through an intermediate activity that contrasts with the expectation of more structured verbal disclosure. Eliciting involvement of the person through relatively nonthreatening and stimulating tasks provides a rapport-building opportunity with individuals from diverse backgrounds (Chandler & Johnson, 1991; Clark, 1995c, 1995d, 1998a, 2001; Lee, 2001). In particular, human figure drawings, sentence completion tasks, and early recollections constitute a coherent and relatively brief appraisal, which yields essential data that readily conforms to a client conceptualization model.

Kissen (1986a) felt that human figure drawings provide an ideal "icebreaker," as most clients respond to the task in a receptive and self-revealing fashion. As is the case with early recollections, the clinical use of drawings entails a minimal amount of time to complete, requires few materials, and is a relatively unstructured procedure (Handler, 1996). From an object relations perspective, the drawings often reveal representations of the self in relationship to others (Kissen, 1986a), and these inferences are compatible with major tripartite facets of the model of the client. As an example, a person completes a human figure with arms raised high and reaching out into the environment. This depiction suggests that the individual has a desire for social acceptance and interaction with others (Cummings, 1986). In another instance, a client draws a diminutive human figure that is less than two inches in size. This minimal degree of graphic expression points to a reduced self-esteem and again relates to the construction of a client conceptualization (Cummings, 1986; Handler, 1996). Such observations assume the quality of a hypothesis and are subject to confirmation or disconfirmation as further data accrues about a person through the assessment and counseling process.

Sentence completion tasks are another selected projective technique that complements human figure drawings and early recollections in formulating a model of a client. Several published protocols with scoring systems are available, and sentence completion formats may also be constructed by practitioners that are pertinent to particular populations (Chandler & Johnson, 1991; Hart, 1986; Holaday, Smith, & Sherry, 2000). In a survey conducted with members of the Society for Personality Assessment, relatively few respondents reported using a formal scoring procedure. Instead, they interpreted sentence completions by relying on their own theoretical orientation and clinical skills (Holaday et al., 2000). Response or completion patterns to sentence stems (the beginning of the sentence) may be compared with typical responses gathered from a practitioner's clientele. This enables a therapist to detect sentence completions that stand out on a comparative basis and appear to be clinically significant. Table 9.1 provides a sentence completion form that I have used in my counseling practice with children and adolescents for many years. In constructing client models, identifiable sentence stems from the assessment protocol relate directly to aspects of the self, others, and events. Relating to the self, various stems are pertinent, such as "I feel . . . ," "I regret . . . ," and "I need. . . ." The construct of others is apparent in such sentence stems as, "Other people . . . ," "My father . . . ," and "Other kids. . . ." Representations of events are detectable among several sentence stems, such as "I am best when . . . ," "The happiest time . . . ," and "School. . . ." Sentence completion tasks are also instrumental in recognizing the operation of defense mechanisms, safeguarding tendencies, and other aspects of personality functioning (Clark, 1998a, 2000).

TABLE 9.1: SENTENCE COMPLETION

NAME: DATE:

1. I feel _____
2. I regret _____
3. Other people _____
4. I am best when _____
5. What bothers me is_____
6. The happiest time _____
7. I am afraid of _____
8. My father _____
9. I dislike to _____
10. I failed _____
11. At home _____
12. Boys _____
13. My mother _____
14. I suffer _____
15. The future _____
16. Other kids _____
17. My nerves are _____
18. Girls _____
19. My greatest worry is _____
20. School_____
21. I need _____
22. What pains me is _____
23. I hate _____
24. Whenever I have to study, I _____
25. I wish _____

As another projective device, early recollections provide continuity within a relatively brief assessment battery that most individuals complete in a total time of approximately 45 minutes. Like the previous two instruments, the unintrusive and participatory quality of the procedure frequently enhances the counseling relationship (Kissen, 1986a, 1986b). Upon completing the elicitation of early recollections, consideration of additional assessment approaches will depend on the needs of the client and the capabilities and resources of practitioners. Other projective techniques, such as the Rorschach and the Thematic Apperception Test (TAT) may be appropriate but require a more extensive and time-consuming evaluation. In regard to the Rorschach, inkblot determinants, such as color, texture, and popular responses suggest inferential material relating to interpersonal functioning. The thematic content and affective expression of an individual's responses on the TAT largely reflect human needs of a social type. In addition to projective techniques, numerous objective tests in the form of self-report inventories provide significant resources with the potential for increasing the counselor's understanding of persons and broadening the conceptualization of a client.

Using the same conceptual structure present in the contextural scoring system for early recollections, objective, interpersonal, and subjective perspectives constitute a means of systematically evaluating multiple sources of client data. In addition to standardized self-report measures, other information may be available to a counselor or therapist that is consistent with an objective perspective as a way of knowing (Rogers, 1964). Particular objective sources might include a practitioner's observation of a client in various locations, such as the classroom, playground, or work site. An individual's functioning relating to mental disorders may also be evaluated through descriptions of diagnostic categories accessible in the *DSM–IV–TR* (2000). In school settings, grades and standardized test results are usually retrievable from cumulative records. From an interpersonal perspective, interactions with a client and observations from third parties, such as a parent, teacher, or employer, are possible sources of information. Further, referral data in the form of written reports, both anecdotal and formal, is often available through various professional resources. In terms of a subjective perspective, a practitioner's intuitive reactions to a client's behavior or information about the person represent a personal way of knowing. It is essential that all such collected data be organized in a fashion that is both efficient and contributes to the conceptualization of a client. In practical terms, this means entering client information in relevant areas relating to self, others, and events. Table 10.2 presents compiled data from a case example in the format of a Contextural Assessment Worksheet.

ENCOURAGEMENT.   In the initial stage, and throughout the counseling experience, a practitioner is able to provide encouragement by expressing faith in a client's potential through various interventions. Supporting the efforts of an individual to assume personal control and engender a sense of competency and self-efficacy is central to the encouragement process (Bandura, 1991; Dinkmeyer & Sperry, 2000). Typically, a discouraged person feels overwhelmed by conditions and has lost hope in the possibility of doing or functioning better (Dreikurs, 1967). Clients at this point tend to employ defensive or evasive tactics in order to protect their tenuous self-esteem and reduce exposure to further failure or painful conflict (Clark, 1998a, 1999a, 2000). As an example, a client engages a safeguarding tendency by expending an extraordinary amount of energy on matters of secondary importance, instead of directly confronting more urgent issues and problems. As long as the person is sufficiently occupied with diverting tasks, he or she is able to avoid the risk of encountering personal insufficiencies in dealing with more consequential concerns.

The task of the counselor or therapist is to transmit to the client a belief in the possibility of pursuing a more challenging way of being. For some clients, this means restoring confidence in their abilities through situational change that reflects a first-order type. These individuals may have lost faith in their capabilities for a period of time but with encouragement are often able to regain a sense of psychological equilibrium and resume a previous level of more purposeful functioning. In other instances, clients maintain ingrained schemas by dogmatically clinging to maladaptive convictions (Mosak & Maniacci, 1998). In this context, therapeutic progress primarily involves executing second-order change through efforts to develop a more structurally sound belief system.

COUNSELOR SELF-DISCLOSURE.   Clients may be encouraged and the counseling relationship enhanced by a practitioner's judicious disclosure of personal experiences or perspectives. Self-disclosures have the potential to improve communication as a person begins to perceive authority figures in mental health roles as less threatening and remote (Watkins, 1990). At the same time, a therapist's disclosure may appear to be intrusive or insensitive and produce an opposite effect by raising doubts about the professional's competency. Self-disclosure also involves a practitioner's personal reactions to a client's behavior in counseling, which is referred to as self-involving statements (Watkins, 1990). A basic principle in the sound application of either type of verbal expression is that disclosures should only be made in the service of engendering a client's development and for enhancing the counseling relationship. Timing considerations include expressing disclosures when a client has a readiness to cognitively and emotionally focus on remarks, and there is evidence of a developing level of trust between the client and counselor (Cormier & Cormier, 1998; Egan, 2002). Even with these general guidelines available, however, a counselor may be uncertain if a disclosure is suitable for a particular client. In this regard, by drawing on inferential data that is available from the emerging model of a client, it becomes possible to estimate more accurately whether a particular comment may be therapeutically appropriate.

In contrasting examples, illustrating the possible effectiveness of self-disclosure, a counselor recalls a particular academic failure from her high school experience in discussions with two different students who are having difficulties in school. In the first instance, Joan reacts with a sense of relief and hope in response to the counselor's personal disclosure. Joan's client model suggests that she perceives others as generally supportive and that she is somewhat capable. Events are challenging, but manageable. Joan feels that if the counselor was able to surmount a setback in an academic subject, perhaps she could do the same. In another case, Sara finds the counselor's comments distressing and largely irrelevant. Sara's client model indicates that she perceives herself as insecure and inferior. Her perception of others is that they are more capable in comparison to herself, and events are frequently disappointing. Sara's negative reaction to the counselor's remarks possibly occurs because the disclosure experience is distant from her discouraged outlook on life. Sara perceives that the counselor has capabilities that she lacks, and a similar successful outcome is unrealistic and simply beyond her grasp. In this respect for Sara, the disclosure of the counselor is seen as dismissive and has a negative effect. Finally, clients such as Sara frequently engage in defensive and evasive maneuvers to protect fragile levels of self-esteem. A practitioner's awareness of this pattern of responses may also enable the more effective use of self-disclosure and other therapeutic interventions.

INTEGRATION STAGE

With a supportive relationship developed through empathic understanding and interactions in the initial period of counseling, therapeutic emphasis begins to shift to a more challenging posture in the middle or integration stage (Patterson & Welfel, 2000). Throughout the middle stage of counseling, the model of a client continues to serve as a conceptual guide to assist in evaluating purposeful change. Initially, treatment focuses on self-defeating conflicts inherent in the functioning of clients that relate to their personal belief systems. Exploring life convictions can be destabilizing for persons, and a practitioner's support is essential in contributing to the construction of more purposeful cognitive structures. Among the counseling interventions that are appropriate in this stage, confrontation, cognitive restructuring, reframing, and interpretation allow for an in-depth exploration of client behavior.

CONFRONTATION.   During the initial stage of counseling, a counselor or therapist attempts to gain an understanding of a client's core convictions and behavioral patterns. For some individuals, this conceptualization appears to be reasonably integrated and adaptive. In other instances, a person's outlook on life is clearly dysfunctional and conflict-laden. In the latter case, a client's disturbed functioning is recognizable through the expression or articulation of maladaptive automatic thoughts that have become known as basic mistakes (Adler, 1931/1958; Dreikurs, 1961; Manaster & Corsini, 1982), irrational ideas (Ellis, 2000), and cognitive distortions (Beck, 1995). As an example, a client named Bob demonstrating marked anxiety states, "I can't seem to focus on anything," "I have so many things I constantly worry about," and "Everything seems to upset me and make me nervous." This broad and unqualified self talk, constitutes confrontation material because it typically contradicts or is inconsistent with other aspects of an individual's behavior or environmental conditions.

To continue with the example in regard to Bob's last statement, a practitioner confronts him about the absolute quality of his perspectives. The therapist states: "You are feeling overwhelmed by it all, but you have also talked about occasions when you have found some escape from your worries." In this instance, the therapist, in a supportive and nonjudgmental tone, challenges Bob by descriptively contrasting his current statement with previous ones. This same approach is used to clarify discrepancies between clients' statements and nonverbal expressions, actions, objective conditions, and omissions of essential material (Clark, 1998a; Ivey & Ivey, 1999). In the case of a person who maintains reasonably adaptive schemas at the core level, a confrontation is usually not particularly threatening. In contrast, clients maintaining dysfunctional belief systems generally experience confrontations as threatening and destabilizing. Consequently, upon challenge it is more likely that these individuals will engage in defensive or evasive tactics. With this understanding in mind, the conceptualization of a client model contributes to the more effective use of confrontation.

COGNITIVE RESTRUCTURING.   Although challenging a client's maladaptive automatic thoughts serves to clarify his or her conflicted functioning, the interactions may not structurally address more fundamental assumptions at the core level (Safran et al., 1986). Another counseling intervention, cognitive restructuring, focuses on transforming an individual's dysfunctional beliefs in a more purposeful direction (Emerson, West, & Gintner, 1991; Meichenbaum, 1977). Essentially, cognitive restructuring involves identifying and examining negative and self-defeating convictions, actively constructing alternative and counterstatements or "counters," and utilizing or practicing the counters both in and outside of counseling and psychotherapy (Beck, 1995; Cormier & Cormier, 1998; Young, 2001). As an approach exclusively focusing on second-order change, more optimum counters are those that are pertinent to, and stimulate change within a client's belief system (Mosak & Maniacci, 1998). Utilizing a model of a client can expedite this effort by considering an individual's long-held perceptions of self, others, and events. At this stage in the counseling process, each schema should be reasonably clear and serve to reflect salient aspects of the cognitive structure of a client.

In order to arrive at an appropriate point for generating counters, it is necessary to evaluate a client's fundamental assumptions, and this transaction can evoke threat. Ingrained convictions developed in childhood are profoundly familiar to an individual, and the prospect of change to new patterns of thinking involves unknown and potentially destabilizing outcomes.

An example of the application of cognitive restructuring in counseling should assist in clarifying the operation of the intervention. To continue with the client, Bob, introduced in the previous confrontation section, it is assumed from the model of a client that he maintains anxiety-laden schemas at the core level. In a collaborative interaction, Bob and the therapist begin to evaluate the logic and credibility of Bob's self-talk or basic mistakes that relate to his life convictions. With an awareness of all of the inferential data available from Bob's client conceptualization, the therapist is able to interact with him at a deep and comprehensive level of understanding. As it becomes apparent, Bob frequently repeats negative statements to himself both in and outside of therapy about his perceived inadequacies. It is at this point, after identifying a dysfunctional automatic thought, that Bob and the therapist agree on a counterstatement in regard to his self-proclaimed, "I have so many things that I constantly worry about." Through discussion, Bob identifies a new counter relating to his perception of self and events: "Some things I choose to worry about, but not everything." This affirmation, with sustained practice, has significant implications in regard to Bob's core meanings. As therapy continues, other basic mistakes evoke further discussion and a therapeutic link to schema representations.

REFRAMING.   As another cognitive intervention, reframing provides a purposeful alternative to a client's constricted frame of reference (Clark, 1998a, 1998b). As a semantic aspect of an interpretation, the essence of meanings of particular assumptions or beliefs are changed in a more constructive direction (Cormier & Cormier, 1998; Levy, 1963). This typically occurs by altering the meaning of experiences or conditions through a relabeling or reclassification procedure. Reframing is most effective when an individual expresses feelings of distress in regard to immediate issues. Consider the previous example of Bob, who experiences anxiety relating to numerous events in his life. In this regard, Bob states, "I still worry about too many things, and it all really gets to me." In response, the counselor relates, "You put yourself down when you say that, and perhaps you are being a little unfair to yourself. A way to look at this in a different light is that you care about a lot of things in your life. If you didn't care, you probably wouldn't give it all so much attention." This reframe contributes to linguistically transforming the meaning of worrying and provides a perspective that is new to Bob, and he therefore begins to consider the implications of the observation. The counselor understands that Bob perceives events as overwhelming and chooses to provide a reformulation in the direction of choice and control. Expressing a reframe as another option to consider, in an inviting and persuasive tone, increases the likelihood of its examination by a client. In Bob's case, the reframe addresses a conceptualization at his core level of functioning, but the intervention can also be useful at peripheral operative levels. For instance, Bob mentions that he continues to live with his parents, even though he is 25 years old. The counselor empathizes with Bob's feelings of discomfort but then points out that many young adults find this a practical arrangement until they are able to become financially established. In this exchange, the counselor's knowledge of Bob's model of a person assists in formulating a reframe that he will likely find feasible and encouraging.

INTERPRETATION. For some clients, it is necessary to explore new frames of reference in terms of motivational factors that explain rather than merely describe their dysfunctional behavior. In the form of a proposition, interpretation transforms an individual's perspectives by relating experiences not previously connected (Clark, 1995a; Ivey & Ivey, 1999; Levy, 1963). In this regard, interpretation involves exploring behavioral patterns and inferring causal links to current functioning. Various theories of counseling and psychotherapy generate inferences through interpretations for the purpose of attempting to resolve enduring conflicts and to promote more integrated client behavior. At a thematical content level, interpretations focus on broad and ingrained personal convictions that influence a client's entire personality functioning. From a therapy orientation perspective, Adler's lifestyle and scripts from transactional analysis represent this conceptualization (Gilliland & James, 1998). The constructional level of interpretation focus emphasizes addressing more intermediate functioning, such as patterns of automatic thoughts, defense mechanisms, safeguarding tendencies, and dreams. It is also possible to conceptualize a situational level of interpretation, which relates to more immediate and contextual conflicts, such as deciding whether to accept a new job that involves a relocation (Clark, 1993, 1995a).

In the continuing example relating to Bob in this chapter, he listens as the counselor expresses a generalization about his behavior, "You find it very difficult to let go of your excessive worry." After a brief discussion and clarification of this point, the counselor concludes the interpretation with a construction, "Could it be that by worrying about so many things, you have found a way in your life of reducing feelings of inadequacy that you experi-

ence? By keeping yourself busy with all of your worries, you manage to dis-
tract yourself from the painful sense of not feeling that good about yourself
that we have talked about?" Bob seems somewhat intrigued by the counselor's statement, and together they discuss at length the implications of this
safeguarding tendency. The essential point is that Bob maintains ingrained
beliefs about his sense of inadequacy and vulnerability in a perceived hostile
environment. By worrying excessively, he is constantly alert to threat, and
the sheer volume of preoccupations possibly keeps his conflicted feelings at a
psychological distance. As Bob attempts to therapeutically reduce his pattern
of worry, this tends to intensify his sense of vulnerability, which, in turn, reinforces his resumption of anxiety-laden behavior. The counselor's rendering
of the interpretation is made with careful forethought and with the benefit of
Bob's model of a person conceptualization. To the extent that an interpretation provides a new perspective and a coherent meaning, the intervention
enables clients to assume more control over their behavior.

ACCOMPLISHMENT STAGE

With progress made toward the constructive integration of client behavior
through the middle period of treatment, therapeutic emphasis shifts to the
development of more adaptive functioning in the final stage of counseling
(Egan, 2002). As individuals construct more accurate and coherent schemas
and perspectives through the counseling process, their readiness increases for
translating change toward more purposeful instrumental actions. The accomplishment stage focuses on encouraging clients to function in more
adaptive ways, and a variety of strategic techniques and interventions are
available to promote action-oriented change (Beck, 1995; Hackney &
Cormier, 2001; Mosak & Maniacci, 1998). The evolving model of a client
continues to guide therapeutic practice, as individuals follow through with
constructive efforts to break constricted and self-defeating patterns. In an example of one intervention, Beck (1995) encourages her patients to complete
"coping cards," which contain written action or coping strategies. Individuals carry the 3 × 5-inch notecards in their pocket or purse or place them in
prominent places in the home or work site. Several times a day, the patient
reads the cards, which serve as prompters or motivational reminders. For example, instructions designed to activate an emotionally constricted person
might include a prompt to express his or her feelings rather than bottle them
up inside. A possible coping strategy relates to the continuing example of
Bob in this chapter. With the counselor's assistance, he decides to write,
"Some things I am going to choose to worry about, and I will talk about
these matters rather than keep them inside," on a card and to read it periodi-
cally during the day and as needed.

APPLICATION ISSUES AND VARIATIONS IN THE USE OF EARLY RECOLLECTIONS

Numerous concerns in the integration of early recollections in counseling and psychotherapy have been a focus of attention in the research literature. In the context of an interpersonal experience, researchers have addressed questions related to predicting and evaluating the relationship between the client and practitioner, and appraising possible changes in client early memories as a result of participating in counseling. The relationship of dreams to early recollections has been a topic of interest in various investigations. Variations in the therapeutic use of early recollections have been a research emphasis relating to such experiential methods as visualization, rescripting, and hypnosis. Applications of early recollections derived from diverse types of group work, such as therapy groups for children and parent education groups, have been another investigative direction.

ISSUES IN THE APPLICATIONS OF EARLY RECOLLECTIONS

The role of early recollections as a predictor of the relationship between a client and the therapist has direct therapeutic implications for the counseling process. Particular considerations include potential for resistance, gender preference, and capacity for transference. Related to these concerns is the interactional component manifested during the collection of early memories that proceeds from the interpersonal style of a practitioner. This issue specifically addresses the possible influence of a counselor on the expression and content of early recollections. In another research direction, dreams have been compared with early memories as an ideographic construction and a source of client data; however, it is important to note that there are important distinctions between the two modes of expression.

PREDICTING THE RELATIONSHIP BETWEEN A CLIENT AND A THERAPIST. Generating hypotheses about the quality of the alliance between a client and a counselor or therapist contributes to sound treatment planning in the counseling experience. Early recollections provide one means for practitioners to explore critical issues that may hinder or advance the therapeutic relationship. Consider, for example, the counseling implications of the following early memory of a client: "I was in the first grade, and the teacher had us draw a picture. I wasn't sure about what to do, so I waited for her to come by my desk. I was afraid to start it myself." The individual's dependent attitude is obvious in this memory, and the tendency may quickly become apparent in therapy and influence transactions in the counseling process. In another instance, a client relates a contrasting memory: "I was playing kick-

ball on the playground, and the teacher said it was time to come in from recess. I didn't want to go in, so I kicked the ball in the woods. She yelled at me
to go and get it. I hid behind some bushes, and the teacher had to come in
and get me. She was really mad, but I fooled her and got to stay out longer."
Thematically, resistance to authority and manipulative tendencies are evident in the individual's recollection. Recognizing the potential operation of
such interpersonal postures can be crucial as a therapist establishes treatment
plans for counseling.

In both examples, each respective client mentions an experience with a female, but in a clearly different light. In the latter instance, a reasonable hypothesis is that the individual may be uncooperative and manipulative with a
female, in contrast to his or her more compliant behavior with a male therapist. This tentative assumption enables a woman practitioner to be alert to
the possibility of the client's engagement of such resistant behaviors. It may
also be, however, that the individual's perspective is not gender-specific and
more broadly relates to people in general. Evaluating further information, including other early memories and additional assessment material, should
provide further insight into a client's schema of other persons. More extensive case examples are also available (Mosak, 1965) that, on the basis of client
early recollections and other appraisal data, serve to predict individual relationships with counselors and therapists. In another framework, specifically
from a psychoanalytic perspective, it may be possible to evaluate a client's potential for transference processing from early memories. It is evident from
the cited examples that both clients maintain conflicted perceptions of authority figures, which may find historical representation in their developmental experiences and immediate interactions in therapeutic treatment.

INTERPERSONAL INFLUENCE ON EARLY RECOLLECTION CONTENT.   In
the process of eliciting early childhood memories, a contemporary research
question emerges relating to a practitioner's social influence on the manifest
content of the memories (Fowler et al., 1996b). As with any assessment device, it is a psychometrically sound principle to attempt to minimize error
variance as it relates to the verbal productions of clients due to the immediate presence of an examiner. Bach (1952) theorized that the formulation
and communication of childhood memories expressed in the therapy process
are influenced by the interpersonal conditions that exist between a client and
therapist. The content of memories, for example, may differ depending on
such relationship variables as degree of trust, quality of rapport, and orientation of the therapist. In an empirical study, Quay (1959) reported that it was
possible to influence the expression of certain types of early memories
through the manipulation of verbal reinforcing stimuli. College student sub-

jects gave a higher proportion of "family" memories after the examiner's use of "uh-huh" as a minimal reinforcer. Through a subtle interpersonal influence, Quay felt that personal and emotionally charged early memories can be manipulated. In contrast to this assertion, Hedvig (1965), in examining the stability of early recollections with children, found no effect on the content of memories when their collection was preceded by success or failure experiences or interactions with friendly, neutral, or hostile examiners.

In another study assessing the interactional component relating to the administration of early memories, Bauserman and Rule (1988) trained volunteer graduate students from a counseling class to assume a particular examiner style. One group of students was instructed to interact in a warm/receptive manner and another group in a cold/administrative style. In collecting early recollections from other graduate students, the "warm" examiners received more solitary and less vivid memories, and the "cold" examiners received more interpersonal and vivid memories. Bauserman and Rule cautioned with respect to their findings that all of the examiners were members of a counseling class, and, by nature, were not congruently cold or business like. From a broader perspective, the interpersonal influence of a practitioner actually begins on meeting a client and continues through various transactions throughout the counseling process. As one specific part of extensive interactions, the elicitation of early recollections must be understood in a particular context. In this regard, cultural forces become a significant contextual aspect to keep in mind when evaluating the interpersonal relationship between the client and counselor. Many clients with orientations representing non-Anglo-American cultures have been found to be more receptive to service delivery with an emphasis on rapport and relationship building (Dana, 1995, 2000). In response to this assumed orientation, the interactive elicitation of early recollections provides an opportunity for practitioners to relate to clients in a more personal and informal style.

POSSIBLE CHANGES IN EARLY RECOLLECTIONS IN COUNSELING.   Another interesting issue that arises in counseling is the question of possible changes in early memories that occur as a consequence of participation in the therapeutic process. Adler (1931/1958) believed that an individual will remember different incidents or will attribute new meanings to memories recalled as his or her lifestyle changes during therapy. In this regard, reported early recollections may change or in some cases will be completely forgotten in accordance with a person's new outlook on life or revisions to his or her previous cognitive organization (Bruhn, 1992a; Dreikurs, 1958, 1967). The question of early memory modification in counseling and psychotherapy is significant because it suggests changes in personality structure in terms of fundamental attitudes and motivations (Saul et al., 1956). If early memories are modifiable through the counseling experience, the changes could possibly present a source for measuring therapeutic progress or detecting subtle processes not previously apparent (Statton & Wilborn, 1991).

In order to investigate possible early recollections changes in counseling, Eckstein (1976) evaluated the early memories of several college females who completed nine months of professional treatment. Employing the Early Recollections Rating Scale (ERRS) (Altman, 1973; Quinn, 1973), Eckstein reported that early memories appear to change significantly with personal growth as a consequence of long-term counseling or therapy. In a related study, Savill and Eckstein (1987) evaluated the early recollections of a group of inpatients in psychiatric treatment and a control group of college students. The authors reported significant changes in the early recollections of the psychiatric group after therapeutic treatment. In particular, this group demonstrated higher levels of social interest as measured on the ERRS. From an object relations perspective, Ryan and Bell (1984) investigated changes in early memories with 63 hospitalized psychiatric patients. Early memories were collected over the course of extensive psychoanalytically oriented psychotherapy and at six-month follow-up. The authors report that a significant difference was found in the direction of positive change in terms of the perceptions of self and others on their early memories for 21 patients from intake to follow-up.

Although the determination of the question of early recollections change over the course of therapy is yet to be established, this variable should not be the essential measure of therapeutic progress. Individuals may also gain an awareness of their maladaptive belief system and with this insight make positive changes in instrumental actions. Therefore, a deliberate choice to act in more constructive ways does not necessarily involve structural cognitive change. As an example, a client may initially maintain ingrained convictions that are consistent with a mood disorder, but with an increasing awareness of his or her dysphoric outlook on life, decide to act in adaptive ways that are more purposeful and life enhancing. In this respect, the client initiates a new behavioral direction in spite of depressive attitudinal functioning at the core level. It is also possible that maintaining purposeful actions over a sustained period of time may have a positive effect on modifying an individual's fundamental belief system.

EARLY RECOLLECTIONS AND DREAMS.   In particular respects, first memories and dreams share common qualities with direct implications for counseling and psychotherapy (Adler, 1936; Kramer, Ornstein, Whitman, & Baldridge, 1967; Krohn & Mayman, 1974). As counseling interventions, each procedure may contribute to the fostering of a therapeutic relationship and to understanding clients by yielding important clinical data (Marcus, 1965; Mosak, 1992; Robbins & Tanck, 1978). Many individuals find early memories and dreams intrinsically interesting, and both approaches may be readily integrated into the counseling process. Dreams and early recollections are also unique constructions of persons that involve a minimal degree of structuring or direction on the part of a counselor or therapist. Although each technique engenders insight into a client's core convictions, this appears to be more the case for recurrent or repeated dreams, in contrast to single instance dreams. Many dreams for individuals occur only one time and may be relatively transient reactions to the problems and preoccupations of daily life (Munroe, 1955). Theories of dream analysis involve diverse conceptualizations, including, among others, Freudian, Adlerian, and Jungian approaches (Clark, 1994b, 1999b). Understandably, Adler emphasized the integration of dreams with early recollections, and it is the Individual Psychology model that provides a comprehensive means for clarifying the correspondence between both processes in the counseling process.

In his numerous references to dreams, Adler (1929/1969, 1931/1958, 1933/1964, 1936) emphasized their meaning in addition to early recollections as a product and expression of an individual's style of life. In this regard, dreams potentially serve a specific problem-solving function of arousing feelings that are coherent with a particular lifestyle (Gold, 1979). Essentially, the purpose or task of a dream, from a perspective of reason and judgment, is not to be understood but to stimulate certain emotions that provide a possible solution to presenting challenges. Upon awakening after dreaming, residual feelings typically linger as motivational energizers to warn, caution, inspire, or fortify the resolve of a person (Adler, 1936; Kaplan, 1985). A client, for example, who perceives others in a distrustful way, encounters a new acquaintance in his waking life who makes a proposal for a collaborative business arrangement. That evening, the client dreams that he gets pushed in front of a speeding train by a stranger dressed in dark clothes. When the client awakens, he experiences fearful and distrustful feelings that prompt him later in the day to reject the business proposition with the prospective partner. The emotional preparation of the dream functions to propel the individual toward a solution of his immediate confronting problem. In this particular instance, the client, who holds a fearful outlook on life, reinforces his core beliefs and maintains psychological equilibrium through the emotions stirred up in his dream. Adler (1936) referred to this quality of dreams to arouse purposeful feelings and emotions as a "residue of mood."

Although dreams may reflect major motivational forces of the personality, they also appear to be influenced by situational struggles and anticipations of daily life (Saul et al., 1956). In contrast to dreams, early memories seem relatively unaffected by the immediate problems and difficulties that persons encounter (Last, 1997). Some theorists (Adler, 1936; Gold, 1979) believe that all dreams reflect an individual's lifestyle and core convictions in the same manner as early recollections, whereas others (Mosak & Maniacci, 1999) assert that dreams involve more immediate, short-range problem solving. Adler (1929/1969, 1936) recognized an especial significance of repeated or recurring dreams in expressing or revealing the lifestyle with greater clarity, in addition to repeating answers to confronting problems. Adler (1936) also believed that the lifestyle is clearly portrayed in impressive dreams that have remained in a person's consciousness for many years. Finally, Dreikurs (1967) felt that dreams from the early childhood period directly reflect the same meaning as early recollections.

VARIATIONS IN THE APPLICATIONS OF EARLY RECOLLECTIONS

Particular experiential methods involving early recollections have emerged that, over an extended period of time, may induce purposeful behavior change. Imagery with rescripting and historical role-plays are the primary approaches that emphasize the therapeutic reexperience of early memories (Arntz & Weertman, 1999). As another experiential approach, hypnosis is controversial due to its application as an age regression technique in recovering early memories in the therapy process. Researchers have also been active in applying early recollections to group work with diverse populations. Early memories have been used in such areas as the selection of group members to enhance the dynamic understanding of individuals in group and to further the development of individual members and the group as a whole.

REEXPERIENCING EARLY RECOLLECTIONS.   A pursuit of various researchers has been to use imagery to rescript pathogenic schemas relating to early recollections (Arntz & Weertman, 1999). A client recalls the experience of an early recollection, and through his or her imagination revises the memory in constructive ways such as asking for help or acting more independently. The approach may also involve intervening in the depiction of the original early recollection interaction through the use of role-play with a counselor or therapist. For example, in an original early recollection, a client feels too ashamed or embarrassed to ask for help. In the revised memory, he or she visualizes making an appropriate request for assistance and then enacts this positive change in a role-play with the therapist. By reappraising the original experiences that contributed to the development of particular schemas, it may be possible to construct new representations or schemas relating to the self and the world (Maniacci, Shulman, Griffith, Powers,

Sutherland, Dushman, & Schneider, 1998). In a specific interpersonal approach, the "Willhite Technique" (Willhite, 1979) involves asking clients to restructure early recollections in such a way as to move from their individual self-concept toward their self-ideal. Through a sequence of steps, clients rework each expressed sentence of their early memories to create a self-ideal narrative. Individuals identify constructive attitudes that they aspire to adopt, and through the counseling process they are encouraged to act on these aspirations in life enhancing ways.

Referring to their experiential method as the "Connexions Focusing Technique," Lew and Bettner (1993) encourage clients to assume an "adult" perspective with respect to their early recollections. By reexperiencing early memories from a more mature and secure developmental stage, individuals are able to recognize options in their original situations that they could not perceive from the vantage point of a young child with limited experiences or knowledge. This structured model also enables clients to understand how they may have developed particular patterns of behavior from early childhood. Using a similar approach, Lingg and Kottman (1991) suggest that a counselor choose an early recollection that most typifies a basic mistake or maladaptive automatic thought under consideration in counseling. A client then visualizes himself or herself as an adult by "entering" the scene of the memory and providing consolation or support to the child image. Other facets of the early recollection are also open to constructive change in order for the individual to feel comfortable and safe. The client then reexamines the basic mistake from the new perspective and attempts to establish more purposeful behavioral patterns to gain a sense of significance and belonging. In another experiential method, Kopp (1998) employs early recollections as metaphors relating to a client's current issue or problem. As an example, an individual's early memory may be metaphorically expressed, "I keep shooting myself in the foot." As a part of a structured interview protocol, the client and the counselor use the metaphor as a vehicle for exploring connections between the client's early recollections and his or her current situation.

EARLY RECOLLECTIONS AND HYPNOSIS.   Hypnosis presents a method for bringing early memories or aspects of memories to consciousness when they may otherwise be unavailable (LeCron, 1963). Warren (1990) analyzed the early recollections of over 300 individuals through the use of hypnosis. He found that the early memories are longer, clearer, and less difficult to evaluate than recollections collected in traditional ways. In a related study with college students, Coram and Hafner (1988) reported that the content of early recollections is qualitatively different after hypnotic induction. Individuals in a hypnotic condition generated increased topics in such content areas as mother, misdeeds, and mastery. The authors observed, however, that early recollections retrieved through hypnosis may be less reliable than nonhypnotic memories. Other researchers have directly cautioned about the malleability of memory, and the possible creation of false memories through inadvertent practitioner suggestions in the hypnotic interview (Fowler, 1994; Lynn, Lock, Myers, & Payne, 1997; Malinoski & Lynn, 1999). In an even more controversial direction, some researchers believe that individuals are able to temporarily regress to an earlier life period of psychological or physiological functioning through hypnosis, while others maintain that the procedure only simulates age regression (DuBreuil, Garry, & Loftus, 1998; Nash, 1987). Therapists who support the use of age regression techniques in hypnosis recognize the therapeutic value of uncovering early trauma and aspects of psychopathology that may not be retrievable through other interventions (Howell, 1965; LeCron, 1963). Others (Berlinger & Briere, 1999; Enns, 2001) reject the utilization of age regression approaches in hypnosis as a risky technique that may possibly generate false memories and lead to client destabilization and decompensation. Adler (1929/1969) maintained a critical view of hypnotism and believed that the procedure should rarely be used. He felt that any therapeutic gains made through hypnotic trances were only temporary, and the approach does not change an individual's fundamental beliefs or style of life.

EARLY RECOLLECTIONS AND GROUP WORK.   Early recollections as a projective technique has been a frequent intervention focus in diverse types of therapeutic groups. The following groups represented in the literature have included an early recollections emphasis: substance abuse, childhood, late adulthood, parent education, family counseling, couple therapy, psychodrama, and art therapy. Introducing early recollections prior to initiating a group or after a group has formed has several distinct advantages. In addition to using other assessment measures in pre-group interviews, early memories may be helpful in determining appropriate member composition of groups and overcoming resistance in the early stages of group counseling or therapy (Kadis, 1958; Rule & McKenzie, 1977). Organizing a therapy group, for example, consisting largely of individuals with dependency issues would likely present a far different dynamic than a group primarily composed of members with a hostile and distrustful outlook on life. Early recollections may also be employed in early group sessions as an experiential exercise in order to increase understanding and cohesiveness among the group members. Generally, the early recollections procedure is a relatively nonthreatening task that can be shared orally or spontaneously within subgroups or with the whole group (Eckstein, 1980). Typically in the operation of small groups, at least one member volunteers to share an early recollection, and the subsequent discussion relating to the meaning of memory evokes empathy from other group participants and improves communication within the group (Kadis, 1958). As is the case with individual treatment, the emerging model of a person serves as a guide for member development through the various stages of group.

In a substance abuse treatment group with adolescents, Mansager, Barnes, Boyce, Brewster, Lertora, Marais, Santos, and Thompson (1995) introduced the topic of early recollections and initially encouraged group members to practice evaluating generic memories. After a period of time, the group participants assessed each other's early recollections and provided reciprocal feedback on the accuracy of various "guesses" or interpretations. The authors found that early recollections were a powerful tool for advancing therapeutic understanding among group members and for promoting each participant's own self-understanding. In a more extensive investigation, Demuth and Bruhn (1997) integrated an early memories procedure in a group therapy program with 30 individuals in treatment for substance abuse in a maximum security prison. As the individuals shared their early memories in small groups, they found commonalities that enabled them to feel less isolated or unique in life perspectives that often reflected a sense of torment or wretchedness. This principle of universality was particularly valued by the group members and contributed to a sense of cohesiveness in the groups. Although the group participants did not necessarily reach a level of core personality change, it was possible for them to instrumentally act differently by creating behavioral options based on their insight into their belief systems.

Early recollections have also been a prominent feature in various therapy groups for children. In an early adolescent female group, Nelson (1986) reported that the task of drawing early recollections was an invaluable activity for developing insights into the lifestyle of group participants and for experiencing and developing empathy. Procedurally, after the group members completed drawings of persons in their family constellations, a therapist would draw a depiction of an early recollection in order to model the procedure. Subsequently, each group participant reported and discussed his or her individual memories. In sharing early recollections in later group discussions, the members found the interactions personal, but sufficiently removed in time to avoid the criticism that may possibly occur when sharing information about present behavior. Frequently, individuals identified with particular themes represented in the early memories, such as a sense of powerlessness and insignificance compared to others. This awareness often led to discussion relating to the implications of either maintaining or possibly changing maladaptive core convictions.

In support of Nelson's observations, Goodnow (1977) recognized the value of drawings to engender the expression of emotions and enable individuals to explore the constructs that they maintain about themselves, others, and events in their lives. Rotter, Horak, and Heidt (1999) also found children's drawings of early recollections in group therapy particularly useful for hypothesizing about a child's perception of life, and with additional data from multiple sources, for developing a comprehensive treatment plan for each individual. Finally, Heidt (1997) discussed her observations relating to the application of early recollections in play therapy groups. Over the course of counseling, Heidt found the approach useful for clarifying counseling goals, formulating treatment plans, and monitoring client progress.

From another life span perspective, early recollections have been a prominent intervention in working with late adulthood groups. Tobin (1976) employed early memories for the purpose of generating data for research on aging. In meeting with various late adulthood groups for the collection of early recollections, Tobin found that the participants were readily engaged in relating their early recollections and that their memories were relatively easy to gather. Typically, the request to reminisce was perceived by the individuals as an interest in their well-being and a recognition of an ability to convey wisdom. This willingness to talk about past life, according to Tobin, contrasts markedly with the resistance that the aged population often demonstrate in response to being asked to complete standard projective tests. Sweeney and Myers (1986) and Sweeney (1990) therapeutically employed early recollections in small groups with older persons, and they reported several advantages in using the approach over traditional life review therapy. In the context of Adlerian lifestyle counseling, early recollections provided an opportunity for structured reminiscence and reflection. Considering that reminiscing is a common activity among the elderly population, the discussion of early childhood memories in a group presents a familiar and a relatively nonthreatening method for evaluating life perspectives. Frequently, themes were uncovered in the memories that prompted a sense of universality and cohesiveness among the group members. In particular, individuals were able to evaluate the meaning that they give to life experiences in the context of supportive peer associations.

Various other group treatment options have received attention in the early recollections literature. As a communication tool in family life classes, Nims and Dinkmeyer (1995) reported that relating early memories stimulated purposeful discussion among family members. The authors also noted the potential of early recollections as a therapeutic tool in family counseling. In couple therapy, Carlson and Dinkmeyer (1999) reported that assessing early recollections provides a unique procedure for understanding each partner's basic perceptions and goals. It is also possible to discern the resources and limitations in the couple system. In psychoeducational parenting sessions, Mansager and Volk (1995) found that early recollections as a projective technique were instrumental in clarifying the parenting style of each of the group participants. As a consequence, rather than emphasizing exclusively a child's misbehavior in the sessions, an examination of the implications of parent styles brought increased critical awareness to the interactions between the parent and child in terms of a systems perspective. In another group context, Maniacci et al. (1998) mentioned an approach in art therapy in which the therapist divides participants into groups, and then the members draw a selected early recollection as if it were their own. The authors also described a psychodramatic approach that involved the therapeutic revision of the early recollections through a corrective group experience.

SUMMARY

Expanding beyond the assessment phase of treatment, consideration is given to varied and innovative applications of early recollections in the counseling process. A focus on client conceptualization provides a theoretical model of a person for guiding therapeutic movement in counseling and psychotherapy. Clarifying first- and second-order change establishes a framework for determining appropriate counseling goals and treatment direction. Conceptualizing the therapy process through three stages enables practitioners to evaluate progress in client development. In the relationship stage, particular interventions promote trust and open communication between the client and the counselor or therapist. In the integration period, the practitioner challenges a client's dysfunctional belief system through various cognitive-behavioral techniques. The accomplishment stage emphasizes breaking self-defeating behavioral patterns and establishing more purposeful instrumental actions. Addressing pertinent issues in the counseling experience, such as early memories and dreams, or reexperiencing early recollections, contributes to a broader understanding of practice considerations. Exploring various types of applications of early recollections with clients beyond traditional individual treatment conveys a sense of the expansive and versatile applications of the projective technique.

Early Recollections in the Counseling Process: A Case Study

"It is the person who remembers—not memory."
—Christa Wolf (1984, p. 118)

SOON AFTER I ARRIVED AT WORK, IN MY POSITION AS A COUNSELOR IN A program for at-risk adolescents, Mrs. Holt appeared at my office door. She was sobbing and quite upset as she tried to talk about her encounter the previous evening with her 15-year-old son. Willie had come home drunk and he "was falling all over the place." In her attempt to talk with him, Willie had put his hand through a pane of glass in the dining room door, and she had to take him to the hospital for medical treatment. They returned home about 4:00 A.M., and at that point Willie went to bed. I was supportive in my interactions with Mrs. Holt, but she hadn't slept all night and her distress was certainly understandable. She had come by to see me because I was about to begin working with Willie in individual counseling. He had recently been referred to our program through a local school district where he was a grade nine student. I had recently met Willie and his mother when I attended a special needs evaluation team meeting where his service plan was formalized.

Willie was present at the planning meeting for about 15 minutes before he went back to his high school class. When I shook his hand to greet him, Willie diverted his eyes to the floor and his handshake was weak. At no time in the meeting did Willie speak, and of the dozen or so adults present, the school counselor was the only person who attempted to engage Willie in conversation. Discussion initially focused on Willie's numerous unexcused absences from school. Even though it was only November, he had exceeded the number of missed days allowed in order to be eligible to receive academic credit for the year. On the infrequent occasions when he did attend school, Willie usually sat in the back of the classroom and avoided speaking to anyone except for one or two other students. Willie rarely completed class or homework assignments, and when he did they were usually done with a minimal degree of care or effort. Willie's achievement test scores were generally below average, but his intelligence scales were above average. I was provided a small packet of additional assessment results, and I noted that Willie had completed, among other measures, self-report inventories for depression and self-esteem. Upon leaving the meeting room, I said to the school counselor, Larry Casey, that Willie looked like a difficult person to get to know. Larry responded, "Check out his early recollections."

A few days after the meeting, Willie began attending his new school program, housed in a wing of an older school building and organized to appeal to students who typically feel alienated from traditional academic instruction. The classes are small, and students usually respond positively to the highly interactive and diverse learning experiences. There are exceptions to this, however, and Willie seemed to be one of them. He sat as far back in the classroom as he could; this is difficult to do considering the class size is six to eight students. As much as the teachers and a few of the students tried to engage him, Willie seemed determined to wait them out and avoid becoming involved. Only in the physical education class, which was concentrating on lifting weights, did Willie make some effort to participate. Beyond his school performance, I wanted to know more about Willie's family background, so I called his mother on the telephone. Willie lives with his mother and an older brother who does well academically in school. Willie's father has not been involved with his family for a number of years and lives in another region of the country. One comment that Mrs. Holt said to me stood out in regard to Willie: "He has an excuse for everything that he does." With the knowledge that I had gathered in speaking with Willie's mother, attending the placement meeting, and learning about Willie's first few days of school, I felt reasonably prepared to meet with him for our initial counseling session.

THE COUNSELING PROCESS

RELATIONSHIP STAGE

As Willie entered my office, he quickly took a seat near my desk. Usually, clients glance around the room or even pick up a toy or two that I place on the corner of my desk. I have an aquarium with several goldfish, and frequently discussion begins with talking about the fish. In other instances, conversation is directed toward the plants, pictures, or posters that I carefully locate around my office. However, none of these materials seemed to draw Willie's attention or interest. Generally, when this occurs with new clients, it suggests to me that they are preoccupied with immediate concerns that preclude more of an environmental focus. With this in mind, I said to Willie that I would like to get to know him and that we would be working together for a number of weeks. After briefly discussing confidentiality issues, I was hoping that Willie would begin to talk. He did not, and I attempted to reflect what I thought were his feelings.

AC: It must not be easy for you to find yourself in a place that is totally new.

WH: Not really.

AC: Oh, I guess then that you sort of expected things to be the way they are around here.

WH: What do you mean?

AC: Well, perhaps you are finding the school about what you thought it would be like.

The discussion proceeded in this generally unproductive direction, and I knew that I was not emotionally connecting with Willie. My process goal early in counseling is to try to develop a relationship with Willie or any other client. At this point, I knew that it was necessary to make a content shift to a new topic. I thought that Willie might have some feelings about his participation in his placement meeting from the previous week. His response to my attempt to be empathic and reflect his feelings about the meeting also seemed to go nowhere. I tried one last time: "It must be difficult to sit in a meeting where a lot of adults plan your future." Willie responded to my seemingly perceptive remark: "Not really."

As our discussion went on like this, I felt determined to touch on a topic that he could relate to with interest. I asked Willie what he enjoyed doing for fun. At this point, he seemed to become somewhat engaged as he began to talk about video games. Usually, I can find some common ground with persons with respect to most areas of life, but I know little about video games and I have made no attempt to learn more about them. I asked Willie to tell me about the games, but since the discussion was so one-sided, he seemed to lose interest quite quickly. As our first counseling session was drawing to a close, I wanted to conclude with a subject that could begin to draw us together. I did recall that Willie had shown some interest in weight lifting in one of his classes. Finally, Willie seemed willing to talk. He stated how he planned to "bulk up" by regularly lifting weights and getting in shape. I disclosed to Willie that I also enjoy weight training, and I talked briefly about my experience. Immediately after my comments, Willie seemed to emotionally withdraw again. Our session had to end at this point, even though I was not pleased with the progress we had made toward building a counseling alliance.

After Willie left my office, I had a few minutes to reflect about our session together. I had hoped to talk about his drinking episode that his mother had brought to my attention. We did not seem to get far with discussing less intimate concerns though, and I thought that it might only hinder our relationship to talk about the incident. Yet, I felt worse when I recalled that not much was accomplished in relationship building, and perhaps I was simply avoiding a potentially uncomfortable issue. I needed to get away, and I went to the exercise room to lift weights.

A few days later, I had an opportunity to observe Willie in the classroom, and his behavior continued to be passive and withdrawn. I was also able to review the psychological data from Willie's files. He had recently completed the Beck Depression Inventory, and his overall score was in the mildly depressed range. The only other current appraisal included the Coopersmith Inventory (Hood & Johnson, 2002), which indicated that Willie had measured low levels of self-esteem in regard to peers, parents, school, and general personal evaluation. In order to build on this material, I did plan to administer a brief personality battery in my next meeting with Willie. This would hopefully yield more specific information that I could use in our counseling sessions and provide a framework for organizing the growing amount of data that I was collecting on Willie.

As Willie entered my office for our second counseling session, he appeared even more subdued than in our initial meeting. I tried to reflect his feelings, "You feel sort of down, and it has been a struggle for you to be here today." This statement seemed to be on target, and for the first time, I saw Willie become emotionally responsive. He stated, "I hate this school. All of the teachers act like kids, and they pretend that they like you." To a degree Willie was accurate that the faculty members attempt to project a youthful attitude, but their interactions are usually sincere in trying to positively relate with the students. I responded to Willie, "This is something that you are not used to and it leaves you feeling uncomfortable." Willie then said, "I don't like dealing with phonies; who needs them?" It began to occur to me that what Willie was saying was plausible in his view, but the perception also serves a possible function of justifying a lack of involvement in the classroom. I was also aware that Willie was beginning to express his feelings, and after concluding our discussion about the teaching staff, I felt that it was an appropriate time to introduce the projective assessment battery.

As we began the projective assessments, Willie initially stated that my request for him to draw a picture of a person was a "waste of time" and that he was not an artist. After reassuring Willie that the artistic quality of the drawing was not important, he slowly drew a small stick figure. Prompting Willie one more time, I asked him to try to draw a full figure. With excessive and faint scribbling, Willie then drew a small drawing of a person. After completing the human figure drawings, I asked Willie to respond to the sentence completion tasks. Willie looked the 25 sentence stems over and began working to fill in the blanks. His interest in the procedure seemed to increase as he proceeded in completing the items.

With about 20 minutes remaining in our session, I asked Willie to provide a set of three of his early recollections. Willie appeared somewhat interested in my request and he began: "I was eating a bowl of cereal at the kitchen table. I must have been fooling with the cereal because it fell on the floor. My father came running into the kitchen and started yelling at me. He made me get on my hands and knees to clean up the mess." When Willie completed his recollection, I asked three follow-up questions relating to details, vividness, and feelings. He responded to each of my questions:

Details: "I particularly remember the bowl of cereal and milk hitting the
    floor with a splat."
Vivid: "My father screaming at me."
Feelings: "I felt stupid and scared."

Willie was also responsive as he reported his second early recollection, and I asked him the same follow-up questions. Willie stated: "I was walking home from school. A couple of big kids were standing on the corner and they started teasing me and calling me names. I started to run as fast as I could, but then I fell and really cut my knee. The boys laughed and then took off."

Details: "My cut knee really hurt."
Vivid: "Running and falling."
Feelings: "Scared."

Willie was mildly enthusiastic in his response to my request for a third memory and additional questions. He reported: "I was sitting at my desk in school in the first grade. The teacher wanted us to write our names on a sheet of paper, but I didn't know how to do it. I started to scribble things on the paper. She asked us to show what we wrote. I didn't want to hold up my paper when the teacher called my name, so I pretended that I hadn't finished."

Details: "Looking at the scribbles on the page and wishing that it was my
    name."
Vivid: "When the teacher called my name to hold up my paper."
Feelings: "Embarrassed and dumb."

When Willie completed his last early recollection, he appeared to be reflecting on the memory, but I recognized that discussing his reactions at this point would be premature. It would be inadvisable to begin an exploratory process before I had an opportunity to gain a more complete understanding of Willie's functioning or, equally important, prior to establishing a reasonalby sound counseling relationship. Instead, with only a few minutes remaining in our session, our discussion turned to the familiar topic of Willie complaining about the school program and his teachers.

After Willie returned to his classroom, I had some time to review his projective material. I considered Willie's human figure drawings first in order to develop inferences. His graphic productions suggest an evasive quality in regard to his stick figure, and the small drawing (less than three inches in height) possibly relates to reduced self-esteem (Handler, 1996). As indicated by his minimal productions, it may well be that Willie restricted his effort or withdrew due to feelings of diminished capacity or adequacy (Leibowitz, 1999). The faint lines that Willie drew may connect to feelings of hesitancy or uncertainty, and the scribbling suggests regressive tendencies. If the drawings represent the self in the environment (Handler, 1996), my conjecture would be that Willie feels inadequate and anxious in a world that evokes evasive and immature behavior. This is a tentative conceptualization and only serves as a starting point in developing a model of a person.

In regard to interpreting the sentence completion tasks, I find it helpful to organize responses in the framework of the self, others, and events. Several of Willie's sentences related prominently to self: "I feel . . . alone." "I suffer . . . but who cares?" "My nerves . . . are tight." "I wish . . . that I could be huge and really strong." With respect to others, particular statements were notable: "Other people . . . give me a hard time." "Other kids . . . don't include me." "Girls . . . could care less about me." "My father . . . has given me nothing." Willie's completion of several sentence stems in relationship to events are also noteworthy: "The happiest time . . . I can't remember." "I failed . . . school because of the dumb teachers." "Whenever I have to study, I . . . avoid it." Drawing inferences from the sentence stem responses, Willie perceives himself as isolated and misunderstood. Others are either rejecting, indifferent, or incompetent. With regard to events, they tend to be adversive, unremarkable, or involve failure experiences. In addition to the inferential material that I write down on a separate sheet of paper, I am able to utilize Willie's prominent responses to sentence stems at a later point in counseling. For example, clarifying Willie's sentence response relating to his father may stimulate or be a springboard for useful discussion content.

In evaluating Willie's early recollections, I use the Early Recollections Interpretation Worksheet as a guide. My preference is to consider one memory at a time and make pertinent notations on the worksheet. With respect to Willie's first memory, from my subjective perspective, he feels inept and fearful after knocking the bowl of cereal on the floor. This reaction essentially occurs due to the harsh and demeaning demands of Willie's father. From an interpersonal perspective, after referring to Table 7.1 of this text, the thematic variables of incompetent and insecure seem to fit Willie's self-representation. Others are hostile and intolerant, and events appear to be distressful and debilitative. In consideration of detail analysis, Willie's auditory sense is prominent due to the "splat" sound. Color is not emphasized, and the location and objects do not seem to be significant. From an objective perspective, I refer to the research literature in chapter 3 of this text in order to consider personality dimensions. Relating to explanatory style, in the memory Willie is insecure and he assumes the role of a victim. Willie also appears anxious in the memory, and his behavior reflects an external locus of control. The last interpretive step is to consider the diagnostic impressions with respect to early recollections in chapter 4. My initial hypothesis is that the presence of fear and threat in Willie's memory suggests some type of anxiety disorder. I ruled out obsessive-compulsive functioning due to a lack of emphasis relating to details and repetition.

Following the same procedures employed in the first early recollection, I began to subjectively evaluate Willie's next memory. Again, his recollection suggests feelings of fear and ineptness. Other people ridicule and intimidate him. He tries to run, but falls down. From an interpersonal perspective, Willie's self-representation is one of incompetence. His perception of others is that they are hostile, and events are overwhelming and destructive. In terms of detail analysis, Willie's cut knee relates to a tactile sense. Other details do not seem significant. From an objective perspective, Willie's memory reflects fearful and threatening content, which is often present in early recollections of individuals with a diagnosis of an anxiety disorder. In order to expand beyond this categorization, I considered other diagnostic impressions. The research relating to early memories and substance abuse also suggests material that is consistent with the content of both of Willie's early recollections. With adult populations and young males in treatment for substance abuse disorders, feelings of inadequacy, isolation, and fear, and a perception of the environment as hostile are common elements.

Willie's third early recollection, from a subjective perspective, presents an anxiety-laden situation in which he perceives himself as inept. He engages both in an avoidance behavior, which appears to work for him, and a type of wishful thinking. With respect to an interpersonal perspective, Willie's self-representation is that he is incapable and insecure. His perception of others (teacher, other students) is that they are capable and events are distressful. The only details that stood out were when Willie heard the teacher call his name and his wish to conceal the writing paper. An objective perspective presents another experience that relates to a diagnostic impression of anxiety and substance related disorders. In regard to explanatory style, Willie demonstrates a passive orientation as he evasively scribbles and delays.

After concluding my evaluation of Willie's third early recollection, it becomes possible to complete the lifestyle syllogism. I find it helpful to reflect back on Willie's set of early recollections and give particular attention to my

TABLE 10.1: EARLY RECOLLECTIONS INTERPRETATION WORKSHEET

NAME: Willie Holt   DATE: December 6, 2001

I. Subjective Perspectives
  A. Early recollection #1: (ER1) Inept and fearful. Harsh and demeaning demands.
  B. Early recollection #2: (ER2) Fearful and inept. Others ridicule and intimidate.
  C. Early recollection #3: (ER3) Embarrassed. "Dumb." Wishful thinking.
II. Interpersonal Perspectives
  A. Thematic Analysis
       1. "I am . . ."
          a. ER1: incompetent and insecure
          b. ER2: incompetent
          c. ER3: incapable and insecure
       2. "Others are . . ."
          a. ER1: hostile and intolerant
          b. ER2: hostile
          c. ER3: capable
       3. "Events are . . ."
          a. ER1: distressful and debilitative
          b. ER2: overwhelming and destructive
          c. ER3: distressful
  B. Detail Analysis
       1. Senses (visual, auditory, tactile, olfactory, and gustatory)
          a. ER1: auditory
          b. ER2: tactile
          c. ER3: auditory
       2. Color
          a. ER1:—
          b. ER2:—
          c. ER3:—
       3. Location
          a. ER1: home (kitchen)
          b. ER2: outside
          c. ER3: school
       4. Objects
          a. ER1:—
          b. ER2:—
          c. ER3: writing paper
III. Objective Perspectives
  A. ER1: Insecure. Victim. Anxious. External locus of control. Anxiety disorder?
  B. ER2: Fearful. Victim. Anxiety disorder? Substance related disorder? (feelings of inadequacy, isolation and fear, hostile environment).
  C. ER3: Passive orientation (explanatory style). Anxiety disorder? Substance related disorder?
IV. Lifestyle Syllogism
  "I am . . . incompetent and insecure."
  "Others are . . . threatening or indifferent."
  "Events are . . . distressful."
  "Therefore, life is . . . often fearful and overwhelming."

analysis of the thematic variables. The following is my formulation of Willie's syllogism: "I am incompetent and insecure. Others are threatening or indifferent. Events are distressful. Therefore, life is often fearful or overwhelming." This rubric serves as a basis for a conceptualization as a model of a person at this point in the counseling process. Table 10.1 presents data relating to Willie that I entered in the Early Recollections Interpretation Worksheet.

As I reflected on the assessment data, I was struck with the sense of isolation and fearfulness inherent in Willie's outlook on life. I thought back on his avoidant and evasive actions, and began to more fully understand how this behavioral pattern possibly serves as a means of a psychological escape. In order to organize the escalating amount of data relating to Willie at this point, I utilized the familiar rubric of self, others, and events in another more comprehensive worksheet. Information pertinent to this framework is drawn from

---

TABLE 10.2: CONTEXTURAL ASSESSMENT WORKSHEET

NAME: Willie Holt   DATE: December 10, 2001

Self
1. Incompetent and insecure (Early Recollections).
2. Mildly depressed (Beck Depression Inventory).
3. Inadequate and anxious (Human Figure Drawings).
4. Isolated and misunderstood (Sentence Completion).
5. Low self-esteem (Coopersmith Inventory).
PERSONAL DATA: Enjoys weight lifting and video games (Interview). Auditory orientation (Early Recollections). Above average intelligence and below average achievement functioning (Standardized Testing). Possible anxiety disorder and/or substance abuse disorder (Early Recollections).

Others
1. Threatening or indifferent (Early Recollections).
2. Rejecting, indifferent, or incompetent (Sentence Completion).
3. Threatening. Evoke evasion and avoidance (Human Figure Drawings).
SOCIAL DATA: Immature and passive functioning indicative of regression as a defense mechanism (Behavioral Observations, Early Recollections, and Sentence Completion). Justifies objectionable behavior with plausible statements that suggest the use of rationalization as defense mechanism (Behavioral Observations and Sentence Completion). Evasive functioning indicative of the safeguarding tendency of hesitating attitude (Behavioral Observations, Human Figure Drawings, and Sentence Completion).

Events
1. Distressful (Early Recollections).
2. Adversive, unremarkable, or involve failure (Sentence Completion).
3. Threatening and evoke evasion and avoidance (Human Figure Drawings).
4. Low self-esteem in relationship to school (Coopersmith Inventory).
ENVIRONMENTAL DATA: Unsatisfactory in all academic classes. High frequency of school absences. Recent incident of alcohol abuse. No contact with father in recent years.

multiple sources such as projective and objective appraisals, behavioral observations, and third-party disclosures. Additional information that is not pertinent to the rubric, I list under personal, social, and environmental entries. All
of this material serves as a basis for a contextural assessment and subsequent
client development in counseling. The early recollections constructs in particular provide an overarching conceptualization for unifying diverse and broad-
based perspectives. Table 10.2 presents compiled data relating to Willie in the
format of a Contextural Assessment Worksheet. As an instructional aid, I
have indicated the source of specific data in parentheses on the sheet.

In my work with clients, I find it particularly helpful to select one of an
individual's early recollections that seems to most clearly capture or represent
his or her dynamic pattern of behavior. For Willie, I chose the last memory
that he disclosed, and I refer to this selection as a "prime early recollection."
The memory portrays Willie in an embarrassing and inferior role because of
his inability to write his name. At the same time, the recollection suggests an
evasive and defensive interaction, as Willie attempts to hide his work from
his teacher. As a prime early recollection, I am able to empathize with Willie
at any point in counseling by visualizing the evocative memory. This understanding also provides an internal goal-directive image to guide the therapeutic process toward establishing more adaptive functioning. Through this
technique, however, I do try to be mindful of Wolf's caution at the beginning of the chapter that, although a memory is significant, what matters
most is the emphasis on the person.

As Willie appeared for his third counseling session, I felt more certain
about understanding him as a result of the assessment process. This knowledge did not, however, have any immediate effect on his behavior, as Willie
immediately began complaining about the teachers in the school program.

> WH: I'm really sick of the teachers around here who act like they are
>   kids. All they want to do is play games.
> AC: It is disappointing to you that they don't measure up to your expec-
>   tations.
> WH: What are you talking about? I don't think that you even know
>   what they are doing.
> AC: Help me to understand what you mean by "playing games."
> WH: It's stupid. They try to get the kids to do the work by pretending
>   their stupid activities are fun. I hate to be treated like a little kid.
> AC: You feel strongly about this, but I don't understand why trying to
>   make learning enjoyable is such a bad thing.
> WH: You really are out of it if you don't get it. I refuse to be manipu-
>   lated to get a reward for doing something.

As our discussion continued, Willie made a further case for his inactivity and unwillingness to participate in the classroom work. In one respect, he presented a somewhat plausible justification for withdrawing from an adverse situation, but for the most part his views were self-defeating. As we talked, I recalled the image of his prime early recollection and his sense of inferiority and evasive reactions. This impression helped me to continue to conceptualize his behavior in terms of discouragement rather than mere excuse-making. At one point, I tried to respond to Willie through his auditory sensory orientation, which seemed prominent in his early recollections. It was one of the first times that I tried to use this technique, and I found it somewhat awkward.

WH: I'm just not going to join in and play their games.
AC: It sounds like you refuse to be led around by anyone.
WH: That's right. I'm not a baby and I won't be treated like one.
AC: I hear what you are saying.

As we continued to talk, it was becoming clearer to me that Willie's model of a person primarily involved the defense of his fragile self-esteem through a type of withdrawal. I was concerned that in acknowledging Willie's perceptions, I might also be reinforcing his self-defeating posture. Yet, I also felt that it was more important at this point to recognize Willie's outlook on life and to convey to him that I have some understanding of his views. Our session time came to a close in much the same way that it began: Willie was complaining, and I was struggling to clarify his feelings and perceptions.

A few days after meeting with Willie, one of his classroom teachers asked me at lunch how things were proceeding with the counseling. I responded, as I usually do, that it takes time to develop a relationship and show some progress. The teacher appeared somewhat irritated by my comment and voiced this by pointing out that if Willie refused to participate in the classroom much longer, he would have to find another school placement because he was a "bad model." In one respect perhaps there was some hope, as the teacher used the term "model" rather than "apple." Immediately, I felt pressure to make a further effort to stimulate Willie to show some willingness to participate and become involved in the program. After lunch, however, as I walked back to my office, I reminded myself about the need to maintain a focus on Willie's model of a person and the importance of not feeling rushed in an effort to effect second-order change prematurely. With all of this in mind, with some degree of urgency I thought about the fourth counseling session scheduled with Willie at the end of the week.

Willie appeared more alert than usual as he walked into my office for our next meeting. He surprised me as he began to discuss doing some work in school. I felt relief as Willie talked, and I tried very carefully to encourage this suggestion of a change in attitude.

WH: Sometimes I get sick of just sitting in class and doing nothing.

AC: This can be more difficult sometimes than doing work.

WH: Well, I don't know about that. What I want to say is that yesterday I started a project in social studies that is kind of interesting.

AC: (Gulp). Yes.

WH: Why are you looking so funny?

AC: Well, I'm. . . .

WH: It's about Vietnam and my father was in the war. Even though my dad is a jerk, I'd like to know more about Vietnam.

AC: This is a fairly big step for you because making an effort in school has never been that easy for you.

WH: Well, it's not like I'm an expert or anything.

Our session continued on in this productive direction, and Willie and I began to explore his uncertainties about his abilities. At the conclusion of our meeting, I went to the lunchroom. I saw the teacher who was critical of the progress being made in counseling, and I know that I had a smug look on my face because Willie seemed for the first time willing to engage in school activities.

As it turned out, my smugness lasted only until Willie began talking in his fifth counseling session. Willie related that he was unable to finish his so-cial studies assignment because it was not clear to him what the teacher's ex-pectations were for the project. When I asked him if he had discussed the problem with the teacher, Willie responded that it would not do any good because the deadline had passed for submitting the work and information on the topic was difficult to locate. I suggested that perhaps he could ask the teacher for a time extension and that there should be quite a bit of material on Vietnam. At this point, Willie looked down to the floor and became emo-tionally withdrawn. I realized that pursuing discussion on the school assign-ment would only detract from our relationship, which I was confident was beginning to develop. At the same time, I knew that Willie's unwillingness to complete academic tasks put his school placement in jeopardy, and progress in this area was central to our work in counseling. For the remainder of our time together, Willie continued to express disenchantment with people and conditions in the school program.

After Willie left my office, I felt fairly discouraged because after five weeks his passive and withdrawn behavior had shown no real change, and his school placement was at-risk. As I thought about Willie, it occurred to me that his most recent behavior in not finishing school assignments was consistent with his general way of functioning. In conceptual terms, he seems to be demonstrating a variation on his evasive and defensive behavioral patterns. Willie's employment of the safeguarding tendency of hesitating attitude and the defense mechanism of rationalization appears recognizable in his tendency to blame other people for his problems and hardships. The response possibly provides a means to avoid or justify failures and to serve a protective function in regard to his low self-esteem. Another safeguarding tendency, distancing complex, may be operating in regard to Willie's sense of apathy, lack of interest, and diminished motivation. His most recent reluctance to follow through on projects is apparently an evasive means to mask perceived deficiencies that might become apparent in a finished product. This reminded me of Willie's prime early recollection in which he felt diminished and used an evasive tactic to avoid further embarrassment. Even though I felt fairly certain about all this, I reminded myself that I needed to be open and receptive to other views that could be helpful in working with Willie.

An interesting and hopeful development occurred in our next meeting as Willie immediately wanted to tell me about a dream that he had had a few times over the past few weeks. I thought that this was a productive direction because it demonstrated a degree of trust for him to be willing to share his dream with me, and it provided a means for Willie to express his feelings. Even more to the point, I was unsure about what we might discuss that would be particularly therapeutic in our sixth counseling session. I did plan to raise the topic of Willie's feelings about his father, whom he had mentioned in the sentence completions, but the dream discussion diverted this possibility. Willie began recalling his dream:

> I'm riding on a really big bicycle on a street, and I don't know where I am. All of a sudden a huge hill appears in front of me, and I ride down the hill. It is frightening because my bike is going really fast, and the brakes don't work. I'm really afraid that I'll fall off. Then the bike starts shaking, and I know that I'm going to get thrown onto the street. Then I wake up and my heart is beating like crazy.

When Willie completed relating his dream, I acknowledged the intensity of his feelings, and we discussed at length the frightening quality of the dream. As we talked it was apparent to me how the dream was congruent with Willie's model of a person with its predominant theme of fear. In his dream he is out of control, and his fearfulness has been intensified. It then occurred to me that Willie has experienced this recurrent dream beginning around the date he was placed in his new school program. Could it be that the dream also functions as a warning to him as a caution not to get involved in an unknown and potentially fearful situation? In this regard the dream may serve a problem-solving purpose that is consistent with the integrity of life attitudes that are also represented in his early recollections. All of this, however, is inferential on my part, and sharing these impressions with Willie at this point would be premature and threatening. Yet, I wanted to take advantage of Willie's expression of fear, and after an extended dream discussion, I decided to self-disclose on a similar out-of-control experience that I had when riding a bicycle as a teenager. Even as I talked, the fear of falling off of a bicycle when speeding down a paved road with a steep incline at a velocity of more than 25 miles per hour resonated within me. Willie seemed to respond positively to my disclosure, and we discussed how such fears can be torturous and long-lasting. As we talked, I was aware that our relationship had progressed to a point where a reasonable degree of trust and open communication was evident. At the same time, I knew that it was therapeutically necessary for me to take advantage of this developing alliance and become more challenging in my counseling efforts.

INTEGRATION STAGE

As we entered the middle period of counseling, I thought about particular conflicts in Willie's behavior that became apparent in the initial therapy phase. My process goal was to enable Willie to become more aware of his conflicted functioning and to progress to a more adaptive behavioral level. Because Willie frequently complained about the inadequacies of other people, I planned to begin our seventh session with a confrontation in the event that he began being critical of others. As Willie began talking, it did not take long for him to arrive at what had become his favorite topic. As usual Willie expressed his dismay about the lack of direction that his teachers provided him in completing assignments. As a response, I confronted Willie by contrasting his present statements and his apparent unwillingness to seek out teachers when they are available. A few weeks ago, I tried to make the same point in the form of a question. This time, through a confrontation, Willie was more responsive.

> AC: You are saying that the teachers are not available, but you have also told me that you don't go to them for help.
> WH: (Pause). I don't know. It's like we talked about last time. I don't bother to ask for things even when I need them.
> AC: This is something you are just not used to doing.

This was a significant comment by Willie, and we returned to an earlier discussion relating to Willie's sense of apathy and passivity. In this session and the next, I used several confrontations in clarifying inconsistencies in Willie's behavior. Yet, even though we were focusing on pertinent issues relating to his conflicted functioning, Willie also expressed feelings of discouragement as he became more aware of what he perceived as personal inadequacies.

In our eighth session, I recognized the importance of progressing beyond those views that had begun to emerge about Willie and his long-held perceptions of the world, which were largely negative and self-defeating. At this point, it was critical to encourage him to develop alternative perspectives relating to his core convictions. It was my intent to employ cognitive restructuring in order to stimulate movement in this direction. This particular counseling intervention directly uses the model of a person in its application. When employing cognitive restructuring, the initial step begins when a client expresses a negative or self-defeating automatic thought in regard to an aspect of his or her outlook on life. It did not take long for Willie to state a basic mistake.

> WH: Things never seem to work out for me like they do for other kids.
> AC: You seem down about this. Are you talking about anything in particular?
> WH: I heard that some of the kids in the school had a party on Saturday night, and I wasn't invited.
> AC: This is disappointing to you.
> WH: Well, sure; I wanted to go.
> AC: You just said, "Things don't work out for me . . . ." Tell me more about that.

We then began talking about how Willie feels insecure and anxious when he does act in a more assertive way. This productive discussion went on for a period of time, and then I introduced the idea of devising a counterstatement to his negative self-talk.

> AC: In some ways, you seem to be telling yourself over and over that you don't measure up.
>
> WH: This is kind of embarrassing, but I think that I do this a lot.
> AC: Would it be possible for you to begin to tell yourself that in some ways, things could work out better for you if you tried to make some changes?
> WH: What do you mean?
> AC: Well, could you begin to say to yourself over and over that you do

have some capabilities and that you are old enough and smart enough
to begin to use them?

WH: I'm not even sure where to begin with all of this.

AC: What about figuring out a statement about yourself that is more
positive than: "Things never seem to work out for me like they do for
other kids."

WH: I'm still not sure.

AC: This is kind of hard for you.

WH: It's not that bad. I'm thinking about, "Things can work out better
for me if I try."

AC: You seem OK with that.

WH: Well, sort of.

AC: It will seem strange and new for a while. What if you write down
what you just said on a note card and repeat it to yourself during the
week?

We then discussed plans for Willie to use the positive counterstatement
or "counter" on a regular and frequent basis between counseling sessions. In
a similar way over the next two meetings, Willie and I had discussions relating to his core convictions about other people and events. This also led to
devising counters in regard to both aspects of his private logic. As we discussed his reactions to evaluating his basic beliefs and formulating counters,
Willie was frequently anxious and uncertain.

As Willie expressed feelings in regard to his belief system, at times he
would point out his discomfort with anxiety. At one point, in an attempt to
transpose the meaning relating to his fearful state, I used a reframe.

WH: We have been working on how I look at things, but thinking and
talking about it is actually making me more nervous.

AC: You feel anxious dealing directly with all of these changes.

WH: You know though, I'm sick of the way things are and I want to
change, but. . . .

AC: I'm wondering if it is possible for you to try to see your nervousness
differently, perhaps in a more positive light.

WH: What do you mean?

AC: What if each time you feel anxious, rather than take it in a negative
way, try to see it as a way to grow and be stronger?

WH: I don't know.

AC: It is hard, but you know how you feel anxious in a good way when
you play video games?

WH: OK.

AC: Well, your tenseness actually helps you play better. Does that make sense to you?

WH: Sort of. You're saying try to put my nervousness to good use in the same way about even more important things.

AC: Yes. Try to understand the tenseness that you feel as something that can be helpful, even when it is not easy to take.

The reframing intervention directly addresses Willie's feelings at the core level. The model of a person continues to guide this therapeutic effort.

In our tenth meeting, Willie raised what he felt was another problem in his attempts to change his behavior. He had already shown some progress in becoming more involved in the classroom and working on some assignments. At the same time, both Willie and I recognized that these changes were rather limited. In response to Willie's initial question, I used the counseling technique of interpretation. Together we attempted to relate the meanings of a recurring dream to his pattern of behavior.

WH: Why is it that I'm still having a hard time with feeling anxious and still continuing to avoid some things?

AC: Even though you have made progress, you are somewhat disappointed.

WH: I am, and I'd like to figure this out better.

AC: Are you still having that dream we talked about a couple of times?

WH: I had it the other night, and I'm still going down the hill out of control, and the brakes don't work on the bicycle.

AC: It seems that each time you have the dream you wake up feeling nervous.

WH: My heart beats like crazy.

AC: I'm wondering if it could be that the dream cautions or alerts you to get anxious about things.

WH: I feel worked up just talking to you about my dream, but what does this have to do with how I act?

AC: Well, perhaps the dream warns you, and then you withdraw or make excuses why you can't do things.

WH: I see what you mean, but I don't act the way I do all the time because of my dream.

AC: True, because you only have the dream from time to time. What the dream seems to do is generate more feelings to plug into what is already there.

WH: The dream then juices me up to get tense. Probably some other things do the same thing. It's starting to make sense to me.

In the next two sessions, we used interpretation to gain an understanding of further aspects of Willie's behavior. One interpretation linked aspects of Willie's fearfulness to his father (represented in Willie's first early memory), but he also expressed a sense of loss in not having his father in his life on a regular basis.

ACCOMPLISHMENT STAGE

To this point in the therapeutic process, Willie seemed to have progressed in developing more constructive core beliefs, and it was time to more fully turn our attention to instrumental actions in the last phase of counseling. Assuming that Willie's outlook on life is relatively less fearful and evasive, he should be in a position to act in ways that are more assertive and active. Willie had already shown some progress toward more adaptive functioning in recent sessions, but this was fairly limited. Willie began in our thirteenth counseling session:

> WH: There's still problems. Sometimes I find myself falling back on my old ways of doing nothing and making excuses.
>
> AC: This is discouraging for you, but you have made some real progress in trying to do more in school.
>
> WH: Well, I think that I've got a better handle on things, but I still struggle with old habits.
>
> AC: They are old ways that seem comfortable for you. I'm wondering if trying out a new idea might help. I'm thinking about something that could wake you up when you find yourself slipping back.
>
> WH: What do you mean?
>
> AC: What if you use some kind of a reminder that you carry with you. Each time you feel that you are about to avoid work, use it to alert yourself about the importance of trying.
>
> WH: That sounds good, but what do I wake myself up with? I have no idea what I could carry around for this.
>
> AC: You like gadgets, like video games.
>
> WH: Yes, but I can't use them for this. I know. I have a watch that has an alarm button. When I feel myself slipping, I'll push the alarm and hear a little beeping noise.

As we continued in this action-oriented phase, Willie and I decided to meet for two more sessions. It was time to conclude our time together, as it was also getting close to the end of the academic year.

OUTCOME

Willie managed to complete his school year with a moderate degree of success. He showed gains in becoming more involved in the classroom and in completing assignments. In our last meeting, our fifteenth counseling session, I once again asked Willie to report his early recollections. The memories were similar to those that he related to me a number of months ago, however, as he spoke to me there was a measurable difference in his emotional reaction. He appeared somewhat less anxious and threatened as he described the memories. There was one content change in the last memory that he shared, which I have referred to as his prime early recollection. In the first accounting of the memory, Willie felt an acute sense of embarrassment when he was not able to write his name, and he used an evasive means to avoid public recognition of this perceived fact. The intensity of his feelings seemed slightly diminished, but he also mentioned that the teacher appeared to smile a little, which made the recollection seem less severe.

As the school year was ending, it was time to consider Willie's educational placement for the fall. I went to an evaluation team meeting for Willie, and many of the same people were present who attended a planning meeting in November, including Mrs. Holt, Willie, and the district school counselor, Larry Casey. Plans were made to allow Willie to return to his district home school in the fall and to enter grade ten. Mrs. Holt said that she was pleased with Willie's progress and thought the teachers were particularly helpful and they made all the difference. As I walked out of the meeting with Mr. Casey, I complained some that Willie's mother did not mention my work for helping him get on track. Larry was understanding about my grumbling, but then he said that he also deserved some credit. I wasn't sure what Larry meant, and he explained, "I told you to check out his early recollections months ago, and I know this definitely helped."

REFERENCES

Ackerknecht, L. K. (1976). New aspects of early recollections (ER) as a diagnostic and thera-peutic device. *The Individual Psychologist, 13,* 44–54.

Acklin, M. W., Bibb, J. L., Boyer, P., & Jain, V. (1991). Early memories as expressions of rela-tionship paradigms: A preliminary investigation. *Journal of Personality Assessment, 57,* 177–192.

Acklin, M. W., Sauer, A., Alexander, G., & Dugoni, B. (1989). Predicting depression using earliest childhood memories. *Journal of Personality Assessment, 53,* 51–59.

Adcock, N. V. (1975). Early memories and sex differences. *New Zealand Psychologist, 4,* 30–34.

Adcock, N. V., & Ross, M. W. (1983). Early memories, early experiences and personality. *Social Behavior and Personality, 11,* 95–100.

Adler, A. (1913). Individualpsychologische ergebnisse bezüglich schlafstörungen [Individual-psychological conclusions regarding sleep disturbances]. *Fortschritte der Medizin, 31,* 925–933.

Adler, A. (1914a). Die individualpsychologie, ihre voraussetzungen und ergebnisse [Indi-vidual psychology, its assumptions and its results]. *Scientia 16,* 74–87.

Adler, A. (1914b). Das problem der "distanz": Über einen grundcharakter der neurose und psychose [The problem of "distance": A basic feature of neurosis and psychosis]. *Interna-tionale Zeitschrift für Individual Psychologie, 1,* 8–16.

Adler, A. (1917). *The neurotic constitution: Outline of a comparative individualistic psychology and psychotherapy* (B. Glueck & J. E. Lind, Trans.). New York: Moffat, Yard. (Original work published 1912)

Adler, A. (1927). *Understanding human nature* (W. B. Wolfe & L. E. Hinsie, Trans.). New York: Greenberg.

Adler, A. (1929). *The case of Miss R.* New York: Greenberg.

Adler, A. (1935). The structure of neurosis. *International Journal of Individual Psychology, 1,* 3–12.

Adler, A. (1936). On the interpretation of dreams. *International Journal of Individual Psy-chology, 2,* 3–16.

Adler, A. (1937a). Position in family constellation influences life-style. *International Journal of Individual Psychology, 3,* 211–227.

Adler, A. (1937b). Significance of early recollections. *International Journal of Individual Psy-chology, 3,* 283–287.

Adler, A. (1947). How I chose my career. *Individual Psychology Bulletin, 6,* 9–11.

Adler, A. (1958). *What life should mean to you* (A. Porter, Ed.). New York: G. Putnam. (Orig-inal work published 1931)

Adler, A. (1964). *Social interest: A challenge to mankind.* New York: Capricorn Books. (Orig-inal work published 1933)

Adler, A. (1968). *The practice and theory of individual psychology* (P. Radin, Trans.). Totowa, NJ: Littlefield, Adams. (Original work published 1920)

Adler, A. (1969). *The science of living* (H. L. Ansbacher, Ed.). Garden City, New York: Anchor Books. (Original work published 1929)

Adler, A. (1982). *The pattern of life* (2nd ed.). (W. B. Wolf, Ed.). Chicago: Alfred Adler Insti-tute of Chicago. (Original work published 1930)

Alessi, H. D., & Ballard, M. B. (2001). Memory development in children: Implications for children as witnesses in situations of possible abuse. *Journal of Counseling & Development, 79,* 398–404.

Allers, C. T., & Golson, J. (1994). Multiple personality disorder: Treatment from an Adlerian perspective. *Individual Psychology: The Journal of Adlerian Theory, Research & Practice, 50,* 262–270.

Allers, C. T., Katrin, S. E., & White, J. F. (1997). Comparison of tape-recorded and hand-written early recollections: Investigating the assumption of equivalence. *Individual Psychology: The Journal of Adlerian Theory, Research & Practice, 53,* 342–346.

Allers, C. T., & Snow, M. (1999). Use of Adlerian assessment techniques in the treatment of dissociative identity disorder: A case study. *The Journal of Individual Psychology, 55,* 162–175.

Allers, C. T., White, J., & Hornbuckle, D. (1990). Early recollections: Detecting depression in the elderly. *Individual Psychology: The Journal of Adlerian Theory, Research & Practice, 46,* 61–66.

Allers, C. T., White, J., & Hornbuckle, D. (1992). Early recollections: Detecting depression in college students. *Individual Psychology: The Journal of Adlerian Theory, Research & Practice, 48,* 324–329.

Allison, R. D., Lichtenberg, J. W., & Goodyear, R. K. (1999). Science and the practice of test interpretation. In J. W. Lichtenberg & R. K. Goodyear (Eds.), *Scientist–practitioner perspectives on test interpretation* (pp.167–182). Boston: Allyn & Bacon.

Altman, K. (1973). *The relationship between social interest dimensions of early recollections and selected counselor variables.* Unpublished doctoral dissertation, University of South Carolina, Columbia, SC.

Altman, K. E., & Rule, W. R. (1980). The relationship between social interest dimensions of early recollections and selected counselor variables. *Journal of Individual Psychology, 36,* 227–234.

American Educational Research Association, American Psychological Association, & National Council on Measurement in Education. (1985). *Standards for educational and psychological testing.* Washington, DC: American Psychological Association.

American Educational Research Association, American Psychological Association, & National Council on Measurement in Education. (1999). *Standards for educational and psychological testing.* Washington, DC: American Psychological Association.

American Psychiatric Association. (2000). *Diagnostic and statistical manual of mental disorders–text revision* (4th ed). Washington, DC: Author.

Anastasi, A., & Urbina, S. (1997). *Psychological testing* (7th ed.). Upper Saddle River, NJ: Prentice Hall.

Ansbacher, H. L. (1947). Adler's place today in the psychology of memory. *Journal of Personality, 15,* 197–207.

Ansbacher, H. L. (1953). Purcell's "memory and psychological security" and Adlerian theory. *Journal of Abnormal Psychology, 48,* 596–597.

Ansbacher, H. L. (1967). Life style: A historical and systematic review. *Journal of Individual Psychology, 23,* 191–203.

Ansbacher, H. L. (1973). Adler's interpretation of early recollections: Historical account. *Journal of Individual Psychology, 29,* 135–145.

Ansbacher, H. L. (1978). An early recollection of Lyndon Johnson: Adlerian considerations. *The Individual Psychologist, 15,* 29–33.

Ansbacher, H. L. (1992). Alfred Adler's concept of community feeling and of social interest and the relevance of community feeling for old age. *Individual Psychology: The Journal of Adlerian Theory, Research & Practice, 48,* 402–412.

Ansbacher, H. L., & Ansbacher, R. R. (Eds.). (1956). *The individual psychology of Alfred Adler: A systematic presentation in selections from his writings.* New York: Harper & Row.

Ansbacher, H. L., & Ansbacher, R. R. (Eds.). (1979). *Superiority and social interest: A collection of later writings* (3rd Rev. ed.). New York: W.W. Norton.

Arbuthnott, K. D., Arbuthnott, D. W., & Rossiter, L. (2001). Guided imagery and memory: Implications for psychotherapists. *Journal of Counseling Psychology, 48*, 123–132.

Arnow, D., & Harrison, R. H. (1991). Affect in early memories of borderline patients. *Journal of Personality Assessment, 56*, 75–83.

Arntz, A., & Weertman, A. (1999). Treatment of childhood memories: Theory and practice. *Behaviour Research and Therapy, 37*, 715–740.

Attarian, P. J. (1978). Early recollections: Predictors of vocational choice. *Journal of Individual Psychology, 34*, 56–62.

Auld, F., & Hyman, M. (1991). *Resolution of inner conflict: An introduction to psychoanalytic therapy*. Washington, DC: American Psychological Association.

Axline, V. M. (1964). *Dibs: In search of self*. New York: Balentine Books.

Bach, G. R. (1952). Some diadic functions of childhood memories. *The Journal of Psychology, 33*, 87–98.

Baldwin, C. (1977). *One to one: Self-understanding through journal writing*. New York: M. Evans.

Bandura, A. (1991). Self-efficacy conception of anxiety. In R. Schwarzer & R. A. Wickland (Eds.), *Anxiety and self-focused attention* (pp. 89–110). New York: Harwood Academic Publishers.

Barclay, C. R. (1986). Schematization in autobiographical memory. In D. C. Rubin (Ed.), *Autobiographical memory* (pp. 82–99). New York: Cambridge University Press.

Barker, S. B., & Bitter, J. R. (1992). Early recollections versus created memory: A comparison for projective qualities. *Individual Psychology: The Journal of Adlerian Theory, Research & Practice 48*, 86–95.

Barrett, D. (1980). The first memory as a predictor of personality traits. *Journal of Individual Psychology, 36*, 136–149.

Barrett, D. (1981). Early recollections of anorexia nervosa patients: Reflections of lifestyle. *Journal of Individual Psychology, 37*, 5–14.

Barrett, D. (1983). Early recollections as predictors of self-disclosure and interpersonal style. *Individual Psychology: The Journal of Adlerian Theory, Research & Practice, 39*, 92–98.

Bartlett, F. C. (1932). *Remembering: A study in experimental and social psychology*. Cambridge, England: Cambridge University Press.

Bauserman, J. M., & Rule, W. R. (1988). Use of subjective information in scientific psychology: II. Contextual influences on production of early recollections. *Perceptual and Motor Skills, 66*, 823–828.

Beck, J. S. (1995). *Cognitive therapy: Basics and beyond*. New York: The Guilford Press.

Benoschofsky, I. (1938). A serdülö leanyok emlékei [Reminiscences of girls in puberty]. *A Budapesti Egyetem Psychologiai Tanulumányai, 2*, 128–133.

Berdach, E., & Bakan, P. (1967). Body position and the free recall of early memories. *Psychotherapy: Theory, Research & Practice, 4*, 101–102.

Berliner, L., & Briere, J. (1999). Trauma, memory, and clinical practice. In L. M. Williams & V. L. Baynard (Eds.), *Trauma and memory* (pp. 3–18). Thousand Oaks, CA: Sage.

Binder, J. L., & Smokler, I. (1980). Early memories: A technical aid to focusing in time-limited dynamic psychotherapy. *Psychotherapy: Theory, Research & Practice, 17*, 52–62.

Bishop, D. R. (1993). Applying psychometric principles to the clinical use of early recollections. *Individual Psychology: The Journal of Adlerian Theory, Research & Practice, 49*, 153–165.

Blonsky, P. (1929). Das problem der ersten kindheitserinnerung und seine bedeutung [The problem of earliest childhood memories and their significance]. *Archive fuer die Gesamte Psychologie, 71*, 369–390.

Bohart, A. C., & Greenberg, L. S. (1997). Empathy: Where are we and where do we go from here? In A. C. Bohart & L. S. Greenberg (Eds.), *Empathy reconsidered: New directions in psychotherapy* (pp. 419–449). Washington, DC: American Psychological Association.

Borden, B. L. (1982). Early recollections as a diagnostic technique with primary age children. *Journal of Individual Psychology, 38,* 207–212.

Bottome, P. (1957). *Alfred Adler: A portrait from life* (3rd ed.). New York: Vangard Press. (Original work published 1939)

Bowers, K. S., & Farvolden, P. (1996). Revisiting a century-old Freudian slip—From suggestion disavowed to the truth repressed. *Psychological Bulletin, 119,* 355–380.

Brewin, C. R., Andrews, B., & Gotlib, I. H. (1993). Psychopathology and early experience: A reappraisal of retrospective reports. *Psychological Bulletin, 113,* 82–98.

Brodsky, P. (1962). The diagnostic importance of early recollections. *American Journal of Psychotherapy, 6,* 484–493.

Brown, E. C. (1972). Assessment from a humanistic perspective. *Psychotherapy: Theory, Research & Practice, 9,* 103–106.

Bruce, D., Dolan, A., & Phillips-Grant, K. (2000). On the transition from childhood amnesia to the recall of personal memories. *Psychological Science, 11,* 360–364.

Bruhn, A. R. (1981). Children's earliest memories: Their use in clinical practice. *Journal of Personality Assessment, 45,* 258–262.

Bruhn, A. R. (1984). Use of early memories as a projective technique. In P. McReynolds & C. J. Chelume (Eds.), *Advances in psychological assessment* (Vol. 6, pp. 109–150). San Francisco: Jossey-Bass.

Bruhn, A. R. (1985). Using early memories as a projective technique—the cognitive perceptual method. *Journal of Personality Assessment, 49,* 587–597.

Bruhn, A. R. (1990a). Cognitive-perceptual theory and the projective use of autobiographical memory. *Journal of Personality Assessment, 55,* 95–114.

Bruhn, A. R. (1990b). *Earliest childhood memories: Theory and application to clinical practice* (Vol. 1). New York: Praeger.

Bruhn, A. R. (1992a). The Early Memories Procedure: A projective test of autobiographical memory, Part 1. *Journal of Personality Assessment, 58,* 1–15.

Bruhn, A. R. (1992b). The Early Memories Procedure: A projective test of autobiographical memory, Part 2. *Journal of Personality Assessment, 58,* 326–346.

Bruhn, A. R. (1995a). Early memories in personality assessment. In J. N. Butcher (Ed.), *Clinical personality assessment: Practical approaches* (pp. 278–301). New York: Oxford University Press.

Bruhn, A. R. (1995b). Ideographic aspects of injury memories: Applying contextual theory to the Comprehensive Early Memories Scoring System-Revised. *Journal of Personality Assessment, 65,* 195–236.

Bruhn, A. R. (1998). Early memories and maladjustment: Comment on Spirrison et al. and recalled age of earliest memory. *Psychological Reports, 82,* 1287–1292.

Bruhn, A. R., & Bellow, S. (1984). Warrior, general, and president: Dwight David Eisenhower and his earliest recollections. *Journal of Personality Assessment, 48,* 371–377.

Bruhn, A. R., & Bellow, S. (1987). The cognitive-perceptual approach to the interpretation of early memories: The earliest memories of Golda Meir. In J. N. Butcher & C. D. Spielberger (Eds.), *Advances in personality assessment* (Vol. 6, pp. 69–87). Hillsdale, NJ: Lawrence Erlbaum.

Bruhn, A. R., & Davidow, S. (1983). Earliest memories and the dynamics of delinquency. *Journal of Personality Assessment, 47,* 476–482.

Bruhn, A. R., & Last, J. (1982). Earliest childhood memories: Four theoretical perspectives. *Journal of Personality Assessment, 46,* 119–127.

Bruhn, A. R., & Schiffman, H. (1982a). Invalid assumptions and methodological difficulties in early memory research. *Journal of Personality Assessment, 46,* 265–267.

Bruhn, A. R., & Schiffman, H. (1982b). Prediction of locus of control stance from the earliest childhood memory. *Journal of Personality Assessment, 46,* 380–390.

Buchanan, L. P., Kern, R., & Bell-Dumas, J. (1991). Comparison of content in created versus actual early recollections. *Individual Psychology: The Journal of Adlerian Theory, Research & Practice, 47*, 348–355.

Burnell, G. M., & Solomon, G. F. (1964). Early memories and ego function. *Archives of General Psychiatry, 11*, 556–567.

Capuzzi, D., & Gross, D. R. (Eds). (1999). *Counseling and psychotherapy: Theories and interventions* (2nd ed.). Upper Saddle River, NJ: Merrill/Prentice Hall.

Carlson, J., & Dinkmeyer, D., Sr. (1999). Couple therapy. In R. E. Watts & J. Carlson (Eds.), *Interventions and strategies in counseling and psychotherapy* (pp. 87–100). Philadelphia: Taylor & Francis.

Carlson, J., & Sperry, L. (2001). Adlerian counseling theory and practice. In D. C. Locke, J. E. Myers, & E. L. Herr (Eds.), *The handbook of counseling* (pp. 171–179). Thousand Oaks, CA: Sage.

Carson, A. D. (1994). Early memories of scientists: Loss of faith in God and Santa Claus. *Individual Psychology: The Journal of Adlerian Theory, Research & Practice, 50*, 149–160.

Caruso, J. C., & Spirrison, C. L. (1994). Early memories, normal personality variation, and coping. *Journal of Personality Assessment, 63*, 517–533.

Caruso, J. C., & Spirrison, C. L. (1996). Reported earliest memory age: Relationships with personality and coping variables. *Personality and Individual Differences, 21*, 135–142.

Cates, J. A. (1999). The art of assessment in psychology: Ethics, expertise, and validity. *Journal of Clinical Psychology, 55*, 631–641.

Chance, J. E. (1957). Some correlates of affective tone of early memories. *Journal of Consulting Psychology, 21*, 203–205.

Chandler, L. A., & Johnson, V. J. (1991). *Using projective techniques with children: A guide to clinical assessment*. Springfield, IL: Charles C Thomas.

Chaplin, M. P., & Orlofsky, J. L. (1991). Personality characteristics of male alcoholics as revealed through their early recollections. *Individual Psychology: The Journal of Adlerian Theory, Research & Practice, 47*, 356–371.

Chesney, S. M., Fakouri, M. E., & Hafner, J. L. (1986). The relationship between early recollections and willingness/unwillingness of alcoholics to continue treatment. *Individual Psychology: The Journal of Adlerian Theory, Research & Practice, 42*, 395–403.

Chess, S. (1951). Utilization of childhood memories in psychoanalytic therapy. *Journal of Child Psychiatry, 2*, 187–193.

Child, I. L. (1940). The relation between measures of infantile amnesia and of neuroticism. *Journal of Abnormal and Social Psychology, 35*, 453–456.

Christie, A. (1977). *Agatha Christie: An autobiography*. New York: Balentine Books.

Claiborn, C. D., & Hanson, W. E. (1999). Test interpretation: A social influence perspective. In J. W. Lichtenberg & R. K. Goodyear (Eds.), *Scientist–practitioner perspectives on test interpretation* (pp. 151–166). Boston: Allyn & Bacon.

Clark, A. J. (1991). The identification and modification of defense mechanisms in counseling. *Journal of Counseling & Development, 69*, 231–236.

Clark, A. J. (1992). Defense mechanisms in group counseling. *Journal for Specialists in Group Work, 17*, 151–160.

Clark, A. J. (1993). Interpretation in group counseling: Theoretical and operational issues. *Journal for Specialists in Group Work, 18*, 174–181.

Clark, A. J. (1994a). Early recollections: A personality tool for elementary school counselors. *Elementary School Guidance and Counseling, 29*, 92–101.

Clark, A. J. (1994b). Working with dreams in group counseling: Advantages and challenges. *Journal of Counseling & Development, 73*, 141–144.

Clark, A. J. (1995a). An examination of the technique of interpretation in counseling. *Journal of Counseling & Development, 73*, 483–490.

Clark, A. J. (1995b). Projective identification in counselling: Theoretical and therapeutic considerations. *Canadian Journal of Counselling, 29*, 37–49.

Clark, A. J. (1995c). Projective techniques in the counseling process. *Journal of Counseling & Development, 73*, 311–316.

Clark, A. J. (1995d). Techniques in the counseling process with adolescents. In K. V. Chandras (Ed.), *Handbook on counseling adolescents, adults and older persons* (pp. 13–22). Alexandria, VA: American Counseling Association.

Clark, A. J. (1997). Projective identification as a defense mechanism in group counseling and therapy. *Journal for Specialists in Group Work, 22*, 85–96.

Clark, A. J. (1998a). *Defense mechanisms in the counseling process*. Thousand Oaks, CA: Sage.

Clark, A. J. (1998b). Reframing: A therapeutic technique in group counseling. *Journal for Specialists in Group Work, 23*, 66–73.

Clark, A. J. (1999a). Safeguarding tendencies: A clarifying perspective. *The Journal of Individual Psychology, 55*, 72–81.

Clark, A. J. (1999b). Theoretical and practical issues in working with children's dreams in counseling. *Journal of Humanistic Education and Development, 37*, 160–168.

Clark, A. J. (2000). Safeguarding tendencies: Implications for the counseling process. *The Journal of Individual Psychology, 56*, 192–204.

Clark, A. J. (2001). Early recollections: A humanistic assessment in counseling. *Journal of Humanistic Counseling, Education and Development, 40*, 96–104.

Clark, A. J. (2002). The defense never rests. In L. B. Golden (Ed.), *Case studies in child and adolescent counseling* (pp. 48–59). Upper Saddle River, NJ: Merrill/Prentice Hall.

Cohen, K. N., & Clark, J. A. (1984). Transitional object attachments in early childhood and personality characteristics in later life. *Journal of Personality and Social Psychology, 46*, 106–111.

Colegrove, F. W. (1899). Individual memories. *American Journal of Psychology, 10*, 228–255.

Colker, J. O., & Slaymaker, F. L. (1984). Reliability of idiographic interpretation of early recollections and their nomothetic validation with drug abusers. *Individual Psychology: The Journal of Adlerian Theory, Research & Practice, 40*, 36–44.

Coram, G. J., & Shields, D. J. (1987). Early recollections of criminal justice majors and nonmajors. *Psychological Reports, 60*, 1287–1290.

Coram, G. J., & Hafner, J. L. (1988). Early recollections and hypnosis. *Individual Psychology: The Journal of Adlerian Theory, Research & Practice, 44*, 472–480.

Cormier, S., & Cormier, B. (1998). *Interviewing strategies for helpers: Fundamental skills and cognitive behavioral interventions* (4th ed.). Pacific Grove, CA: Brooks/Cole.

Corsini, R. J., & Wedding, D. (Eds.). (2000). *Current psychotherapies* (6th ed.). Itasca, IL: F. E. Peacock.

Cowan, N., & Davidson, G. (1984). Salient childhood memories. *Journal of Genetic Psychology, 145*, 101–107.

Craddick, R. A. (1972). Humanistic assessment: A reply to Brown. *Psychotherapy: Theory, Research & Practice, 9*, 107–110.

Crook, G. H. (1925). Memory of infantile life—A scrap of personal experience. *Journal of Abnormal and Social Psychology, 20*, 90–91.

Crook, M. N., & Harden, L. (1931). A quantitative investigation of early memories. *Journal of Social Psychology, 2*, 252–255.

Crovitz, H. F., & Quina-Holland, K. (1976). Proportion of episodic memories from early childhood by years of age. *Bulletin of the Psychonomic Society, 7*, 61–62.

Cummings, J. A. (1986). Projective drawings. In H. M. Knoff (Ed.), *The assessment of child and adolescent personality* (pp. 199–244). New York: The Guilford Press.

Dana, R. H. (1995). Impact of the use of standard psychological assessment on the diagnosis and treatment of ethnic minorities. In J. F. Aponte, R. Y. Rivers, & J. Wohl (Eds.), *Psycho-*

logical interventions and cultural diversity (pp. 57–73). Boston: Allyn and Bacon.

Dana, R. H. (2000). Culture and methodology in personality assessment. In I. Cuéllar & F. A. Paniagua (Eds.), *Handbook of multicultural mental health: Assessment and treatment of diverse populations* (pp. 97–120). San Diego, CA: Academic Press.

Davidow, S., & Bruhn, A. R. (1990). Earliest memories and the dynamics of delinquency: A replication study. *Journal of Personality Assessment, 54*, 601–616.

Demuth, P. W., & Bruhn, A. R. (1997). The use of the early memories procedure in a psychotherapy group of substance abusers. *International Journal of Offender Therapy and Comparative Criminology, 41*, 24–35.

Dinkmeyer, D., Jr., & Sperry, L. (2000). *Counseling and psychotherapy: An integrated, individual psychology approach* (3rd ed.). Upper Saddle River, NJ: Merrill/Prentice Hall.

Douglas, C. (2000). Analytical psychotherapy. In R. J. Corsini & D. Wedding (Eds.), *Current psychotherapies* (6th ed., pp. 99–132). Itasca, IL: F. E. Peacock.

Dowd, E. T., & Kelly, F. D. (1980). Adlerian psychology and cognitive-behavior therapy: Convergences. *Journal of Individual Psychology, 36*, 119–135.

Doyle, R. E. (1998). *Essential skills and strategies in the helping process* (2nd ed.). Pacific Grove, CA: Brooks/Cole.

Dreikurs, R. (1958). Minor psychotherapy, a practical psychology for physicians. *Transactions of the Academy of Psychosomatic Medicine, 5*, 253–260.

Dreikurs, R. (1961). The Adlerian approach to therapy. In M. I. Stein (Ed.), *Contemporary psychotherapies* (pp. 80–94). New York: The Free Press of Glencoe.

Dreikurs, R. (1967). *Psychodynamics, psychotherapy, and counseling: Collected papers of Rudolph Dreikurs*. Chicago: Alfred Adler Institute of Chicago.

DuBreuil, S. C., Garry, M., & Loftus, E. F. (1998). Tales from the crib: Age regression and the creation of unlikely memories. In S. J. Lynn & K. M. McConkey (Eds.), *Truth in memory* (pp. 137–160). New York: The Guilford Press.

Dudycha, G. J., & Dudycha, M. M. (1933a). Adolescents' memories of preschool experiences. *Journal of Genetic Psychology, 42*, 468–480.

Dudycha, G. J., & Dudycha, M. M. (1933b). Some factors and characteristics of childhood memories. *Child Development, 4*, 265–278.

Dudycha, G. J., & Dudycha, M. M. (1941). Childhood memories: A review of the literature. *Psychological Bulletin, 38*, 668–682.

Dutton, W. A., & Newlon, B. J. (1988). Early recollections and sexual fantasies of adolescent sex offenders. *Individual Psychology: The Journal of Adlerian Theory, Research & Practice, 44*, 85–94.

Eacott, M. J. (1990). Memory for the events of early childhood. *Current Directions in Psychological Science, 8*, 46–49.

Eacott, M. J., & Crawley, R. A. (1998). The offset of childhood amnesia: Memory for events that occurred before age 3. *Journal of Experimental Psychology: General, 127*, 22–33.

Eckstein, D. (1999). An early recollections skill building workshop. *The Journal of Individual Psychology, 55*, 437–448.

Eckstein, D., Baruth, L., & Mahrer, D. (Eds.). (1982). *Life style: What it is and how to do it* (2nd ed.). Dubuque, IA: Kendall/Hunt.

Eckstein, D. G. (1976). Early recollection changes after counseling: A case study. *Journal of Individual Psychology, 32*, 212–223.

Eckstein, D. G. (1980). The use of early recollections in group counseling. *Journal for Specialists in Group Work, 5*, 87–92.

Eckstein, D. G., & Springer, T. P. (1981). Early recollections and social interest in psychology students. In L. G. Baruth & D. G. Eckstein (Eds.), *Life style: Theory, practice, and research* (pp. 132–134). Dubuque, IA: Kendall/Hunt.

Edwards, D. J. A. (1990). Cognitive therapy and the restructuring of early memories through guided imagery. *Journal of Cognitive Psychotherapy: An International Quarterly, 4,* 33–50.

Egan, G. (2002). *The skilled helper: A problem-management and opportunity-development approach to helping* (7th ed.). Pacific Grove, CA: Brooks/Cole.

Eisengart, S. P., & Faiver, C. M. (1996). Intuition in mental health counseling. *Journal of Mental Health Counseling, 18,* 41–52.

Eisenstein, V. W., & Ryerson, R. (1951). Psychodynamic significance of the first conscious memory. *Bulletin of the Menninger Clinic, 15,* 213–220.

Ellenberger, H. F. (1970). *The discovery of the unconscious: The history and evolution of dynamic psychiatry.* New York: Basic Books.

Elliot, D., Amerikaner, M., & Swank, P. (1987). Early recollections and the Vocational Preference Inventory as predictors of vocational choice. *Individual Psychology: The Journal of Adlerian Theory, Research & Practice, 43,* 353–359.

Elliot, W. N., Fakouri, M. E., & Hafner, J. L. (1993). Early recollections of criminal offenders. *Individual Psychology: The Journal of Adlerian Theory, Research & Practice, 49,* 68–75.

Ellis, A. (2000). Rational emotive behavior therapy. In R. J. Corsini & D. Wedding (Eds.), *Current psychotherapies* (6th ed., pp. 168–204). Itasca, IL: F. E. Peacock.

Emerson, P., West, J. D., & Gintner, G. G. (1991). An Adlerian perspective on cognitive restructuring and treating depression. *Journal of Cognitive Psychotherapy: An International Quarterly, 5,* 41–53.

Enns, C. Z. (2001). Some reflections on imagery and psychotherapy implications. *Journal of Counseling Psychology, 48,* 136–139.

Epstein, R. (1963). Social class membership and early childhood memories. *Child Development, 34,* 503–508.

Ewen, R. B. (1998). *An introduction to theories of personality* (5th ed.). Mahwah, NJ: Lawrence Erlbaum.

Faidley, A. J., & Leitner, L. M. (1993). *Assessing experience in psychotherapy: Personal construct alternatives.* Westport, CT: Praeger.

Fakouri, C. H., Fakouri, M. E., & Hafner, J. L. (1986). Early recollections of women preparing for nursing careers. *Perceptual and Motor Skills, 63,* 264–266.

Fakouri, M. E., & Hafner, J. L. (1984). Early recollections of first-borns. *Journal of Clinical Psychology, 40,* 209–213.

Fakouri, M. E., & Hafner, J. L. (1994). Adlerian-oriented early recollection studies: What do we ask? *Individual Psychology: The Journal of Adlerian Theory, Research & Practice, 50,* 170–172.

Fakouri, M. E., Hartung, J. R., & Hafner, J. L. (1985). Early recollections of neurotic depressive patients. *Psychological Reports, 57,* 783–786.

Fakouri, M. E., & Zucker, K. B. (1987). The affective components of early recollections and current social perceptions: Are they related? *Individual Psychology: The Journal of Adlerian Theory, Research & Practice, 43,* 18–23.

Farrell, R. A. (1984). Deviance imputations, early recollections and the reconstruction of self. *International Journal of Social Psychiatry, 30,* 189–199.

Feichtinger, F. (1943). Early recollections in neurotic disturbances. *Individual Psychology Bulletin, 3,* 44–51.

Ferguson, E. D. (1964). The use of early recollections for assessing life style and diagnosing psychopathology. *Journal of Projective Techniques and Personality Assessment, 28,* 403–412.

Finn, S. E., & Tonsager, M. E. (1997). Information-gathering and therapeutic models of assessment: Complimentary paradigms. *Psychological Assessment, 9,* 374–385.

Forer, L. K. (1977). The use of birth order information in psychotherapy. *Journal of Individual Psychology, 33,* 105–113.

Fowler, C. (1994). A pragmatic approach to early childhood memories: Shifting the focus from truth to clinical utility. *Psychotherapy, 31*, 676–686.

Fowler, C., Hilsenroth, M. J., & Handler, L. (1995). Early memories: An exploration of theoretically derived queries and their clinical utility. *Bulletin of the Menninger Clinic, 59*, 79–98.

Fowler, C., Hilsenroth, M. J., & Handler, L. (1996a). A multimethod approach to assessing dependency: The Early Memory Dependency Probe. *Journal of Personality Assessment, 67*, 399–413.

Fowler, C., Hilsenroth, M. J., & Handler, L. (1996b). Two methods of early memories data collection: An empirical comparison of the projective yield. *Assessment, 3*, 63–71.

Fowler, C., Hilsenroth, M. J., & Handler, L. (1998). Assessing transitional phenomena with the transitional object memory probe. *Bulletin of the Menninger Clinic, 62*, 455–475.

Fowler, J. C., Hilsenroth, M. J., & Handler, L. (2000). Martin Mayman's early memories technique: Bridging the gap between personality assessment and psychotherapy. *Journal of Personality Assessment, 75*, 18–32.

Francis, M. (1995). Childhood's garden: Memory and meaning of gardens. *Children's Environments, 12*, 183–191.

Freeman, A., & Urschel, J. (1997). Individual psychology and cognitive behavior therapy: A cognitive therapy perspective. *Journal of Cognitive Psychotherapy: An International Quarterly, 11*, 165–179.

Freud, A. (1966). *The ego and the mechanisms of defense* (Rev. ed.). New York: International Universities Press. (Original work published 1936)

Freud, S. (1953). Three essays on the theory of sexuality. In J. Strachey (Ed. and Trans.), *The standard edition of the complete psychological works of Sigmund Freud* (Vol. 7, pp. 135–243). London: Hogarth. (Original work published 1905)

Freud, S. (1955). A childhood recollection from Dichtung und Wahrheit. In J. Strachey (Ed. and Trans.), *The standard edition of the complete psychological works of Sigmund Freud* (Vol. 17, pp. 147–156). London: Hogarth. (Original work published 1917)

Freud, S. (1957). Leonardo da Vinci and a memory of his childhood. In J. Strachey (Ed. and Trans.), *The standard edition of the complete psychological works of Sigmund Freud* (Vol. 11, pp. 63–137). London: Hogarth. (Original work published 1910)

Freud, S. (1960). The psychopathology of everyday life. In J. Strachey (Ed. and Trans.), *The standard edition of the complete psychological works of Sigmund Freud* (Vol. 6, pp. 43–52). London: Hogarth. (Original work published 1901)

Freud, S. (1962). The aetiology of hysteria. In J. Strachey (Ed. and Trans.), *The standard edition of the complete psychological works of Sigmund Freud* (Vol. 3, pp. 191–221). London: Hogarth. (Original work published 1896)

Freud, S. (1962). Screen memories. In J. Strachey (Ed. and Trans.), *The standard edition of the complete psychological works of Sigmund Freud* (Vol. 3, pp. 303–322). London: Hogarth. (Original work published 1899)

Fried, E. (1989). *Active/passive: The crucial psychological dimension.* New York: Brunner/Mazel. (Original work published 1970)

Friedberg, R. L. (1975). Early recollections of homosexuals as indicators of their life styles. *Journal of Individual Psychology, 31*, 196–204.

Friedman, J., & Schiffman, H. (1962). Early recollections of schizophrenic and depressed patients. *Journal of Individual Psychology, 18*, 57–61.

Friedmann, A. (1935). First recollections of school. *International Journal of Individual Psychology, 1*, 111–116.

Friedmann, A. (1950). Early childhood memories of mental patients: Preliminary report. *Individual Psychology Bulletin, 8*, 111–116.

Friedmann, A. (1952). Early childhood memories of mental patients. *Journal of Child Psychiatry, 2*, 266–269.

Gilliland, B. E., & James, R. K. (1998). *Theories and strategies in counseling and psychotherapy* (4th ed.). Boston: Allyn and Bacon.

Ginter, E. J., & Bonney, W. (1993). Freud, ESP, and interpersonal relationships: Projective identification and the Möbius interaction. *Journal of Mental Health Counseling, 15,* 150–169.

Glover, E. (1929). The "screening" function of traumatic memories. *International Journal of Psychoanalysis, 10,* 90–93.

Goethe, J. W. (1872). *The auto-biography of Goethe: Truth and poetry: From my own life* (J. Oxenford, Trans.). London: Bell & Daldy. (Original work published 1811)

Gold, E. & Neisser, U. (1980). Recollections of kindergarten. *The Quarterly Newsletter of the Laboratory of Comparative Human Cognition, 2,* 77–80.

Gold, L. (1979). Adler's theory of dreams: An holistic approach to interpretation. In B. B. Wolman (Ed.), *Handbook of dreams: Research, theories, and applications* (pp. 319–341). New York: Van Nostrand Reinhold.

Goldman, L. (1990). Qualitative assessment. *The Counseling Psychologist, 18,* 205–213.

Goodman, G. S., & Clarke-Stewart, A. (1991). Suggestibility in children's testimony: Implications for sexual abuse investigations. In J. Doris (Ed.), *The suggestibility of children's recollections: Implications for eyewitness testimony* (pp. 92–105). Washington, DC: American Psychological Association.

Goodnow, J. (1977). *Children drawing.* Cambridge, MA: Harvard University Press.

Gordon, K. (1928). A study of early memories. *The Journal of Delinquency, 12,* 129–132.

Greenacre, P. (1949). A contribution to the study of screen memories. *Psychoanalytic Study of the Child, 3–4,* 73–84.

Grunberg, J. (1989). Early recollections and criminal behavior in mentally-ill homeless men. *Individual Psychology: The Journal of Adlerian Theory, Research & Practice, 45,* 289–299.

Gushurst, R. S. (1971). The technique, utility, and validity of life style analysis. *The Counseling Psychologist, 3,* 30–40.

Hackney, H. L., & Cormier, L. S. (2001). *The professional counselor: A process guide to helping* (4th ed.). Boston: Allyn and Bacon.

Hadfield, J. A. (1928). The reliability of infantile memories. *British Journal of Medical Psychology, 8,* 87–111.

Hafner, J. L., & Fakouri, M. E. (1978). Early recollections, present crises, and future plans in psychotic patients. *Psychological Reports, 43,* 927–930.

Hafner, J. L., Corotto, L. V, & Fakouri, M. E. (1980). Early recollections of schizophrenics. *Psychological Reports, 46,* 408–410.

Hafner, J. L., & Fakouri, M. E. (1984a). Early recollections of individuals preparing for careers in clinical psychology, dentistry, and law. *Journal of Vocational Behavior, 24,* 236–241.

Hafner, J. L., & Fakouri, M. E. (1984b). Early recollections and vocational choice. *Individual Psychology: The Journal of Adlerian Theory, Research & Practice, 40,* 54–60.

Hafner, J. L., Fakouri, M. E., & Chesney, S. M. (1988). Early recollections of alcoholic women. *Journal of Clinical Psychology, 44,* 302–306.

Hafner, J. L., Fakouri, M. E., & Etzler, D. R. (1986). Early recollections of individuals preparing for careers in chemical, electrical, and mechanical engineering. *Individual Psychology: The Journal of Adlerian Theory, Research & Practice, 42,* 360–366.

Hafner, J. L., Fakouri, M. E., & Labrentz, H. L. (1982). First memories of "normal" and alcoholic individuals. *Individual Psychology: The Journal of Adlerian Theory, Research & Practice, 38,* 238–244.

Hafner, J. L., Fakouri, M. E., Ollendick, T. H., & Corotto, L. V. (1979). First memories of "normal" and of schizophrenic, paranoid-type individuals. *Journal of Clinical Psychology, 35,* 731–733.

Hall, G. S. (1899). Note on early memories. *Pedagogical Seminary, 6,* 485–512.

Hampl, P. (1981). *A romantic education*. Boston: Houghton Mifflin.

Hanawalt, N. G., & Gebhardt, L. J. (1965). Childhood memories of single and recurrent incidents. *Journal of Genetic Psychology, 107*, 85–89.

Handler, L. (1996). The clinical use of drawings. In C. S. Newmark (Ed.), *Major psychological assessment instruments* (2nd ed., pp. 206–293). Boston: Allyn & Bacon.

Hankoff, L. D. (1987). The earliest memories of criminals. *International Journal of Offender Therapy and Comparative Criminology, 31*, 195–201.

Harder, D. W. (1979). The assessment of ambitious–narcissistic character style with three projective tests: The Early Memories, TAT, and Rorschach. *Journal of Personality Assessment, 43*, 23–32.

Hart, D. H. (1986). The sentence completion techniques. In H. M. Knoff (Ed.), *The assessment of child and adolescent personality* (pp. 245–272). New York: The Guilford Press.

Hayes, S. C., Nelson, R. O., & Jarrett, R. B. (1987). The treatment utility of assessment: A functional approach to evaluating assessment quality. *American Psychologist, 42*, 963–974.

Hedvig, E. B. (1963). Stability of early recollections and Thematic Apperception stories. *Journal of Individual Psychology, 19*, 49–54.

Hedvig, E. B. (1965). Children's early recollections as a basis for diagnosis. *Journal of Individual Psychology, 21*, 187–188.

Heidt, H. M. (1997). Using drawings of early recollections to facilitate life style analysis for children in play therapy. In H. G. Kaduson & C. E. Schaefer (Eds.), *101 favorite play therapy techniques* (pp. 327–332). Northvale, NJ: Jason Aronson.

Heinemann, E. (1939). Das erste schuljahr in der erinnerung des erwachsenen [Adults' recollections of their first year of school]. *Zeitschrift fuer Kinderforschung, 48*, 22–71.

Henderson, E. N. (1911). Do we forget the disagreeable? *The Journal of Philosophy, Psychology and Scientific Methods, 8*, 432–437.

Hennig, R. (1937). Die zahl der datierbaren erinnerungen eines menschenlebens [The number of datable memories in a human life]. *Zeitschrift fuer Psychologie, 140*, 330–356.

Henri, V. (1895a). On our earliest recollections of childhood. *Psychological Review, 2*, 215–216.

Henri, V. (1895b). Our earliest memories. *American Journal of Psychology, 7*, 303–305.

Henri, V., & Henri, C. (1896). Enquête sur les premiers souvenirs de l'enfance [Inquiry into the first memories of childhood]. *Année Psychologique, 3*, 184–198.

Henri, V., & Henri, C. (1898). Earliest recollections. *Popular Science Monthly, 53*, 108–115.

Hersztejn-Korzeniowa, H. (1935). O Najwcześniejszych wspomnieniach z dzieciństwa [On the memory of the earliest childhood experiences]. *Kwartalnik Psychologiczny, 7*, 243–274.

Holaday, M., Smith, D. A., & Sherry, A. (2000). Sentence completion tests: A review of the literature and results of a survey of members of the Society for Personality Assessment. *Journal of Personality Assessment, 74*, 371–383.

Holmes, D. S. (1965). Security feelings and affective tone of early recollections: A re-evaluation. *Journal of Projective Techniques & Personality Assessment, 29*, 314–318.

Holmes, D. S., & Watson, R. I. (1965). Early recollection and vocational choice. *Journal of Consulting Psychology, 29*, 486–488.

Hood, A. B., & Johnson, R. W. (2002). *Assessment in counseling: A guide to the use of psychological assessment procedures* (3rd ed.). Alexandria, VA: American Counseling Association.

Horner, A. J. (1997). Belief systems and the analytic work. *American Journal of Psychoanalysis, 57*, 75–78.

Horowitz, M. J. (1991). Person schemas. In M. J. Horowitz (Ed.), *Person schemas and maladaptive interpersonal patterns* (pp. 13–31). Chicago: University of Chicago Press.

Horton, C. B., & Cruise, T. K. (1997). Clinical assessment of child victims and adult survivors of child maltreatment. *Journal of Counseling & Development, 76*, 94–104.

Howe, M. L. (2000). *The fate of early memories: Developmental science and the retention of childhood experiences.* Washington, DC: American Psychological Association.

Howell, R. J. (1965). A verified childhood memory elicited during hypnosis. *American Journal of Clinical Hypnosis, 8,* 141–142.

Howes, M., Siegel, M., & Brown, F. (1993). Early childhood memories: Accuracy and affect. *Cognition, 47,* 95–119.

Huyghe, P. (1985, September). Voices, glances, flashbacks: Our first memories. *Psychology Today, 19,* 48–52.

Hyer, L., Woods, M. G., & Boudewyns, P. A. (1989). Early recollections of Vietnam veterans with PTSD. *Individual Psychology: The Journal of Adlerian Theory, Research & Practice, 45,* 300–312.

Hyman, I. E., Jr., & Pentland, J. (1996). The role of mental imagery in the creation of false childhood memories. *Journal of Memory and Language, 35,* 101–107.

Ilgenfritz, C. W. (1979). Ann: A case of dependency and depression. In H. A. Olson (Ed.), *Early recollections: Their use in diagnosis and psychotherapy* (pp. 321–324). Springfield, IL: Charles C Thomas.

Ivey, A. E. (1991). *Developmental strategies for helpers: Individual, family and network interventions.* Pacific Grove, CA: Brooks/Cole.

Ivey, A. E., D'Andrea, M., Ivey, M. B., & Simek-Morgan, L. (2002). *Theories of counseling and psychotherapy: A multicultural perspective* (5th ed.). Boston: Allyn and Bacon.

Ivey, A. E., & Ivey, M. B. (1999). *Intentional interviewing and counseling: Facilitating client development in a multicultural society* (4th ed.). Pacific Grove, CA: Brooks/Cole.

Ivimey, M. (1950). Childhood memories in psychoanalysis. *American Journal of Psychoanalysis, 10,* 38–47.

Jackson, M., & Sechrest, L. (1962). Early recollections in four neurotic diagnostic categories. *Journal of Individual Psychology, 18,* 52–56.

Janoe, E., & Janoe, B. (1979). Using early recollections with children. In H. A. Olson (Ed.), *Early recollections: Their use in diagnosis and psychotherapy* (pp. 230–234). Springfield, IL: Charles C Thomas.

Jones, J. V., Jr., & Lyddon, W. J. (1997). Adlerian and constructivist psychotherapies: A constructivist perspective. *Journal of Cognitive Psychotherapy: An International Quarterly, 11,* 195–210.

Josselson, R. (1982). Personality structure and identity status in women as viewed through early memories. *Journal of Youth and Adolescence, 11,* 293–299.

Josselson, R. (2000). Stability and change in early memories over 22 years: Themes, variations, and cadenzas. *Bulletin of the Menninger Clinic, 64,* 462–481.

Kadis, A. L. (1958). Early childhood recollections as aids in group psychotherapy. *Journal of Individual Psychology, 13,* 182–187.

Kadis, A. L., Greene, J. S., & Freedman, N. (1952). Early childhood recollections—An integrative technique of personality test data. *The American Journal of Individual Psychology, 53,* 31–42.

Kadis, A. L., & Lazarsfeld, S. (1948). The respective roles of "earliest recollections" and "images." *American Journal of Psychotherapy, 2,* 250–255.

Kahana, R. J., Weiland, I. H., Snyder, B., & Rosenbaum, M. (1953). The value of early memories in psychotherapy. *The Psychiatric Quarterly, 27,* 73–82.

Kal, E. F. (1994). Reaction to "Applying psychometric principles to the clinical use of early recollections" by D. Russell Bishop. *Individual Psychology: The Journal of Adlerian Theory, Research & Practice, 50,* 256–261.

Kaplan, H. B. (1985). A method for the interpretation of early recollections and dreams. *Individual Psychology: The Journal of Adlerian Theory, Research & Practice, 41,* 525–532.

Karliner, R., Westrich, E. K., Shedler, J., & Mayman, M. (1996). Bridging the gap between psychodynamic and scientific psychology: The Aldelphi Early Memory Index. In J. M.

Masling & R. F. Bornstein (Eds.), *Psychoanalytic perspectives on developmental psychology* (pp. 43–67). Washington, DC: American Psychological Association.

Karoly, P. (1993). Goal systems: An organizing framework for clinical assessment and treatment planning. *Psychological Assessment, 5,* 273–280.

Katan, M. (1975). Childhood memories as contents of schizophrenic hallucinations and delusions. *Psychoanalytic Study of the Child, 30,* 357–374.

Kelly, G. A. (1991a). *The psychology of personal constructs: Vol. 1. A theory of personality.* London: Routledge. (Original work published 1955)

Kelly, G. A. (1991b). *The psychology of personal constructs: Vol 2. Clinical diagnosis and psychotherapy.* London: Routledge. (Original work published 1955)

Kennedy, H. E. (1950). Cover memories in formation. *Psychoanalytic Study of the Child, 5,* 275–284.

Kern, R. M., & Eckstein, D. (1997). The early recollections role reversal technique. *Individual Psychology: The Journal of Adlerian Theory, Research & Practice, 53,* 407–417.

Kihlstrom, J. F., & Harackiewicz, J. M. (1982). The earliest recollection: A new survey. *Journal of Personality, 50,* 134–148.

Kissen, M. (1986a). Object relations aspects of human figure drawings. In M. Kissen (Ed.), *Assessing object relations phenomena* (pp. 175–191). Madison, CT: International Universities Press.

Kissen, M. (1986b). Combined use of human figure drawings and the early memories test in assessing object relations phenomena. In M. Kissen (Ed.), *Assessing object relations phenomena* (pp. 193–205). Madison, CT: International Universities Press.

Knapp, P. H. (1991). Self-other schemas: Core organizers of human experience. In M. J. Horowitz (Ed.), *Person schemas and maladaptive interpersonal patterns* (pp. 81–102). Chicago: The University of Chicago Press.

Knapp, S., & VandeCreek, L. (2000). Recovered memories of childhood abuse: Is there an underlying professional consensus? *Professional Psychology: Research and Practice, 31,* 365–371.

Kohut, H. (1977). *The restoration of the self.* New York: International Universities Press.

Kopp, R. R. (1998). Early recollections in Adlerian and metaphor therapy. *The Journal of Individual Psychology, 54,* 480–486.

Kopp, R. R., & Der, D. (1979). Humanistic psychological assessment in psychotherapy. In H. A. Olson (Ed.), *Early recollections: Their use in diagnosis and psychotherapy* (pp. 29–38). Springfield, IL: Charles C Thomas.

Kopp, R. R., & Der, D. (1982). Level of activity in adolescents' early recollections: A validity study. *Individual Psychology: The Journal of Adlerian Theory, Research & Practice, 38,* 213–222.

Kopp, R. R., & Dinkmeyer, D. (1975). Early recollections in life style assessment and counseling. *The School Counselor, 23,* 22–27.

Korner, A. F. (1965). Theoretical considerations concerning the scope and limitations of projective techniques. In B. I. Murstein (Ed.), *Handbook of projective techniques* (pp. 23–34). New York: Basic Books.

Kramer, M., Ornstein, P. H., Whitman, R. M., & Baldridge, B. J. (1967). The contribution of early memories and dreams to the diagnostic process. *Comprehensive Psychiatry, 8,* 344–374.

Kris, E. (1956). The recovery of childhood memories in psychoanalysis. *Psychoanalytic Study of the Child, 11,* 54–88.

Kroger, J. (1990). Ego structuralization in late adolescence as seen through early memories and ego identity status. *Journal of Adolescence, 13,* 65–77.

Krohn, A., & Mayman, M. (1974). Object representations in dreams and projective tests. *Bulletin of the Menninger Clinic, 38,* 445–466.

Lachman, F. M. (1996). How many selves make a person? *Contemporary Psychoanalysis, 32,* 595–614.

LaFountain, R. M. (1996). Social interest: A key to solutions. *Individual Psychology: The Journal of Adlerian Theory, Research & Practice, 52,* 150–157.

LaFountain, R. M., & Garner, N. E. (1998). *A school with solutions: Implementing a solution-focused/Adlerian-based comprehensive school counseling program.* Alexandria, VA: American School Counselor Association.

LaFountain, R. M., & Bartos, R. B. (2002). *Research and statistics made meaningful in counseling and student affairs.* Pacific Grove, CA: Brooks/Cole.

Laird, D. A. (1935). What can you do with your nose? *Scientific Monthly, 41,* 126–130.

Langs, R. J. (1965a). Earliest memories and personality: A predictive study. *Archives of General Psychiatry, 12,* 379–390.

Langs, R. J. (1965b). First memories and characterologic diagnosis. *Journal of Nervous and Mental Disease, 141,* 318–320.

Langs, R. J. (1967). Stability of earliest memories under LSD-25 and placebo. *Journal of Nervous and Mental Disease, 144,* 171–184.

Langs, R. J., Rothenberg, M. B., Fishman, J. R., & Reiser, M. F. (1960). A method for clinical and theoretical study of the earliest memory. *Archives of General Psychiatry, 3,* 523–534.

Laser, E. D. (1984). The relationship between obesity, early recollections, and adult life-style. *Individual Psychology: The Journal of Adlerian Theory, Research & Practice, 40,* 29–35.

Laskowitz, D. (1961). The adolescent drug addict: An Adlerian view. *Journal of Individual Psychology, 17,* 68–79.

Last, J. M. (1997). The clinical utilization of early childhood memories. *American Journal of Psychotherapy, 51,* 376–386.

Last, J. M., & Bruhn, A. R. (1983). The psychodiagnostic value of children's earliest memories. *Journal of Personality Assessment, 47,* 597–603.

Last, J. M., & Bruhn, A. R. (1985). Distinguishing child diagnostic types with early memories. *Journal of Personality Assessment, 49,* 187–192.

LeCron, L. M. (1963). The uncovering of early memories by ideomotor responses to questioning. *International Journal of Clinical and Experimental Hypnosis, 11,* 137–142.

Lee, R. S. (2001). A modified life style assessment and its use in the school setting. *The Journal of Individual Psychology, 57,* 298–309.

Lehmann, H. (1966). Two dreams and a childhood memory of Freud. *Journal of the American Psychoanalytic Association, 14,* 388–405.

Leibowitz, M. (1999). *Interpreting projective drawings: A self psychological approach.* Philadelphia: Taylor & Francis.

Levy, J. (1965). Early memories: Theoretical aspects and application. *Journal of Projective Techniques & Personality Assessment, 29,* 281–291.

Levy, J., & Grigg, K. A. (1962). Early memories: Thematic-configurational analysis. *Archives of General Psychiatry, 7,* 57–69.

Levy, L. H. (1963). *Psychological interpretation.* New York: Holt, Rinehart & Winston.

Lew, A., & Bettner, B. L. (1993). The connexions focusing technique for using early recollections. *Individual Psychology: The Journal of Adlerian Theory, Research & Practice, 49,* 166–184.

Lewy, E., & Rapaport, D. (1944). The psychoanalytic concept of memory and its relation to recent memory theories. *Psychoanalytic Quarterly, 13,* 16–41.

Lieberman, M. G. (1957). Childhood memories as a projective technique. *Journal of Projective Techniques, 21,* 32–36.

Lingg, M., & Kottman, T. (1991). Changing mistaken beliefs through visualization of early recollections. *Individual Psychology: The Journal of Adlerian Theory, Research & Practice, 47,* 255–260.

Liotti, G. (1987). Structural cognitive therapy. In W. Dryden & W. L. Golden (Eds.), *Cognitive behavioral approaches to psychotherapy* (pp. 92–128). London: Hemisphere.

Lombardi, D. N., & Angers, W. P. (1967). First memories of drug addicts. *The Individual Psychologist, 5*, 7–13.

Lord, D. B. (1982). On the clinical use of children's early recollections. *Individual Psychology: The Journal of Adlerian Theory, Research & Practice, 38*, 198–206.

Lord, M. M. (1971). Activity and affect in early memories of adolescent boys. *Journal of Personality Assessment, 35*, 448–456.

Lundy, A., & Potts, T. (1987). Recollection of a transitional object and needs for intimacy and affiliation in adolescents. *Psychological Reports, 60*, 767–773.

Lyddon, W. J. (1990). First- and second-order change: Implications for rationalist and constructivist cognitive therapies. *Journal of Counseling & Development, 69*, 122–127.

Lyddon, W. J., & Satterfield, W. A. (1994). Relation of client attachment to therapist first- and second-order change assessments. *Journal of Cognitive Psychotherapy: An International Quarterly, 8*, 233–242.

Lynn, S. J., Lock, T. G., Myers, B., & Payne, D. G. (1997). Recalling the unrecallable: Should hypnosis be used to recover memories in psychotherapy? *Current Directions in Psychological Science, 6*, 79–83.

Mahoney, M. J. (2000). Core ordering and disordering processes: A constructive view of psychological development. In R. A. Neimeyer & J. D. Raskin (Eds.), *Constructions of disorder: Meaning-making frameworks for psychotherapy* (pp. 43–62). Washington, DC: American Psychological Association.

Malinoski, P., Lynn, S. J., & Sivec, H. (1998). The assessment, validity, and determinants of early memory reports: A critical review. In S. J. Lynn & K. M. McConkey (Eds.), *Truth in memory* (pp. 109–136). New York: The Guilford Press.

Malinoski, P. T., & Lynn, S. J. (1999). The plasticity of early memory reports: Social pressure, hypnotizability, compliance, and interrogative suggestibility. *International Journal of Clinical and Experimental Hypnosis, 47*, 320–345.

Manaster, G. J. (1977). Birth order: An overview. *Journal of Individual Psychology, 33*, 3–8.

Manaster, G. J., Berra, S., & Mays, M. (2001). Manaster–Perryman Early Recollections scoring manual: Findings and summary. *The Journal of Individual Psychology, 57*, 413–419.

Manaster, G. J., & Corsini, R. J. (1982). *Individual psychology: Theory and practice*. Itasca, IL: F.E. Peacock.

Manaster, G. J., & King, M. (1973). Early recollections of male homosexuals. *Journal of Individual Psychology, 29*, 26–33.

Manaster, G. J., & Perryman, T. B. (1974). Early recollections and occupational choice. *Journal of Individual Psychology, 30*, 232–237.

Manaster, G. J., & Perryman, T. B. (1979). Manster–Perryman Manifest Early Recollections scoring manual. In H. A. Olson (Ed.), *Early recollections: Their use in diagnosis and psychotherapy* (pp. 347–353). Springfield, IL: Charles C Thomas.

Maniacci, M., Shulman, B., Griffith, J., Powers, R. L., Sutherland, J., Dushman, R., & Schneider, M. F. (1998). Early recollections: Mining the personal story in the process of change. *The Journal of Individual Psychology, 54*, 451–479.

Mansager, E., Barnes, M., Boyce, B., Brewster, J. D., Lertora, H. J., III, Marais, F., Santos, J., & Thompson, D. (1995). Interactive discussion of early recollections: A group technique with adolescent substance abusers. *Individual Psychology: The Journal of Adlerian Theory, Research & Practice, 51*, 413–421.

Mansager, E., & Volk, R. (1995). The application of early recollections in intense psycho-educational parenting sessions. *Individual Psychology: The Journal of Adlerian Theory, Research & Practice, 51*, 375–385.

Marcus, K. (1965). Early childhood experiences remembered by adult analysands. *Journal of Analytical Psychology, 10*, 163–172.

Marcus, H. (1980). The self in thought and memory. In D. M. Wegner & R. R. Vallacher (Eds.), *The self in social psychology* (pp. 102–130). New York: Oxford University Press.

Marcus, M. B., Manaster, G. J., & Spencer, D. (1999). Client and counselor-trainee early recollections: A manifest content comparison. *The Journal of Individual Psychology, 55*, 82–90.

Markowsky, G. J., & Pence, A. R. (1997). Looking back: Early adolescents' recollections of their preschool day care experiences. *Early Child Development and Care, 135*, 123–143.

Martin, P. A. (1959). One type of earliest memory. *Psychoanalytic Quarterly, 28*, 73–77.

Maslow, A. (1966). *The psychology of science: A reconnaissance.* New York: Harper & Row.

Maslow, A. H. (1942). The dynamics of psychological security–insecurity. *Character and Personality, 10*, 331–344.

Masson, J. M. (1984). *The assault on truth: Freud's suppression of the seduction theory.* New York: Farrar, Strauss and Giroux.

May, R. (1953). *Man's search for himself.* New York: W.W. Norton.

Mayman, M. (1968). Early memories and character structure. *Journal of Projective Techniques & Personality Assessment, 32*, 303–316.

Mayman, M., & Faris, M. (1960). Early memories as expressions of relationship paradigms. *American Journal of Orthopsychiatry, 30*, 507–520.

McCabe, A., Capron, E., & Peterson, C. (1991). The voice of experience: The recall of early childhood and adolescent memories by young adults. In A. McCabe & C. Peterson (Eds.), *Developing narrative structure* (pp. 137–173). Hillsdale, NJ: Lawrence Erlbaum.

McCarter, R. E., Schiffman, H. M., & Tomkins, S. S. (1961). Early recollections as predictors of Tomkins-Horn Picture Arrangement Test performance. *Journal of Individual Psychology, 17*, 177–180.

McFarland, M. (1988). Early recollections discriminate persons in two occupations: Medical technology and nursing. *Individual Psychology: The Journal of Adlerian Theory, Research & Practice, 44*, 77–84.

McKelvie, W. H. (1979). Career counseling with early recollections. In H. A. Olson (Ed.), *Early recollections: Their use in diagnosis and psychotherapy* (pp. 99–118). Springfield, IL: Charles C Thomas.

McLaughlin, J. J., & Ansbacher, R. R. (1971). Sane Benjamin Franklin: An Adlerian view of his autobiography. *Journal of Individual Psychology, 27*, 189–207.

McNamee, S. (1996). Psychotherapy as a social construction. In H. Rosen & K. T. Kuehlwein (Eds.), *Constructing realities: Meaning-making perspectives for psychotherapists* (pp. 115–137). San Francisco: Jossey-Bass.

Meichenbaum, D. (1977). *Cognitive-behavior modification: An integrative approach.* New York: Plenum.

Melchert, T. P. (1996). Childhood memory and a history of different forms of abuse. *Professional Psychology: Research and Practice, 27*, 438–446.

Melchert, T. P. (1998). Family of origin history, psychological distress, quality of childhood memory, and content of first and recovered childhood memories. *Child Abuse & Neglect, 22*, 1203–1216.

Merler, G. (1992). Individual psychology and the literary text: Stendhal's early recollections. *Individual Psychology: The Journal of Adlerian Theory, Research & Practice, 48*, 41–52.

Miles, C. (1893). A study of individual psychology. *American Journal of Psychology, 6*, 534–558.

Mitchell, S. A. (1988). *Relational concepts in psychoanalysis: An integration.* Cambridge, MA: Harvard University Press.

Monahan, R. T. (1983). Suicidal children's and adolescents' responses to Early Memories Test.

Journal of Personality Assessment, 47, 258–264.

Morawski, C. (1990). Early recollections: A key to success in reading and language arts. *Canadian Journal of English Language Arts, 12*, 34–47.

Morawski, C. M., & Brunhuber, B. S. (1993). Early recollections of learning to read: Implications for prevention and intervention in reading difficulties. *Reading Research and Instruction, 32*, 35–48.

Morran, D. K., Kurpius, D. J., Brack, G., & Rozecki, T. G. (1994). Relationship between counselors' clinical hypotheses and client ratings of counselor effectiveness. *Journal of Counseling & Development, 72*, 655–660.

Mosak, H. H. (1958). Early recollections as a projective technique. *Journal of Projective Techniques, 22*, 302–311.

Mosak, H. H. (1965). Predicting the relationship to the psychotherapist from early recollections. *Journal of Individual Psychology, 21*, 77–81.

Mosak, H. H. (1969). Early recollections: Evaluation of some recent research. *Journal of Individual Psychology, 25*, 56–63.

Mosak, H. H. (1992). The "traffic cop" function of dreams and early recollections. *Individual Psychology: The Journal of Adlerian Theory, Research & Practice, 48*, 319–323.

Mosak, H. H. (2000). Adlerian psychotherapy. In R. J. Corsini & D. Wedding (Eds.), *Current psychotherapies* (6th ed., pp. 54–98). Itasca, IL: F. E. Peacock.

Mosak, H. H., & Kopp, R. R. (1973). The early recollections of Adler, Freud, and Jung. *Journal of Individual Psychology, 29*, 157–166.

Mosak, H. H., & Maniacci, M. P. (1998). *Tactics in counseling and psychotherapy*. Itasca, IL: F. E. Peacock.

Mosak, H. H., & Maniacci, M. P. (1999). *A primer of Adlerian psychology: The analytic-behavioral-cognitive psychology of Alfred Adler*. Philadelphia: Taylor & Francis.

Mosak, H. H., Schneider, S., & Mosak, L. E. (1980). *Life style: A workbook*. Chicago: Alfred Adler Institute.

Mullen, M. K. (1994). Earliest recollections of childhood: A demographic analysis. *Cognition, 52*, 55–79.

Munroe, R. L. (1955). *Schools of psychoanalytic thought: An exposition, critique, and attempt at integration*. New York: Holt, Rinehart & Winston.

Murray, H. A. (1938). *Explorations in personality*. New York: Oxford Universities Press.

Myer, R., & James, R. K. (1991). Using early recollections as an assessment technique with children. *Elementary School Guidance and Counseling, 25*, 228–232.

Nash, M. (1987). What, if anything, is age regressed about hypnotic age regression? A review of the empirical literature. *Psychological Bulletin, 102*, 42–52.

Neimeyer, G. J., & Rareshide, M. B. (1991). Personal memories and personal identity: The impact of ego identity development on autobiographical memory recall. *Journal of Personality and Social Psychology, 60*, 562–569.

Nelson, A. (1986). The use of early recollection drawings in children's group therapy. *Individual Psychology: The Journal of Adlerian Theory, Research & Practice, 42*, 288–291.

Nelson, K. (1990). Remembering, forgetting, and childhood amnesia. In R. Fivush & J. A. Hudson (Eds.), *Knowing and remembering in young children* (pp. 301–316). New York: Cambridge University Press.

Nelson, K. (1993). The psychological and social origins of autobiographical memory. *Psychological Science, 4*, 7–14.

Nichols, C. C., & Feist, J. (1994). Explanatory style as a predictor of earliest recollections. *Individual Psychology: The Journal of Adlerian Theory, Research & Practice, 50*, 31–39.

Niederland, W. G. (1965). The role of the ego in the recovery of early memories. *Psychoanalytic Quarterly, 34*, 564–571.

Nigg, J. T., Lohr, N. E., Westen, D., Gold, L. J., & Silk, K. R. (1992). Malevolent object representations in borderline personality disorder and major depression. *Journal of Abnormal Psychology, 101,* 61–67.

Nigg, J. T., Silk, K. R., Westen, D., Lohr, N. E., Gold, L. J., Goodrich, S., & Ogata, S. (1991). Object representations in the early memories of sexually abused borderline patients. *American Journal of Psychiatry, 148,* 864–869.

Nikelly, A. G., & Verger, D. (1971). Early recollections. In A. G. Nikelly (Ed.), *Techniques for behavior change* (pp. 55–60). Springfield, IL: Charles C Thomas.

Nims, D., & Dinkmeyer, D., Jr. (1995). Early recollections as a communication tool between generations. *Individual Psychology: The Journal of Adlerian Theory, Research & Practice, 51,* 406–412.

Noonan, K. A. (1981). *Coping with illness.* Albany, NY: Delmar.

Oberholzer, E. (1931). An infantile cover-memory—A fragment of an analysis. *Journal of Nervous and Mental Disease, 74,* 212–213.

Olson, H. A. (Ed.). (1979a). *Early recollections: Their use in diagnosis and psychotherapy.* Springfield, IL: Charles C Thomas.

Olson, H. A. (1979b). Robert: A case of schizoaffective psychosis. In H. A. Olson (Ed.), *Early recollections: Their use in diagnosis and psychotherapy* (pp. 313–320). Springfield, IL: Charles C Thomas.

Olson, H. A. (1979c). Techniques of interpretation. In H. A. Olson (Ed.), *Early recollections: Their use in diagnosis and psychotherapy* (pp. 69–82). Springfield, IL: Charles C Thomas.

Olson, H. A. (1979d). To score or not to score. In H. A. Olson (Ed.), *Early recollections: Their use in diagnosis and psychotherapy* (pp. 156–159). Springfield, IL: Charles C Thomas.

Opedal, L. E. (1935). Analysis of the earliest memory of a delinquent. *International Journal of Individual Psychology, 1,* 52–58.

Orgler, H. (1952). Comparative study of two first recollections. *American Journal of Individual Psychology, 10,* 27–30.

Orgler, H. (1965). *Alfred Adler: The man and his work.* New York: Capricorn Books. (Original work published 1939)

Orlofsky, J., & Frank, M. (1986). Personality structure as viewed through early memories and identity status in college men and women. *Journal of Personality and Social Psychology, 50,* 580–586.

Paniagua, F. A. (1994). *Assessing and treating culturally diverse clients: A practical guide.* Thousand Oaks, CA: Sage.

Papanek, H. (1972). The use of early recollections in psychotherapy. *Journal of Individual Psychology, 28,* 169–176.

Parrott, L. (1992). Earliest recollections and birth order: Two Adlerian exercises. *Teaching of Psychology, 19,* 40–42.

Patterson, L. E., & Welfel, E. R. (2000). *The counseling process* (5th ed.). Pacific Grove, CA: Brooks/Cole.

Pattie, F. A., & Cornett, S. (1952). Unpleasantness of early memories and maladjustment of children. *Journal of Personality, 20,* 315–321.

Pepinsky, H. B. (1947). Application of informal projective methods in the counseling interview. *Educational and Psychological Measurement, 7,* 135–140.

Pepinsky, H. B., & Pepinsky, P. B. (1954). *Counseling: Theory and practice.* New York: Ronald Press.

Person, E. S., & Klar, H. (1994). Establishing trauma: The difficulty distinguishing between memories and fantasies. *Journal of the American Psychoanalytic Association, 42,* 1055–1081.

Peterson, C., Buchanan, G. M., & Seligman, M. E. P. (1995). Explanatory style: History and evolution of the field. In G. M. Buchanan & M. E. P. Seligman (Eds.), *Explanatory style* (pp. 1–20). Hillsdale, NJ: Lawrence Erlbaum.

Piaget, J. (1929). *The child's conception of the world.* New York: Harcourt, Brace.

Piers, C. C. (1999). Remembering trauma: A characterological perspective. In L. M. Williams & V. L. Baynard (Eds.), *Trauma and memory* (pp. 57–65). Thousand Oaks, CA: Sage.

Piotrowski, C., & Keller, J. W. (1984). Psychological testing: Trends in masters' level counseling psychology programs. *Teaching of Psychology, 11*, 244–245.

Piotrowski, C., Sherry, D., & Keller, J. W. (1985). Psychodiagnostic test usage: A survey of the Society for Personality Assessment. *Journal of Personality Assessment, 49*, 115–119.

Plank, E. N. (1953). Memories of early childhood in autobiographies. *Psychoanalytic Study of the Child, 8*, 381–393.

Plank, E. N. (1959). Memories of infancy. *Child–Family Digest, 18*, 21–23.

Plewa, R. (1935). The meaning in childhood recollections. *International Journal of Individual Psychology, 1*, 88–101.

Plottke, P. (1949). First memories of "normal" and of "delinquent" girls. *Individual Psychology Bulletin, 7*, 15–20.

Plutchik, R., Platman, S. R., & Fieve, R. R. (1970). Stability of the emotional content of early memories in manic-depressive patients. *British Journal of Medical Psychology, 43*, 177–181.

Potwin, E. B. (1901). Study of early memories. *Psychological Review, 8*, 596–601.

Powell, R.A., & Boer, D.P. (1994). Did Freud mislead patients to confabulate memories of abuse? *Psychological Reports, 74*, 1283–1298.

Powers, R. L., & Griffith, J. (1987). *Understanding life-style: The psycho-clarity process.* Chicago: The Americas Institute of Adlerian Studies.

Purcell, K. (1952). Memory and psychological security. *Journal of Abnormal and Social Psychology, 47*, 433–440.

Pustel, G., Sternlicht, M., & Siegel, L. (1969). Pleasant vs. unpleasant early childhood recollections of institutionalized adolescent and adult retardates. *Journal of Clinical Psychology, 25*, 110–111.

Quay, H. (1959). The effect of verbal reinforcement on the recall of early memories. *Journal of Abnormal and Social Psychology, 59*, 254–257.

Quinn, J. (1973). *Predicting recidivism and type of crime from early recollections of prison inmates.* Unpublished doctoral dissertation, University of South Carolina, Columbia, SC.

Rabbit, P., & McInnis, L. (1988). Do clever old people have earlier and richer first memories? *Psychology and Aging, 3*, 338–341.

Rabin, A. I. (1981). Projective methods: A historical introduction. In A. I. Rabin (Ed.), *Assessment with projective techniques: A concise introduction* (pp. 1–22). New York: Springer.

Rabin, A. I. (Ed.). (1986). *Projective techniques for adolescents and children.* New York: Springer.

Reichlin, R. E., & Niederehe, G. (1980). Early memories: A comprehensive bibliography. *Journal of Individual Psychology, 36*, 209–218.

Reimanis, G. (1965). Relationship of childhood experience memories to anomie later in life. *Journal of Genetic Psychology, 106*, 245–252.

Reimanis, G. (1974). Anomie, crime, childhood memories, and development of social interest. *Journal of Individual Psychology, 30*, 53–58.

Robbins, P. R., & Tanck, R. H. (1978). Early memories and dream recall. *Journal of Clinical Psychology, 34*, 729–731.

Robbins, P. R., & Tanck, R. H. (1994). Depressed mood and early memories: Some negative findings. *Psychological Reports, 75*, 465–466.

Rogers, C. (1964). Toward a science of a person. In T. W. Wann (Ed.), *Behaviorism and phenomenology: Contrasting bases for modern psychology* (pp. 109–140). Chicago: University of Chicago Press.

Rogers, G. W., Jr. (1977). Early recollections and college achievement. *Journal of Individual Psychology, 33*, 233–239.

Rogers, G. W., Jr. (1982). Predicting college achievement from early recollections. *Individual*

Psychology: The Journal of Adlerian Theory, Research & Practice, 38, 50–54.

Roland, C. B. (1993). Exploring childhood memories with adult survivors of sexual abuse: Concrete reconstruction and visualization techniques. *Journal of Mental Health Counseling, 15*, 363–372.

Rom, P. (1965). Goethe's earliest recollection. *Journal of Individual Psychology, 21*, 189–193.

Ross, B. M. (1991). *Remembering the personal past: Descriptions of autobiographical memory.* New York: Oxford University Press.

Roth, H., & Nicholson, C. L. (1990). Earliest school recollections as a diagnostic device for identifying successfully or unsuccessfully mainstreamed violent and assaultive youth. *Journal of Offender Counseling, Services & Rehabilitation, 15*, 117–129.

Rotter, J. C., Horak, R. A., Jr., & Heidt, H. M. (1999). Incorporating children's drawings as early recollections in Adlerian psychotherapy. *The Journal of Individual Psychology, 55*, 316–327.

Rubin, D. C. (2000). The distribution of early childhood memories. *Memory, 8*, 265–269.

Rubin, D. C., & Schulkind, M. D. (1997). Distribution of important and word-cued autobiographical memories in 20-, 35-, and 70-year-old adults. *Psychology and Aging, 12*, 524–535.

Rule, W. R. (1972). *The relationship between early recollections and selected counseling and lifestyle characteristics.* Unpublished doctoral dissertation, University of South Carolina, Columbia, SC.

Rule, W. R. (1991–1992). Personal adjustment variables in early recollections and recalled parental strictness–permissiveness. *Imagination, Cognition and Personality, 11*, 143–148.

Rule, W. R. (1992). Associations between personal problems and therapeutic intervention, early recollections and gender. *Individual Psychology: The Journal of Adlerian Theory, Research and Practice, 48*, 119–128.

Rule, W. R., & Jarrell, G. R. (1983). Intelligence and earliest memory. *Perceptual and Motor Skills, 56*, 795–798.

Rule, W. R., & McKenzie, D. H. (1977). Early recollections as a variable in group composition and in facilitative group behavior. *Small Group Behavior, 8*, 75–82.

Rule, W. R., & Traver, M. D. (1982). Early recollections and expected leisure activities. *Psychological Reports, 51*, 295–301.

Ryan, E. R., & Bell, M. D. (1984). Changes in object relations from psychosis to recovery. *Journal of Abnormal Psychology, 93*, 209–215.

Safran, J. D., & Segal, Z. V. (1990). *Interpersonal process in cognitive therapy.* New York: Basic Books.

Safran, J. D., Vallis, T. M., Segal, Z. V., & Shaw, B. F. (1986). Assessment of core cognitive processes in cognitive therapy. *Cognitive Therapy and Research, 10*, 509–526.

Sargent, H. (1945). Projective methods: Their origins, theory, and application in personality research. *Psychological Bulletin, 42*, 257–293.

Sattler, J. M., & Brandon, R. A. (1967). Early recollections related to anxiety and introversion–extroversion. *Journal of Consulting Psychology, 31*, 107.

Saul, L. J., Snyder, T. R., Jr., & Sheppard, E. (1956). On earliest memories. *Psychoanalytic Quarterly, 25*, 228–237.

Saunders, L. M. I., & Norcross, J. C. (1988). Earliest childhood memories: Relationship to ordinal position, family functioning, and psychiatric symptomatology. *Individual Psychology: The Journal of Adlerian Theory, Research & Practice, 44*, 95–105.

Savill, G. E., & Eckstein, D. G. (1987). Changes in early recollections as a function of mental status. *Individual Psychology: The Journal of Adlerian Theory, Research & Practice, 43*, 3–17.

Schachtel, E. G. (1947). On memory and childhood amnesia. *Psychiatry, 10*, 1–26.

Schmideberg, M. (1950). Infant memories and constructions. *Psychoanalytic Quarterly, 19*, 468–481.

Schrecker, P. (1973). Individual psychological significance of first childhood recollections. *Journal of Individual Psychology, 29*, 146–156.

Schwartz, A. E. (1984–1985). Earliest memories: Sex differences and the meaning of experience. *Imagination, Cognition & Personality, 4*, 43–52.

Searleman, A., & Herrmann, D. (1994). *Memory from a broader perspective*. Boston: McGraw-Hill.

Segal, Z. V. (1988). Appraisal of the self-schema construct in cognitive models of depression. *Psychological Bulletin, 103*, 147–162.

Seligman, L. (1996). *Diagnosis and treatment planning in counseling* (2nd ed.). New York: Plenum.

Shedler, J., Mayman, M., & Manis, M. (1993). The illusion of mental health. *American Psychologist, 48*, 1117–1131.

Shulman, B. H. (1962). The family constellation in personality diagnosis. *Journal of Individual Psychology, 18*, 35–47.

Shulman, B. H. (1985). Cognitive therapy and the individual psychology of Alfred Adler. In M. J. Mahoney & A. Freeman (Eds.), *Cognition and psychotherapy* (pp. 243–258). New York: Plenum.

Shulman, B. H., & Mosak, H. H. (1977). Birth order and ordinal position: Two Adlerian views. *Journal of Individual Psychology, 33*, 114–121.

Shulman, B. H., & Mosak, H. H. (1988). *Manual for life style assessment*. Bristol, PA: Accelerated Development.

Simmel, E. (1925). A screen-memory in statu nascendi. *International Journal of Psychoanalysis, 6*, 454–457.

Singer, J. L., & Salovey, P. (1991). Organized knowledge structures and personality: Person schemas, self schemas, prototypes, and scripts. In M. J. Horowitz (Ed.), *Person schemas and maladaptive interpersonal patterns* (pp. 33–79). Chicago: University of Chicago Press.

Singer, J. L., & Salovey, P. (1993). *The remembered self: Emotion and memory in personality*. New York: Free Press.

Slap, J. W., & Saykin, A. J. (1983). The schema: Basic concept in a nonmetapsychological model of the mind. *Psychoanalysis and Contemporary Thought, 6*, 305–325.

Slavik, S. (1991). Early memories as a guide to client movement through life. *Canadian Journal of Counselling, 25*, 331–337.

Smith, M. E. (1952). Childhood memories compared with those of adult life. *Journal of Genetic Psychology, 80*, 151–182.

Sobel, D. (1990). A place in the world: Adults' memories of childhood's special places. *Children's Environments Quarterly, 7*, 5–12.

Spengler, P. M., Strohmer, D. C., Dixon, D. N., & Shivy, V. A. (1995). A scientist–practitioner model of psychological assessment: Implications for training, practice and research. *The Counseling Psychologist, 23*, 506–534.

Sperry, L., & Carlson, J. (1996). *Psychopathology and psychotherapy: From DSM-IV diagnosis to treatment* (2nd ed.). Philadelphia: Taylor & Francis.

Spirrison, C. L., Schneider, I. M., Hartwell, J. A., Carmack, R. W., & D'Reaux, R. A. (1997). Early memories and maladjustment. *Psychological Reports, 18*, 227–233.

St. Clair, M. (2000). *Object relations and self psychology: An introduction* (3rd ed.). Belmont, CA: Brooks/Cole.

Statton, J. E., & Wilborn, B. (1991). Adlerian counseling and the early recollections of children. *Individual Psychology: The Journal of Adlerian Theory, Research & Practice, 47*, 338–347.

Stein, D. J. (1992). Schemas in the cognitive and clinical sciences: An integrative construct. *Journal of Psychotherapy Integration, 2*, 45–63.

Sulloway, F. J. (1996). *Born to rebel: Birth order, family dynamics, and creative lives*. New York: Pantheon.

Sweeney, T. J. (1990). Early recollections: A promising technique for use with older people. *Journal of Mental Health Counseling, 12*, 260–269.

Sweeney, T. J. (1998). *Adlerian counseling: A practitioner's approach* (4th ed.). Philadelphia: Taylor & Francis.

Sweeney, T. J., & Myers, J. E. (1986). Early recollections: An Adlerian technique with older people. *Clinical Gerontologist, 4*, 3–12.

Taylor, J. A. (1975). Early recollections as a projective technique: A review of some recent validation studies. *Journal of Individual Psychology, 31*, 213–218.

Terner, J., & Pew, W. L. (1978). *The courage to be imperfect: The life and work of Rudolph Dreikurs.* New York: Hawthorn Books.

Terr, L. (1988). What happens to early memories of trauma? A study of twenty children under age five at the time of documented traumatic events. *Journal of the American Academy of Child and Adolescent Psychiatry, 27*, 96–104.

Thatcher, P. (1944). Early recollection in a case of juvenile delinquency. *Individual Psychology Bulletin, 4*, 59–60.

Thompson, G. G., & Witryol, S. L. (1948). Adult recall of unpleasant experiences during three periods of childhood. *Journal of Genetic Psychology, 72*, 111–123.

Thorne, F. (1975). The life style analysis. *Journal of Clinical Psychology, 31*, 236–240.

Titchener, E. B. (1900). Early memories. *American Journal of Psychology, 11*, 435–436.

Tobey, L. H., & Bruhn, A. R. (1992). Early memories and the criminally dangerous. *Journal of Personality Assessment, 59*, 137–152.

Tobin, S. S. (1976). The earliest memory as data for research in aging. In D. Kent, R. Kastenbaum, & S. Sherwood (Eds.), *Research planning and action for the elderly: The power and potential of social science* (pp. 252–275). New York: Behavioral Publications.

Tobin, S. S., & Etigson, E. (1968). Effect of stress on earliest memory. *Archives of General Psychiatry, 19*, 435–444.

Tolor, A., & Fazzone, R. A. (1966). Early memories as indicators of ego functioning. *Psychological Reports, 19*, 979–983.

Tuch, R. H. (1999). The construction, reconstruction, and destruction of memory in the light of social cognition. *Journal of the American Psychoanalytic Association, 47*, 153–186.

Tulving, E. (1985). Memory and consciousness. *Canadian Psychology, 26*, 1–12.

Tylenda, B., & Dollinger, S. J. (1987). Is the earliest childhood memory special? An examination of affective characteristics of autobiographical memories. *Journal of Social Behavior and Personality, 2*, 361–368.

Usher, J. A., & Neisser, U. (1993). Childhood amnesia and the beginnings of memory for four early life events. *Journal of Experimental Psychology: General, 122*, 155–165.

Verger, D. M., & Camp, W. L. (1970). Early recollections: Reflections of the present. *Journal of Counseling Psychology, 17*, 510–515.

Vettor, S. M., & Kosinski, F. A. (2000). Work-stress burnout in emergency medical technicians and the use of early recollections. *Journal of Employment Counseling, 37*, 216–227.

Wagenheim, L. (1960). First memories of "accidents" and reading difficulties. *American Journal of Orthopsychiatry, 30*, 191–195.

Waldfogel, S. (1948). The frequency and affective character of childhood memories. *Psychological Monographs, 62* (4, Whole No. 291).

Wang, Q. (2001). Culture effects on adults' earliest childhood recollection and self-description: Implications for the relation between memory and the self. *Journal of Personality and Social Psychology, 81*, 220–233.

Warren, C. (1982). The relationship between early recollections and behavior patterns. *Individual Psychology: The Journal of Adlerian Theory, Research & Practice, 38*, 223–237.

Warren, C. (1987). Earliest recollection analysis: An intrapersonal technique of communication therapy. *Individual Psychology: The Journal of Adlerian Theory, Research & Practice, 43*,

24–35.

Warren, C. (1990). Use of hypnogogic reverie in collection of early recollections. *Individual Psychology: The Journal of Adlerian Theory, Research & Practice, 46*, 317–323.

Watkins, C. E., Jr. (1984). Using early recollections in career counseling. *Vocational Guidance Quarterly, 32*, 271–276.

Watkins, C. E., Jr. (1985). Early recollections as a projective technique in counseling: An Adlerian view. *American Mental Health Counselors Association Journal, 7*, 32–40.

Watkins, C. E., Jr. (1990). The effects of counselor self-disclosure: A research review. *The Counseling Psychologist, 18*, 477–500.

Watkins, C. E., Jr. (1992a). Adlerian oriented early memory research: What does it tell us? *Journal of Personality Assessment, 59*, 248–263.

Watkins, C. E., Jr. (1992b). Research activity with Adler's theory. *Individual Psychology: The Journal of Adlerian Theory, Research & Practice, 48*, 107–108.

Watkins, C. E., Jr. (2000). Some final thoughts about using tests and assessment procedures in counseling. In C. E. Watkins, Jr. & V. L. Campbell (Eds.), *Testing and assessment in counseling practice* (2nd ed., pp. 547–555). Mahwah, NJ: Lawrence Erlbaum.

Watkins, C. E., Jr., Campbell, V. L., Hollifield, J., & Duckworth, J. (1989). Projective techniques: Do they have a place in counseling psychology training? *The Counseling Psychologist, 17*, 511–513.

Watkins, C. E., Jr., & Guarnaccia, C. A. (1999). The scientific study of Adlerian theory. In R. E. Watts & J. Carlson (Eds.), *Interventions and strategies in counseling and psychotherapy* (pp. 207–230). Philadelphia: Taylor & Francis.

Watkins, C. E., Jr., & Schatman, M. E. (1986). Using early recollections in child psychotherapy. *Journal of Child and Adolescent Psychotherapy, 3*, 207–213.

Watson, J. C., Goldman, R., & Vanaerschot, G. (1998). Empathic: A postmodern way of being. In L. S. Greenberg, J. C. Watson, & G. Lietaer (Eds.), *Handbook of experiential psychotherapy* (pp. 61–81). New York: The Guilford Press.

Watts, R. E., & Carlson, J. (Eds.). 1991). *Interventions and strategies in counseling and psychotherapy*. Philadelphia: Taylor & Francis.

Watts, R. E., & Engels, D. W. (1995). The life task of vocation: A review of Adlerian research literature. *TCA Journal, 23*, 9–20.

Weiland, I. H., & Steisel, I. M. (1958). An analysis of manifest content of the earliest memories of children. *Journal of Genetic Psychology, 92*, 41–52.

Westen, D. (1998). The scientific legacy of Sigmund Freud: Toward a psychodynamically informed psychological science. *Psychological Bulletin, 124*, 333–371.

Westman, A. S. (1995). First memories seem quite complete but when the event happened is recalled least frequently. *Psychological Reports, 77*, 543–546.

Westman, A. S., & Orellana, C. (1996). Only visual impressions are almost always present in long-term memories, and reported completeness, accuracy, and verbalizability of recollections increase with age. *Perceptual and Motor Skills, 83*, 531–539.

Westman, A. S., & Wautier, G. (1994a). Early autobiographical memories are mostly nonverbal and their development is more likely continuous than discrete. *Psychological Reports, 74*, 655–656.

Westman, A. S., & Wautier, G. (1994b). Early memories are only fragments but make life more comprehensible or enhance social solidarity and are frequently verbalizable. *Psychological Reports, 75*, 387–393.

Westman, A. S., & Westman, R. S. (1993). First memories are nonverbal and emotional, not necessarily talked about or part of a recurring pattern. *Psychological Reports, 73*, 328–330.

Westman, A. S. Westman, R. S., & Orellana, C. (1996). Earliest memories and recall by modality usually involve recollections of different memories: Memories are not amodal. *Perceptual and Motor Skills, 82*, 1131–1135.

Willhite, R. G. (1979). "The Willhite": A creative extension of the early recollection process. In H. Olson (Ed.), *Early recollections: Their use in diagnosis and psychotherapy* (pp. 108–130). Springfield, IL: Charles C Thomas.

Williams, E. L., & Manaster, G. J. (1990). Restricter anorexia, bulimic anorexia, and bulimic women's early recollection and Thematic Apperception Test response. *Individual Psychology: The Journal of Adlerian Theory, Research & Practice, 46,* 93–107.

Williams, R. L., & Bonvillian, J. D. (1989). Early childhood memories in deaf and hearing college students. *Merrill-Palmer Quarterly, 35,* 483–497.

Winthrop, H. (1958). Written descriptions of the earliest memories: Repeat reliability and other findings. *Psychological Reports, 4,* 320.

Wohl, J. (1989). Integration of cultural awareness into psychotherapy. *American Journal of Psychotherapy, 43,* 343–355.

Wolf, C. (1984). *Patterns of childhood* (U. Molinaro & H. Rappolt, Trans.). New York: The Noonday Press.

Wolfman, C., & Friedman, J. (1964). A symptom and its symbolic representation in earliest memories. *Journal of Clinical Psychology, 20,* 442–444.

Wolman, R. N. (1970). Early recollections and the perception of others: A study of delinquent adolescents. *Journal of Genetic Psychology, 116,* 157–163.

Wynne, R. D., & Schaffzin, B. (1965). A technique for the analysis of affect in early memories. *Psychological Reports, 17,* 933–934.

Yeats, W. B. (1927). *Autobiographies: Reveries over childhood and youth and the trembling of the veil.* New York: Macmillan.

Young, M. E. (2001). *Learning the art of helping: Building blocks and techniques* (2nd ed.). Upper Saddle River, NJ: Merrill/Prentice Hall.

Zarski, J. (1981). The Early Recollections Rating Scale: Development and applicability in research. In L. G. Baruth & D. G. Eckstein (Eds.), *Life style: Theory, practice, and research* (2nd ed., pp. 106–108). Dubuque, IA: Kendall/Hunt.

ABOUT THE AUTHOR

Arthur J. Clark is a professor and coordinator of the Counseling and Development Program at St. Lawrence University in Canton, New York. He received his doctorate in counseling from Oklahoma State University in 1974 and has held positions as a school counselor, director of guidance, and school psychologist. His professional experience also includes counseling in a substance abuse treatment center and maintaining a private practice as a licensed psychologist. Dr. Clark is an editorial board member of the *Journal of Counseling and Development* and has been on the editorial boards of *Elementary School Guidance and Counseling* and the *Journal for Specialists in Group Work*. He holds memberships in the American Counseling Association and the American Psychological Association. His numerous publications in counseling and psychology include the book, *Defense Mechanisms in the Counseling Process* (1998), published by Sage Publications. He currently resides in Canton, New York, with his wife, Marybeth, and their daughters, Heather, Tara, and Kayla.

INDEX